Communicating with XML

Airi Salminen · Frank Tompa

Communicating with XML

 Springer

Airi Salminen
Department of Computer Science
and Information Systems
University of Jyväskylä
Jyväskylä, Finland
airi.salminen@jyu.fi

Frank Tompa
David R. Cheriton School
of Computer Science
University of Waterloo
Waterloo, ON, Canada
fwtompa@uwaterloo.ca

ISBN 978-1-4899-9380-9   ISBN 978-1-4614-0992-2 (eBook)
DOI 10.1007/978-1-4614-0992-2
Springer New York Dordrecht Heidelberg London

Printed on acid-free paper

Springer is part of Springer Science+Business Media (www.springer.com)

Preface

XML (Extensible Markup Language) is the *lingua franca* in contemporary networked environments. It is intended to support communication between software modules, particularly on the Web, as well as communication between people involved in developing new XML-based solutions. Developing the new solutions for a specific domain or for a particular organization requires understanding the capabilities and challenges of XML-based information management. This understanding should be shared by professionals with various backgrounds, including technological experts and experts in a particular domain or organizational environment.

The book aims to provide understanding of the possibilities and challenges of XML in building new information management solutions in networked organizations. It first describes the special features of Web communication and introduces XML fundamentals. Then it examines the benefits of adopting XML in an organization and introduces various types of XML use: XML in document management; XML as a format for metadata, including metadata for the Semantic Web; and XML in support of data interchange between software applications and organizations. The challenges of adopting XML in large-scale information migration are examined at the end of the book. The book provides several case studies of the adoption of XML.

This book is particularly suitable for a course offered by departments or schools of Information Studies, Information Systems, or Information Technology. It is also suitable for courses offered by departments or schools in related fields, including Computer Science, Library Studies, and Business. In addition, this book also serves as a guide to practice for professionals in information or communication technologies.

Airi Salminen and Frank Tompa

Contents

1 Setting the Stage 1
    1.1 Web Communications 2
    1.2 Markup 3
    1.3 Markup Languages 6
    1.4 Document Type Definition 10
    1.5 Types of XML Use 11
        1.5.1 Documents and Web Pages 12
        1.5.2 Other Primary Data 13
        1.5.3 Metadata 14
        1.5.4 Data Interchange and Web Services 15
    1.6 Case Study: Communicating Via News Feeds 16
    References 19

2 Fundamentals 21
    2.1 Formal Grammars 22
    2.2 Processors and Applications 24
    2.3 XML Documents 27
        2.3.1 Logical Structure 27
        2.3.2 Physical Structure 33
        2.3.3 Character Encoding 37
    2.4 Declaring and Constraining Structures 38
        2.4.1 DTD and Markup Declarations 38
        2.4.2 Element Type Declarations 40
        2.4.3 Attribute List Declarations 43
        2.4.4 Entity and Notation Declarations 46
        2.4.5 XML Processor Treatment of Entities and References 48
        2.4.6 XML Schema 52
        2.4.7 RELAX NG 61

  2.5 Processing Models.. 62
       2.5.1 Stream Processing 63
       2.5.2 Tree Processing.. 64
       2.5.3 Comparing Stream and Tree Processing................... 66
  References 66

3 **Why Use XML?**.. 69
  3.1 Collaborative Standardization 70
       3.1.1 Standardization at W3C.. 71
       3.1.2 Sectoral Standardization... 72
  3.2 XML Family of Languages 73
       3.2.1 Classification of the XML Languages...................... 74
       3.2.2 XML Accessories 75
       3.2.3 XML Transducers.. 76
       3.2.4 XML Applications... 77
  3.3 Variety of Software... 84
  3.4 Application-Independent Data Assets..................................... 85
  3.5 Web-Enabled Access... 86
  3.6 Interoperability 87
  3.7 Case Study: Business Applications 88
  References 90

4 **Document Management**.. 93
  4.1 Structured Documents 94
       4.1.1 Structure Versus Content Versus Layout 94
       4.1.2 Characteristics of Structured Document Management........ 95
  4.2 Transformations and XSLT 96
  4.3 Rendering 100
       4.3.1 Rendering with CSS 102
       4.3.2 Rendering with XSL... 104
  4.4 Information Retrieval 104
       4.4.1 Indexing.. 105
       4.4.2 Retrieval Effectiveness and Ranking 107
       4.4.3 Querying XML Data.. 108
  4.5 Case Study: Storing and Accessing Dictionaries 109
  References 111

5 **Data-Centric and Multimedia Components** 113
  5.1 Data Types in XML Schema 114
       5.1.1 Classification of Data Types.................................. 115
       5.1.2 Facets.. 117
       5.1.3 Type Hierarchy 119
       5.1.4 Example: Data Type Definitions
              for the UK Government... 120
  5.2 Numeric Data 121
  5.3 Dates and Time.. 122

5.4	Graphics and Multimedia Data	123
	5.4.1 Scalable Vector Graphics	123
	5.4.2 Multimedia	130
5.5	Scientific Data	135
	5.5.1 Mathematical Data	135
	5.5.2 Geospatial Data	139
5.6	Data for Humanities and Social Sciences	141
	5.6.1 Electronic Books	142
	5.6.2 Text Encoding Initiative	143
	References	145
6	**Metadata**	**149**
6.1	XML as Metadata and XML for Metadata	150
6.2	Resource Discovery	152
6.3	Dublin Core	153
6.4	Resource Management	154
	6.4.1 Learning Object Metadata	155
	6.4.2 Metadata for Records Management	156
	6.4.3 Metadata for Preservation	158
6.5	RDF: Resource Description Framework	158
6.6	Semantic Web	162
	References	166
7	**Data Interchange**	**169**
7.1	EDI	170
7.2	Frameworks for Business Interactions	173
	7.2.1 ebXML	174
	7.2.2 RosettaNet	175
	7.2.3 Industry-Specific Frameworks	176
7.3	Web Services	178
7.4	Security in Data Interchange	179
7.5	The Status of Interchange Standards	182
	References	183
8	**Adopting XML for Large-Scale Information**	**185**
8.1	Persistent Storage of XML Data	186
	8.1.1 Special Characteristics and Requirements	186
	8.1.2 XML Management Solutions	191
	8.1.3 Migration into XML Format	194
8.2	When Not to Use XML	195
	8.2.1 Not to Replace Database Technology Universally	196
	8.2.2 Not to Replace Other Proven Technologies Arbitrarily	196
	8.2.3 Risks in the Development and Deployment of New XML Applications	197

8.3   Case Study: Government Applications 198
        8.3.1   The Case of the Finnish Parliament
                 and Government Ministries 198
        8.3.2   The Case of Massachusetts... 201
  8.4   Conclusions 202
  References 203

Appendix A   Introduction to XHTML 207

Appendix B   History of XML... 209
B.1   Origins of the Internet 209
B.2   Origins of SGML 210
B.3   From the Internet to the World Wide Web 210
B.4   From SGML to XML 211
Historical Readings... 214

Appendix C   Extended Backus-Naur Form (EBNF) 215

Index.. 217

List of Figures

Fig. 1.1 Typical business card.. 4
Fig. 1.2 Page image from HTML 6
Fig. 1.3 Example of HTML markup.. 7
Fig. 1.4 Example of descriptive XML markup... 8
Fig. 1.5 Element hierarchy for the XML document in Fig. 1.4................... 9
Fig. 1.6 XML encoding for the business card in Fig. 1.1 9
Fig. 1.7 Viewing a blog by means of a feed reader
(With permission of Laila Lalami) 17
Fig. 1.8 The XML code for the blog feed shown in Fig. 1.7 18
Fig. 1.9 An example of an Atom feed, extracted from a feed
from www.w3c.org 19

Fig. 2.1 The processing context of an XML document 25
Fig. 2.2 A physical structure with three entities 34
Fig. 2.3 A schema with an anonymous complex type definition................. 56
Fig. 2.4 A schema with a named complex type definition.......................... 56
Fig. 2.5 A schema with references to global elements 57
Fig. 2.6 A schema with an attribute declaration 59
Fig. 2.7 XML document as a tree 64

Fig. 3.1 Levels of XML standardization.. 70
Fig. 3.2 The idealized recommendation process at W3C 71
Fig. 3.3 XML family of languages 73

Fig. 4.1 The three facets of a structured document................................... 94
Fig. 4.2 Example XSLT template 98
Fig. 4.3 Example XSLT program.. 100
Fig. 4.4 The rhymes from Example 2.2 as an XHTML document............... 101
Fig. 4.5 Screen dump of the document from Fig. 4.4 rendered
by Firefox 101
Fig. 4.6 An XML document with a reference to a CSS style sheet............. 103
Fig. 4.7 The rhymes.css style sheet 103

Fig. 4.8   The document from Fig. 4.6 as shown by Firefox using
the style sheet in Fig. 4.7 103
Fig. 4.9   Interactive information retrieval environment 105
Fig. 4.10   Encoding for a hypothetical dictionary entry 110
Fig. 4.11   Rendering of a hypothetical dictionary entry 110

Fig. 5.1   The built-in XSD data types 115
Fig. 5.2   Possible combinations of classes of simple data types 117
Fig. 5.3   Constraining facets 118
Fig. 5.4   Type hierarchy for the built-in data types 119
Fig. 5.5   Type definitions from http://www.govtalk.gov.uk/core 120
Fig. 5.6   An SVG document example from the SVG specification
rendered by Mozilla Firefox 128
Fig. 5.7   The page source of the document shown in Fig. 5.6 128
Fig. 5.8   Example of a dialog in VoiceXML 133
Fig. 5.9   MathML data inside XHTML and rendered
by Mozilla Firefox 136
Fig. 5.10   MathML and SVG data inside XHTML rendered
by the Amaya editor/browser 138
Fig. 5.11   Geographic information copied in the KML format
from the Google Earth 3D image to the WordPad text editor 140
Fig. 5.12   "A Christmas Carol" by Charles Dickens downloaded
in the EPUB format from project Gutenberg and displayed
by Firefox's EPUB reader 143

Fig. 6.1   TEI markup of a piece of William Wordsworth's poem [32] 150
Fig. 6.2   Dublin Core description in the XHTML source page
of the DCMI home page at http://dublincore.org/ 153
Fig. 6.3   A piece of a LOM XML instance 157
Fig. 6.4   Related RDF statements as a graph 160
Fig. 6.5   The XML syntax for the graph in Fig. 6.4 161
Fig. 6.6   External RDF metadata description of the DCMI
home page at http://dublincore.org/index.shtml.rdf 162

Fig. 7.1   Business interaction between two partners over the Internet 173
Fig. 7.2   An example of a SAML assertion 181

Fig. 8.1   XML document without explicit modeling
of the real-world data 187

List of Tables

Table 2.1 The five possible combinations of entity types 36
Table 2.2 Contexts for referencing entities and characters........................... 49

Table 3.1 XML accessories 75
Table 3.2 XML transducers 76
Table 3.3 XML applications for Web publishing 79
Table 3.4 XML applications for metadata and Semantic Web.................... 80
Table 3.5 XML applications for Web communication and services 82
Table 3.6 XML applications for non-textual data 83
Table 3.7 Government interoperability frameworks...................................... 87

Table 5.1 Markup languages for scientific data.. 135

Table 6.1 W3C case studies serving primarily semantic search
and data integration 164
Table 6.2 W3C case studies serving other semantic applications 165
Table 6.3 Public ontologies and vocabularies used
in the case studies of [40] 166

Table 7.1 Standards for data interchange and security
in Great Britain and New Zealand.. 183

Table 8.1 Summarization of Bourret's XML database
product listings [6] 191

List of Tables

Chapter 1
Setting the Stage

Abstract The World Wide Web is a communications network that provides connections among individuals, corporations, and government agencies. In order to exchange written information, the communicating parties must agree on how documents will be represented. This is achieved through a common understanding of markup. XML, the extensible markup language, provides mechanisms to describe document structures, and its use is becoming increasingly widespread, not only for representing conventional documents, but also Web pages, graphics and other notations, metadata representing document features, traditional business data, and services available on the Web.

Keywords Data interchange • Document type definition • Markup languages • Metadata • Web communications • Web services • Web syndication • World Wide Web

The *World Wide Web*, also known as *WWW* or *the Web*, has drastically changed how people, communities, and computers communicate with each other. Instead of calling or visiting a travel agency to book a flight, we contact a travel service on the Web, the travel service contacts flight services of various air carriers, and the aggregated service provides us with information about the schedules and prices. If we decide to purchase a ticket, we submit our credit card data to a service that contacts our credit card company and subsequently sends us confirmation about an e-ticket. Family members living in different continents share family photos and diaries daily by means of blogging and other social media. People and organizations communicate within e-community, e-business, e-commerce, e-economy, e-government, e-democracy, e-learning, e-terrorism, and other Internet-based networks. Five years ago few people knew the term blogging or social media; now millions of people and companies utilize those technologies in their communication. In 5 years there may be communication capabilities available that we cannot imagine today.

A core requirement to the evolution of this e-world has been the invention and development of languages suitable for the communication that connects people, organizations, communities, and computers.

A. Salminen and F. Tompa, *Communicating with XML*,
DOI 10.1007/978-1-4614-0992-2_1, © Springer Science+Business Media, LLC 2011

The *Extensible Markup Language*, better known by its acronym XML, has been called the *lingua franca* of Internet communication. Most Internet users never need to know anything about XML: they are still able to use the services, tools, and resources available. On the other hand, all those who are involved in finding and developing new ways to use Web technologies in organizations should understand the advantages and challenges of adopting XML. This does not concern people building technical solutions only. The deployment of XML requires the development of new languages for the needs of communities and organizations. The development of a new solution cannot be done by technical people alone. It requires people having knowledge about the domain, its needs and communication practices, and the ways in which information is structured and presented within that domain. Development of new solutions is often a challenging collaborative effort involving people with varying backgrounds and expertise.

In this chapter we will show why XML evolved, what is special about XML as compared to earlier ways to present digital information, and what kinds of capabilities it offers. We introduce the core concepts of XML without going into detail. First, in Sect. 1.1 we briefly introduce the history of Web communication. Presentation of information in XML is based on the use of *markup*. In Sect. 1.2 we introduce the principles of markup and various types of markup. Section 1.3 compares XML as a *markup language* to its predecessors, SGML (Standard Generalized Markup Language) [3] and HTML (HyperText Markup Language). XML is a metalanguage facilitating the definition of special markup languages for special needs and application domains. The definition mechanism is introduced in Sect. 1.4. In Sect. 1.5 we introduce the principal types of XML use, and at the end of the chapter we introduce a case study illustrating how XML supports communication via news feeds.

1.1 Web Communications

Computers were originally regarded primarily as a means to calculate trajectories and to evaluate various scientific and financial computations efficiently. Communications between networks of computers started with the introduction of ARPANET in the U.S. in the late 1960s, and grew rapidly over the next two decades. The resulting integrated network, the Internet, provides a pervasive infrastructure to share computing resources. The creation of ARPANET was activated by the cold war competition between the United States and the Soviet Union, but the resulting network technology was soon adopted by universities all over the world in addition to U.S. defense organizations. On top of this infrastructure, Tim Berners-Lee proposed "a universal linked information system, in which generality and portability are more important than fancy graphics techniques and complex extra facilities" [1]. The resulting World Wide Web now allows participants from around the world to share data resources, including simple text or complex multimedia documents, pictures, music, videos, and discussions. Hundreds of millions of people speaking and writing dozens of languages, thousands of various kinds of organizations, and hundreds of different software applications are connected to each other. Thus, efficient processing power and a huge number of resources became accessible worldwide.

This technology has spawned new kinds of communities and businesses, but effective use of the resources requires flexible communication capabilities between various parties using their own languages.

Internet communication takes place between people, between software applications, and between people and software applications. Both natural and formal languages are needed in this complex communication environment. In a commercial transaction, for example, several natural and formal languages and several translation steps may be needed. For example, a buyer requests some information from an online catalog; the database system managing the catalog checks the inventory from the database system in which supplies are recorded; this triggers a message to the human stock manager, who sends an email message to his supervisor. When Tim Berners-Lee developed the Web, he designed the *HyperText Markup Language (HTML)*[1] and the *HyperText Transport Protocol (HTTP)* to provide a simple means to ship documents among any types of machine running various operating systems. However, HTML provides facilities to describe data in terms of headings, paragraphs, and various typographic conventions; it does not allow the expression of meaningful information units commonly used within a particular community and for a particular class of applications.

Thus if data is exchanged using HTML, communications between software applications is often hindered by the differences in data representations. This is a great barrier for effective use of the Internet, particularly for business purposes. By the mid-1990s, it became urgent to find some common rules for representing information and information structures within the Internet and for exchanging information between applications over the Internet. Those rules were developed by the World Wide Web Consortium (W3C) and expressed in a language called the *Extensible Markup Language (XML)* and in a set of related languages we will call the *XML family of languages*. XML offers a common syntactic framework to use both natural and formal languages for Web communications. Specifications for HTML, XML, and all other languages in the XML family are published on the W3C website [6].

1.2   Markup

For two humans to communicate, they must agree to use a particular medium, such as telephone or surface mail, and they must express their messages using a common language and common vocabulary. Similarly passing information from one software application to another requires that both agree to use certain communication channels and protocols and to represent the information content using certain conventions. HTTP (used in conjunction with many other communications protocols)

---

[1] A brief introduction to XHTML, a variant of HTML based on XML, is provided in Appendix A.

Fig. 1.1 Typical business card

and HTML provide one mechanism that could be used. However, as mentioned above, HTML is not suited to describe how various units of information fit together into meaningful structures.

Consider how you might wish to represent your contact information, such as what is printed on the business card shown in Fig. 1.1. Whose card is this? Which part represents the name of the city? Is a fax number included? We can answer these and similar questions because we know the meanings of some words, some well-understood proper nouns are included, and we are familiar with the encoding conventions used on such a card. Because natural language processing is too imprecise and too inefficient for most applications software, computer-to-computer communications must rely solely on using encoding conventions to distinguish the information components of the transmitted data.

Perhaps the information content from this card is already stored in a database, a spreadsheet, or some other application program's store. To send the data to another application, possibly sitting on some other computer, it would have to be extracted from the first application's store, bundled as a data "package," shipped to the other machine, unbundled, and stored in the second application's store. The first application might be written in COBOL and the second one in Java; the first store might represent a phone number as one large integer, and the second one might represent it using separate integers for country code and area code; the first machine might store an integer in the space used by four characters and the second one in the space used by six characters. With so many discrepancies, how can these applications communicate?

The simplest solution is to transmit all the information as character data, which uses standard encodings (typically ASCII or Unicode) on most systems. For example, rather than sending the number 145 as an integer, one can send the character '1' followed by the character '4' followed by the character '5'.

Consider again the information provided on the business card in Fig. 1.1. The content can easily be represented as a sequence of characters:

logowww.3ballsafloat.comDana LeeSenior Sales RepresentativeNorth American Division3 Balls Afloat1010 Main StreetToronto, ON M3W 1A1dana.lee@3ballsafloat.com+1-416-555-0123

However, as this clearly illustrates, not only must all content be encoded as characters, but the structural information must be encoded as well. Various cultures and languages have developed spacing and layout conventions for presenting many types of documents: that's what makes the business card easy to read, and what gives distinctive looks to newspapers, novels, plays, poems, dictionaries, parts catalogs, and business correspondence.

If the content of a document is to be stored in a computer memory using a sequence of characters, the layout is best represented by embedded *markup*, special symbols that are interleaved with the content to delineate units of text, just as punctuation does. This markup can be of any form, and can, in fact use symbols that are different from all conventional characters. The first task is merely to delineate the units:

logo|www.3ballsafloat.com|Dana Lee|Senior Sales Representative|North American Division |3 Balls Afloat|1010 Main Street|Toronto, ON M3W 1A1|dana.lee@3ballsafloat.com|+1-416-555-0123

However, this does not provide as much information as was present on the business card. Therefore, in addition to providing delimiters, a markup can also include formatting information, illustrated here after each '|' and ending with ':':

logo|blue type:www.3ballsafloat.com|new line, bold:Dana Lee|new line:Senior Sales Repres entative|new line:North American Division|space:3 Balls Afloat|new line:1010 Main Street|n ew line:Toronto, ON M3W 1A1|space, blue type, underscored:dana.lee@3ballsafloat.com|n ew line:+1-416-555-0123

Of course, another way to represent this data is via HTML:

<img alt="3 Balls Afloat logo" src="logo.gif"><font color="blue">www.3ballsafloat.com</font >
Dana Lee
Senior Sales Representative
North American Division<sp> 3 Balls Afloat
1010 Main Street
Toronto, ON M3W 1A1<sp><font color="blue"><u> dana.lee@3ballsafloat.com</u></font>
+1-416-555-0123

Notice that HTML uses conventional, albeit rarely used, characters '<' and '>' to separate the markup from the content. In particular, the markup shown here consists of start- and end-*tags* for each data unit. Every tag begins with a left angle bracket and ends with a right angle bracket, separating the tag (markup) from the content. By using conventional characters as delimiters, we can be sure that the symbols will be represented identically on all computers, regardless of which operating systems are deployed. (To make this unambiguous, however, we need another convention to use when we wish to transmit those delimiters – namely, the angle brackets – as part of information content).

Fig. 1.2 Page image from HTML

Those of you who are familiar with HTML might argue that this is not a faithful representation for this data. An alternative HTML encoding is:

```
<table><tr><td width="250" align="center"><img alt="3 Balls Afloat logo"  src="logo.gif" alig
n="middle"><font  color="blue"><b>www.3ballsafloat.com</b></font></td><td><b>Dana Le
e</b><br>Senior Sales Representative<br>North American Division<p><address>3 Balls A
float<br>1010 Main Street<br>Toronto, ON M3W 1A1</address></p><p><a href="mailto:d
ana.lee@3ballsafloat.com">dana.lee@3ballsafloat.com</a> <br>+1-416-555-0123</p> </td
></tr></table>
```

If this data were sent over the Web, the recipient could view the page using a browser, as in Fig. 1.2. To produce such a representation, a table is used to separate the logo into a separate column, an address tag is introduced to delineate the address fields on the card, and the email address is tagged as a link instead of just showing its typography. The revised version, therefore, conveys more information to a human reader or to a recipient program, by using markup that better describes the content. However, some layout information remains in the markup, and this inhibits reading the content.

1.3 Markup Languages

The markup intended for computers must be formal and systematic. With well-designed markup languages the rules for the identification and interpretation of markup are so clear that it is possible to develop computer programs to identify and interpret the markup. Text written in a markup language consists of two kinds of text pieces: markup and primary content. HTML is an example of a markup language.

```
<html>
  <head><title>University of Jyv&auml;skyl&auml;</title></head>
  <body>
    <h2>Faculties</h2>
    <ul>
      <li>Humanities
      <li>Information Technology
      <li>Social Sciences
    </ul>
    <br>
    <address>admin@jyu.fi</address>
  </body>
</html>
```

Fig. 1.3 Example of HTML markup

The markup rules of HTML have been defined in the HTML specification published by W3C. For example, in the HTML text:

```
<h1>Faculty members</h1>
```

the tags <h1> and </h1> represent markup and Faculty members is the primary content.

Figure 1.3 illustrates more HTML markup, shown in this example using bold text. Most of the markup consists of element tags. For most elements there is both a *start-tag* at the beginning of the element and a matching *end-tag* at the end of the element, including an identical *element name* preceded by a slash. For example, <html> matches </html> and <ul> matches </ul>. On the other hand, the three list item elements and the line break element are represented by start-tags only (<li> and <br>, respectively). The markup ä in the title element is a *character entity reference* instructing the software reading the markup to replace it by the letter ä from the Scandinavian alphabet.

The HTML 4.01 specification defines 91 element types for use in HTML documents. End-tags may be omitted for 15 of the elements (such as li in the example), and 13 so-called empty elements (including br) are forbidden to have end-tags.

In the Web environment, the reading of HTML text takes place in two phases. First a *browser* reads the marked up text, interprets the markup, and displays the primary content on a screen. After that the human user of the browser reads the primary content from the screen. Because HTML elements are nested hierarchically, the contents of an HTML document are often stored and displayed with "pretty printing" (as in Fig. 1.3) to improve human readability of the marked up text; the extra "white space" in the text is ignored by Web browsers.

As clear as the HTML markup seems to be, there is a problem. The markup indicates that there is a list of items in a section with heading Faculties, but are these the names of the faculties or are they the names of the professors teaching in the faculties, or are they the names of the suppliers of services to the faculties? Appropriate descriptions are not being provided by the markup.

On the other hand, the markup denoted by <address> and </address> clearly *describes* the text piece between those two markup symbols; it does not merely

```
<university>
        <name>University of Jyväskylä</name>
        <faculties>
                <faculty>Humanities</faculty>
                <faculty>Information Technology</faculty>
                <faculty>Social Sciences</faculty>
        </faculties>
        <contact_email>admin@jyu.fi</contact_email>
</university>
```

Fig. 1.4 Example of descriptive XML markup

convey how to present the text on the screen or on paper. The advantages of such *descriptive markup* were recognized in the 1980s, and explained most eloquently in an article by James Coombs et al. [2]. They point out that the inclusion of *presentational markup*, such as punctuation characters and spacing, is part of our writing system. In computer representations, some of this markup is preserved. However, some aspects, such as vertical spacing, font changes, and line justification, cannot be represented directly. Instead we can use *procedural markup*: explicit commands placed into the text where vertical space is to be inserted, where the font should change from arial to courier, or the typeface changed to italic or bold, and so forth.

Most of HTML markup is procedural. An application program can subsequently read the text and use the embedded markup to determine how to render the document on a printed page. However, if a human reader or a recipient program wishes to process the content in some way other than producing a print version, such formatting commands interfere with the reading of the text; it is far better to describe what role each component in the text represents. HTML provides some facilities for descriptive markup (e.g., <p> for paragraph, <h1> for a major-level heading, <address> for representing contact information), but many tags are purely procedural (e.g., <br> for a line break, <i> for italic text) and many components that you may wish to describe have no corresponding tags in HTML.

XML and its predecessor SGML are alternative markup languages that allow users to include whatever tag names are desired. By using XML instead of HTML, users are not limited in their choice of element names. Thus the content of the document in Fig. 1.3 can be given by "pure" descriptive markup, providing complete information about the content, not about the way it should be presented. An example of such descriptive markup is given in Fig. 1.4.

With this approach, a human reader can recognize that the list of elements nested within the faculties element indicates names of individual faculties and that the address provided is an e-mail address rather than a physical address. This advantage over HTML, however, brings with it a cost: some process must convert the descriptive markup to a procedural or presentational markup before the document content can be properly rendered on a screen or on paper. On the other hand, such conversion can be adapted to the target medium to produce alternative output suitable for very small displays or even output suitable for media that support animation or audio reception. Supporting such re-use of information resources for multiple purposes is one of the benefits of using the descriptive markup capabilities found in XML.

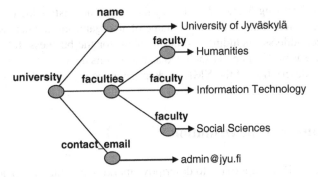

Fig. 1.5 Element hierarchy for the XML document in Fig. 1.4

```
<card>
  <url img="logo.jpg">www.3ballsafloat.com</url>
  <name>
    <forename>Dana</forename>
    <surname>Lee</surname>
  </name>
  <position>
    <title>Senior Sales Representative</title>
    <division>North American Division</division>
  </position>
  <address>
    <org>3 Balls Afloat</org>
    <street>
      <streetnum>1010</streetnum>
      Main Street
    </street>
    <city>Toronto</city>
    <province>ON</province>
    <postalcode>M3W1A1</postalcode>
  </address>
  <email>dana.lee@3ballsafloat.com</email>
  <phone>+1-416-555-0123</phone>
</card>
```

Fig. 1.6 XML encoding for the business card in Fig. 1.1

XML was developed to represent information in the form of structured documents for applications on the Internet. It is a restricted form of SGML. For example, unlike HTML and SGML, XML requires that all elements are terminated by end-tags, which simplifies processing. As a result, the syntax of the markup language makes it possible to ensure that elements are properly nested within each other, resulting in a hierarchical organization of the elements, as illustrated in Fig. 1.5.

Applying the ideas of descriptive markup to the business card example from the previous section results in the XML representation shown in Fig. 1.6. In this encoding, which again uses tags *not* available in HTML, each data unit is explicitly marked to indicate its information content. It is clear which part of the data represents the person's name, and furthermore which is the forename and which is the surname.

Even though the string 3 Balls Afloat has syntactic characteristics identical to 1010 Main Street, it is clear that the first is the name of an organization, whereas the latter is a full street address, including a street number, for the business. It is now also clear that there is no fax number included as part of this data.

A detailed description of the XML markup language is included in Chap. 2.

1.4 Document Type Definition

XML adopted SGML's approach to descriptive markup, in which the placement of tags is controlled by a *document type definition*, or DTD. The chief role of a document type definition is to serve as a *prescriptive* grammar to control the creation of new materials. As well as constraining new material, a DTD also constrains the complete collection of material. Therefore, DTDs can be regarded as *schemas* for information repositories much like database schemas. In SGML, every document required an associated DTD cataloging the names of elements allowed to appear in the document, which elements may be nested inside which other elements, whether elements can appear once only or whether they can repeat arbitrarily often, and the order in which nested elements can occur. For example, the document in Fig. 1.4 can be associated with a grammar that specifies that the outermost element is university, that it must contain three elements (a name, faculties, and contact_email element, in that order), that faculties contains one or more faculty elements, and that name, faculty, and contact_email elements contain text data only.

Such a grammar or schema can also be used *descriptively* to inform new users about the data organization and to direct search and display tools to particular sections of the text. For example, a DTD can inform a new user of a large document collection concerning music that the element name to use to search for the name of a singer is artist, that artists may be associated with either whole CDs or individual tracks, and that several artists might be associated with any given track. This information will help the user to formulate sensible queries and help interpret where misunderstandings produce empty responses for what seem to be sensible queries.

In fact, a major strength of XML stems from its use by a widespread community of colleagues and business partners. Such a community can establish how they will share data by defining a schema appropriate to their needs and subsequently creating documents that match the schema, using XML tools to enforce compliance. One example of such a community includes humanists, some of whom created the TEI collection of schemas for exchanging scholarly documents. Government bodies have created a schema entitled the Governmental Markup Language for encoding public sector documents in the European Community and a collection of schemas for representing US Congressional documents. Scientists have defined the Chemical Markup Language, the Systems Biology Markup Language, the Materials Property Data Markup Language, the Physics Markup Language, and the Astronomical Markup Language, among others. Business sectors have defined the Steel Markup Language for the steel industry, PetroXML for the petroleum industry, and AgXML for the grain and oilseed industry, among others. The schemas for each of these initiatives serve to document the consensus reached by the community regarding what elements are important to record in documents and how that recording should take place. Those schemas prescribe how documents should be created and describe what to expect to see in those documents, and therefore they form the grammar underlying meaningful communication.

1.5 Types of XML Use

The designers of XML wished to improve upon both SGML and HTML when used to represent the vast variety of data for Internet applications. The intent was to adopt from each of the two languages the features best suited to the needs of the time. The goals included:

- The capability to describe Internet resources and their relationships (like HTML);
- The capability to define information structures for various kinds of business sectors (unlike HTML, like SGML);
- A format formal enough for computers and clear enough to be human-legible (like SGML);
- Rules simple enough to allow easy building of software (unlike SGML, like HTML); and
- Strong support for diverse natural languages (unlike SGML).

The widespread adoption of XML indicates that these goals were well-chosen and that apparently they have been realized.

The most obvious target for adopting XML is to replace SGML and HTML for representing documents in applications that depend on the Web. Not only do such documents constitute the contents of home pages and the huge Web sites to which they are connected, but they also comprise the content of the *Deep Web*, stored in backend document databases. This primary application is introduced in Sect. 1.5.1 and then described in more detail in Chap. 4.

Internet applications, however, depend on many more types of data than simple text documents. Therefore XML has been adopted to represent other basic forms of data, from video and audio to chemical structures and biomedical data. These uses of XML are introduced in Sect. 1.5.2 and illustrated to a greater extent in Chap. 5.

Organizations rely not only on primary information in the form of text, multimedia data, and special-purpose data. In addition, organizations require access to metadata assets, which are related to the primary information assets. For example, metadata includes information about the creation of an item of data (who created it, when was it created, and why was it created). The purpose of metadata is to facilitate or support the management of the primary information assets. Applications of XML for metadata storage and management is described in Sect. 1.5.3 and elaborated in Chap. 6.

Finally, XML is also used to transmit data among diverse Internet applications. If an application stores its data in XML form, it can easily ship it out or receive new fragments of XML data. However, even programs that do not store their data and metadata as XML have adopted XML as one of their formats for input and output; they merely need to convert the XML to and from their internal data format. Furthermore, XML is also used to encode the communications messages that envelop the data. These uses of XML are introduced in Sect. 1.5.4 and described in more detail in Chap. 7.

1.5.1 Documents and Web Pages

Documents have used various forms of markup for as long as they have been stored in computer systems. In the 1980s, SGML began to influence several domains including book publishing (through the Association of American Publishers), military procurement and technical documentation (through the US Department of Defense's CALS initiative), and various transportation and communications industries. More recently these and subsequent initiatives have transferred their focus to using XML in place of SGML. Therefore today XML is used to represent documents being prepared for commercial publication, for technical documentation in all industries, and to represent scholarly texts.

In addition to managing traditional documents, XML is also adept at representing Web documents. The original definition of HTML as an SGML application has been upgraded to XHTML, which is an XML application, and modern Web browsers support XHTML directly. Not only are many stored Web pages derived from data stored in XML, but XML and XHTML are also used as "export" forms for presenting data from backend databases through a Web browser. Thus XML and XHTML have become standard formats for publishing information through the World Wide Web.

Using XML as a document format allows an organization to adopt the approach of *structured documents* for its document management. In this approach, a set of documents of a specific type is characterized through specification by a DTD or another schema definition language such as XML Schema proposed by W3C. The set of documents matching a schema can then be regarded as a database instance for that schema. The constraints defined in the schema are enforced either at the time of document creation or at the time a document is stored in the repository. Searches for particular documents or parts of documents use the information structure expressed in the schema, greatly improving the precision of search engines in finding documents that match users' queries. External representations for the documents or their parts are typically specified by separate style sheets.

Managing documents with a structured documents approach has well-known benefits. The approach supports

- Consistency and correctness,
- Rich information retrieval capabilities,
- Information reuse and multi-channel publishing,

- Independence from particular software providers, and
- Long-term accessibility to information.

To achieve these benefits, the adoption of XML must be supplemented by several other tools. Processors for the style languages CSS and XSL are available for presenting the data through various viewers. The transformation language XSLT is available to specify transductions needed for the reuse of data and to tailor documents for publication in various channels. For querying the data, processors for the XQuery language, applications interfaces based on the Document Object Model (DOM), and XSLT processors can be deployed.

To store documents in XML form, repositories can be divided into two broad categories: those managed by native systems and those relying on relational database systems. Native systems are designed especially for the management of XML data. Complete systems include capabilities to define, create, store, validate, manipulate, publish, and retrieve XML documents and their parts. Some native systems, such as the Astoria XML Content Management Solution, are comprehensive document management systems with front-ends for users to work with documents. Others, such as Software AG's Tamino XML Server, provide software packages intended for building applications to manage XML data.

In the second form of repository, a relational or object-oriented database system is extended to support XML data. All current commercial database systems provide some XML support, including Oracle's XML DB, IBM's DB2 pureXML, and Microsoft's SQLXML. When conventional database systems were first used for XML, the data model of the original system was typically extended to encompass XML data, but the extensions defined simplified tree models rather than rich XML documents. More recently, however, relational database vendors have developed extensions that encompass XML more fully. In some approaches, whole documents can be stored either externally as independent files or internally in a column of a table. Elements and attributes can also be stored separately in side tables, which can be accessed independently or used for selecting whole documents. DTDs, which are typically stored in a special table, can be associated with XML documents and used to validate them.

1.5.2   Other Primary Data

XML databases are used for storing not only documents but also other kinds of data. Simple data types, such as numerics, logical values, dates, and times, may be declared in a schema language such as XML Schema, and stored in documents as simply as storing text strings. In fact, XML Schema defines a hierarchy of 45 built-in data types that are available for use in any document.

Many documents also need to include digital media information, such as pictures, videos, and audio clips. Such data is incorporated through entity references (where, for example, &DreamHouse; refers to the declared entity

```
<!ENTITY DreamHouse SYSTEM "../DreamHouse.gif" NDATA gif>)
```

in which case the data is connected to an XML document much as an attachment to an email message. When multimedia data is involved, XML can serve to tie video and audio together or to sequence pictures and audio into a slide show, using the Synchronized Multimedia Integration Language (SMIL).

Other complex data can also be represented by encoding component parts as nested elements within an XML document. For example, the Mathematical Markup Language (MathML) specifies how to represent complex mathematical equations, the Systems Biology Markup Language (SBML) specifies how to encode models of biochemical reaction networks, and the Chemical Markup Language (CML) specifies how to encode chemical molecular structures. XML has also been adopted outside the sciences: the Geography Markup Language (GML) specifies how to encode geographical features, MusicXML specifies how to encode musical scores, and HL7 v2.xml specifies how to encode health information.

1.5.3   Metadata

Metadata about documents and other primary information assets must be treated with as much care as the primary assets themselves. Such metadata includes who created or acquired the primary assets, when it was acquired, where it resides, who may use it, who *has* used it, and other information useful for managing the primary assets effectively. Metadata related to resources other than documents is also important. For example, for being able to use XML as a data interchange format between a set of software systems, data about the systems is needed. The following are examples of metadata:

- Information about each document in an organization's archive, including the author, date of creation, version, and keywords for each document;
- Access control, distribution information, and retention information for each active document in an organization;
- Information about the Web resources useful to an organization, including the Web address, publisher, publishing date, and expiry date for each of the resources;
- The schemas for the XML documents in an organization;
- The relational and other database schemas of the organization;
- Transaction logs for an organization, whether related to document updates or inventory control;
- A dictionary of essential terms used in the organization.

When data and its associated metadata share the same information format, both may be stored together. For example, the metadata associated with an HTML page is often stored in the <head> section of the page and the data itself is stored in the <body> section. If the metadata does not share a form with the data it describes, or if the metadata is voluminous and often retrieved independently of the associated data, then it is preferable to store it separately. For example, a dictionary of essential terms is often stored as a separate catalog, perhaps accessed via software that is designed to manipulate ontologies.

In Web communities there is a wide interest towards *semantic metadata* as a means to help people and computers to communicate better. Semantic metadata is not a new invention. Keywords have been traditionally used to describe the content of publications, thus providing some semantic information about the content. Ontologies represent refinements for this kind of metadata. An ontology describes the concepts and their relationships of a domain. For example, a music ontology might define concepts such as "Instrument", "Oboe", "Musician", and "Person", the relationship "Is A" between "Oboe" and "Instrument" as well as between "Musician" and "Person", and the relationship "To Play" between "Musician" and "Instrument". Clear definitions of concepts and their relationships have been regarded important for sharing common understanding of a domain even before the use of computers. However, if ontologies are intended to be used by computers, they must be defined in a formal way. The W3C has developed languages supporting the extension of the current Web to the *Semantic Web*, where the usability of heterogeneous resources, be they accessible on the Internet or in the intranets or extranets of organizations, is improved by metadata resources describing properties of resources in a standardized way.

1.5.4 Data Interchange and Web Services

Data is typically created and maintained within some department of an organization. Historically, it was very difficult for an organization to ensure that the data was accessible to other organizational units, and so each unit created and maintained independent copies of the same data. A major advantage of employing database management systems was to provide a centralized home for all data, thus permitting multiple units within an organization to share data. However, many organizations still suffer from data "silos" because of using incompatible hardware or software or because data managers are over-zealous in guarding the storage of their data.

Flexible data interchange is important in contemporary global and local networks connecting heterogeneous systems, data resources, and organizations. Following are typical alternatives for data interchange:

- Integration of systems by a common user interface,
- Integration of services by a portal,
- Data transmission between software systems within an organization, or
- Data transmission between software systems among distinct organizations.

With the growth of high-speed networks to connect the machines within one organization and to connect machines between organizations, there has been a rise in the growth of intranets and extranets, respectively. Before the advent of XML, data exchange between organizations was supported by electronic data interchange (EDI) standards. Because XML was designed to facilitate data exchange across the Internet, it is also well-suited to facilitate data exchange within an organization and between collaborative organizations. Thus traditional EDI standards have been gradually replaced by XML-based formats, both in commerce and in public administration.

An example of a public domain service utilizing XML for data exchange is Suomi.fi, a portal providing access to e-government services in Finland. In the portal the various public services are classified and described. Information related to various counties is automatically updated daily by the interconnection of the portal and a system controlled by the county union. In this interconnection, data is exchanged in XML form, using a document type developed especially for this purpose.

Not only is data encoded in XML, but the transactions themselves often use XML encodings. The Simple Object Access Protocol (SOAP) is an XML standard developed by W3C to describe which transaction is to be invoked on a remote machine and which parameters are to be used in executing the transaction. When the transaction has been completed on the remote machine, its success or failure is transmitted back to the first machine again using SOAP, which provides mechanisms to pass data back to the first machine as well. From this basis, users can establish an arbitrary network of computations involving exchanges of data among several machines within one room or dispersed across the Internet.

Capitalizing on this idea, service centers can be established at various sites across a network. Each center provides a specific service, such as finding appropriate travel arrangements or purchasing particular supplies, that is available to any users on the Web, including software agents as well as human users. XML is typically used to describe such Web services, often using the Web Services Description Language (WSDL). Other XML tools, such as Universal Description, Discovery, and Integration (UDDI) provide facilities for software agents to discover what services might be available and how to prepare data appropriately for moving the output of one service to the correct form for input to another.

1.6   Case Study: Communicating Via News Feeds

Technology for news feeds has served as an important contributor to the evolution from the original Web of interlinked HTML pages to the Web of social communities. A feed provides a form of summary of a Web site, or a portion of that site. As the content of the site is updated, the new information is transmitted to subscribers, much like syndicated broadcast or news. For such *Web syndication*, the content contributor for a site allows users to subscribe to a *feed*, which transmits updated versions of the contents to be read via software known as *feed readers* or *feed aggregators*. The reader software may be integrated into other software such as a Web browser. Figure 1.7 shows an Internet Explorer window where the user has opened a blog feed.

At a minimum, a feed includes a title, a description, and a link to the source site. Usually the feed also contains a list of items, such as a list of news from a news site, a list of events published on a university site, or a list of entries from a blog. Content providers and subscribers interchange feeds using standard XML-based formats. For example, Fig. 1.8 shows the XML format for the feed shown in Fig. 1.7.

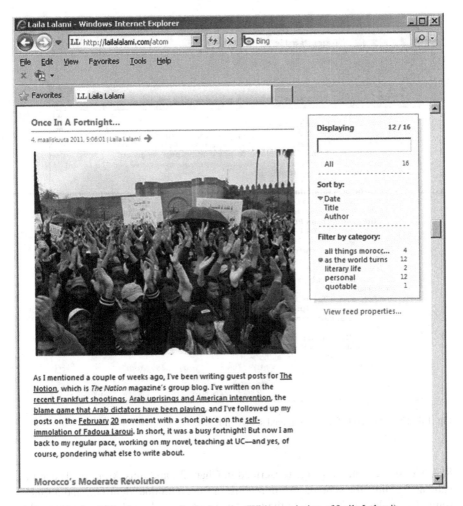

Fig. 1.7 Viewing a blog by means of a feed reader (With permission of Laila Lalami)

Several feed formats have been proposed, including RSS and Atom. The basic structure of feeds is the same in all formats, but there are differences in details and in the terminology. The RSS family of standards started with RSS 0.9, which was developed by Netscape in 1999. Possibly the version in widest use today is RSS 2.0 (*Really Simple Syndication*), which is published by the RSS Advisory Board [5]. RSS 1.0 (also known as *RDF Site Summary*) is a competing format defined using XML Schema and based on RDF, both of which are introduced in Chap. 3.

The Atom syndication format, proposed as an alternative to RSS, was published by the Internet Engineering Task Force (IETF) as RFC 4287 in 2005 [4]. In place of elements named channel and item in an RSS document, Atom includes element names feed and entry, respectively. Atom is formally defined by means of the

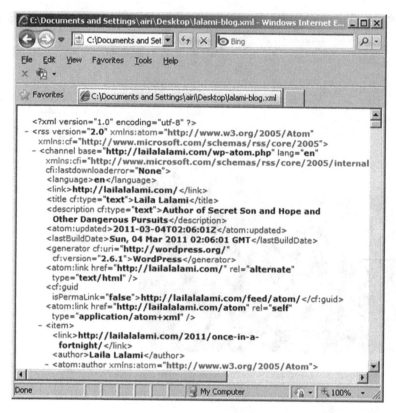

Fig. 1.8 The XML code for the blog feed shown in Fig. 1.7

RELAX NG schema language (described in Chap. 2), and thus Atom feeds can be validated against the schema. Atom requires a title, a unique identifier, and a time-stamp for the last update at both the feed level and for each feed entry. An example of the XML format for an Atom feed, representing a subset of a news feed for W3C emanating from the site at http://www.w3c.org/, is shown in Fig. 1.9.

In spite of the variety of feed formats, the use of feeds has continually expanded. The possibility to automatically export the content descriptions from various sites in the form of tagged text enables the aggregation of data and the creation of new services, for example, news sites providing latest news from a variety of newspapers. Page designers and authors can also embed feeds in their pages to form *mashups*, based on materials imported from external content providers.

In summary, news feeds illustrate both the difficulties and the benefits related to using XML. The difficulties arise from the difficulty of standards development and the evolution of many standards for the same purpose. Nevertheless, many benefits ensue from adopting the open textual data format provided by XML.

```
<?xml version="1.0" encoding="utf-8"?>
<feed xmlns="http://www.w3.org/2005/Atom">
   <title>W3C News</title>
   <link rel="alternate" type="text/html" href="http://www.w3.org/" />
   <link rel="self" type="application/atom+xml" href="http://www.w3.org/News/atom.xml" />
   <id>tag:www.w3.org,2008-09-29://4</id>
   <updated>2011-03-08T14:58:59Z</updated>
<entry>
   <title>Last Call: Ontology for Media Resources 1.0</title>
   <link rel="alternate" type="text/html"
         href="http://www.w3.org/News/2011.html#entry-9030" />
   <id>tag:www.w3.org,2011://4.9030</id>
   <published>2011-03-08T14:58:30Z</published>
   <updated>2011-03-08T14:58:30Z</updated>
   <summary>The Media Annotations Working Group has published a Last....</summary>
   <author>
      <name>W3C Staff</name>
   </author>
   <content type="html" xml:lang="en" xml:base="http://www.w3.org/">
      ...
   </content>
</entry>
</feed>
```

Fig. 1.9 An example of an Atom feed, extracted from a feed from www.w3c.org

References

1. Berners-Lee, T.: Information management: a proposal (March 1989, updated May 1990) http://www.w3.org/History/1989/proposal.html, Cited 5 Mar 2011.
2. Coombs, J.H., Renear A.H., DeRose, S.J.: Markup systems and the future of scholarly text processing. Communications of the ACM **30**, 11, 933–947 (1987).
3. Goldfarb, C.F.: The SGML Handbook. Y. Rubinsky (ed) Oxford University Press, Oxford, UK (1990).
4. Nottingham, M., Sayre, R. (eds): The Atom syndication format. Network Working Group, Request for Comments 4287, Proposed standard (December 2005) http://tools.ietf.org/html/rfc4287, Cited 9 March 2011.
5. RSS Advisory Board, RSS 2.0 Specification. http://www.rssboard.org/rss-specification, Cited 11 Mar 2011.
6. W3C, All Standards and Drafts. http://www.w3.org/TR/, Cited 5 Mar 2011.

Chapter 2
Fundamentals

Abstract The primary purpose of the chapter is to introduce the basics for reading and writing text with XML markup. The logical structure of an XML document includes primarily nested elements, some of which have associated attributes. A document type definition (DTD) can be included to constrain the contents and structure of the document. The concepts of *well-formedness* and *validity* of documents are defined. Two alternative constraining mechanisms, XML Schema and RELAX NG, are introduced and compared to DTDs. Finally, the two standard processing models for XML, one based on streams and one based on trees, are introduced. Although not all details of XML are covered, the chapter provides some literacy with respect to XML specifications, so that the complete language can be learned as necessary.

Keywords DTD • Formal grammars • Logical structure • Namespaces • Physical structure • Processing models • RELAX NG • Schema languages • XML documents • XSD

Chapter 1 introduced markup and some of the basic ideas and uses of XML. This chapter describes XML in more detail and how it is processed by computers. Like HTML, the unit of communication when using XML is a document.

The abbreviation XML comes from the name *Extensible Markup Language*. XML was developed initially for representing information in the context of the Internet. When using XML, software applications store and exchange data in the form of documents. Within those documents, structural elements are named and marked up in a systematic way to facilitate applications' processing of the elements. XML is a restricted form of SGML,[1] an older markup language.

The rules constraining all XML documents are defined in XML specifications published by the World Wide Web Consortium (W3C) as W3C Recommendations [23].

---

[1] SGML, the Standard Generalized Markup Language, was accepted as ISO standard 8879 in 1986 [16] and later augmented by supplements [17].

A. Salminen and F. Tompa, *Communicating with XML*,
DOI 10.1007/978-1-4614-0992-2_2, © Springer Science+Business Media, LLC 2011

The first W3C Recommendation for XML was published in 1998 [5]. Since then, four new editions of version 1.0 have been published, in 2000, 2004, 2006, and 2008. These four specifications do not define a new language version but provide corrections for errors discovered after publication of the previous edition. A new version 1.1 of XML was published in February 2004 [6], with a second edition in 2006.

The history leading to the development of XML, as well as the history of XML itself, is summarized in Appendix B. The XML development at W3C is closely related to both software development for processing XML and applications development activities where XML-related representation and communication languages are developed around the world for various communities and application areas. We describe the development process for W3C specifications in Sect. 3.1.

We start this chapter by first introducing the way XML and XML-based languages utilize formal grammar rules to define constraints for languages. In Sect. 2.2 we introduce the processing context of XML documents, which is needed to understand the role of various XML document components in XML communication. Then in Sect. 2.3 we give an overview of the data structure called *XML document*. The definition capabilities included in XML documents are described in Sect. 2.4. Finally, Sect. 2.5 introduces two alternative processing models for XML documents: stream processing and tree processing.

2.1   Formal Grammars

Natural and formal languages are both important in Web communications. Natural languages are used by humans to communicate among themselves; no technology need be involved unless the humans are separated from each other in space or time. For a particular natural language, there may be written rules for building valid sentences in the language, but the rules do not cover the full variety of expressions used by people. Furthermore, people can use a natural language long before they learn to articulate its rules.

XML documents very often include parts written in a natural language, but XML itself and the XML-based markup languages are formal languages, defined by formal grammars. A *formal language* is a set of character strings for which the characters are taken from a given alphabet and concatenated into strings according to exact rules. The language consisting of all positive numbers (that is, strings of digits, such as 301992, 7, and 4124) is an example of a formal language: we can define exact rules for testing whether or not a string belongs to the language. The following are other examples of formal languages:

- SGML, HTML, XML, and other markup languages deriving from SGML
- C, Java, C++, and other programming languages
- Algebraic expressions
- Roman numerals
- Social security identifiers
- Genetic code

The examples show that formal languages are usually developed by a group of people for a specific purpose, such as for computer programming or to represent information in computers. Such languages are developed to facilitate communication with a computer and between computers. Formal languages however seem to evolve also without human activities. The genetic code is an example that exists in nature and is documented as a formal language by humans.

The syntax of formal languages is often specified by a *formal grammar*. A formal grammar (or simply *grammar*) describes the strings of the language by a set of *production rules* (also simply called *rules* or *productions*). *Extended Backus–Naur Form* or *EBNF form* is a notation commonly used to describe such rules. EBNF is used in the XML specifications to describe the acceptable expressions that make up XML. The notation is introduced in the XML specification and in Appendix C of this book.

Each rule in the XML grammar describes one named part, using the form

symbol ::= expression

The symbol on the left is the name of the part, and the expression on the right describes the structure of the part. As examples, some productions of the XML 1.0 specification are shown here, where the number in brackets refers to the number of the production in the full specification.

[1]	document	::= prolog element Misc*
[3]	S	::= (#x20 | #x9 | #xD | #xA)+
[22]	prolog	::= XMLDecl? Misc* (doctypedecl Misc*)?
[27]	Misc	::= Comment | PI | S
[39]	element	::= EmptyElementTag | Stag content Etag
		[WFC: Element Type Match]
		[VC: Element Valid]

The first production defines the structure of an XML document. The order of the components on the right side is significant: the notation A B means that A comes before B. Thus, a document always contains a prolog followed by an element. After the element there are zero or more occurrences of parts called Misc, the potential omission or repetition being indicated by the *metasymbol* * (*asterisk*).

Production 3 defines the white space used in XML markup between structural components. It consists of space characters (#x20), tabs (#x9), carriage returns (#xD), or line feeds (#xA). Symbols of the form #xN in the XML syntactic notation refer to a particular Unicode character having code value corresponding to the hexadecimal integer N. Alternatives are separated in the production by the metasymbol | (*pipe*). The parentheses are used to group one part of the rule, and the metasymbol + (*plus*) following the ending parenthesis indicates that whatever is represented by the group can be repeated one or more times. Thus in XML, whitespace can be any string of one or more characters, each chosen from any of the four alternatives. Note that unlike the constituents of Production 1, the order of the individual characters comprising white space is not constrained.

Production rule 22 shows that a prolog may begin with an XML declaration (XMLDecl), where the metasymbol ? (*question mark* or *query*) shows that this part is not mandatory. The following Misc may occur zero or more times (indicated by the metasymbol *). At the end of the prolog there can be a document type declaration (doctypedecl) followed by zero or more Misc occurrences, again the ? indicating that this group is optional. Since none of the three components of a prolog are mandatory, a prolog can be an empty string (that is, a string consisting of no characters at all).

The part called Misc is defined in production 27, which specifies one of three alternatives: Misc is either a comment, a processing instruction (PI), or white space (S).

Production 39 defines an element. According to the production, an element is either an empty-element tag or it consists of a start-tag, content, and end-tag, in that order. Production 39 shows also the notation for associating two special kinds of constraints with productions: *well-formedness constraints* of the form [WFC: ...] and *validity constraints* of the form [VC: ...]. This production is associated with a well-formedness constraint called Element Type Match (which specifies that an element's end-tag must match the element type in the start-tag) and a validity constraint called Element Valid (which specifies the conditions for the validity of an element). The concepts well-formed and valid are introduced in the next section.

The document type definition (DTD) mechanism of XML is a tool for describing the production rules for a particular XML language. The DTD, together with the rules expressed in the XML specification, defines a formal language. Some of the notations used in the production rules of the XML specification are also used in DTDs to define the structure of elements. In defining element structures, for example, the metasymbols (,), ?, |, *, and + are used to refer to grouping, optionality, alternatives, and iteration, just as they are in the XML rules. This is elaborated in Sect. 2.4.2.

2.2 Processors and Applications

The XML specifications from W3C describe not only the structure of XML documents but also some essential aspects of the behavior of computer programs that process XML documents. There are two types of software modules mentioned in the specifications. A software module called an *XML processor* is used to read XML documents. The XML processor is not an independent software module but always works with another software module called an *application*. The XML processor provides the application access to the content and structure of documents (see Fig. 2.1). Although functionally distinct, often the XML processor is embedded as part of the application.

As explained in Chap. 1, an XML document contains marked up text and possibly other forms of data linked to the text by entity references. The XML processor reads the marked up text, separates the markup from other content, and checks that the text conforms to the rules defined for all XML documents in the XML specifications. Those rules are called *well-formedness rules* and documents fulfilling the

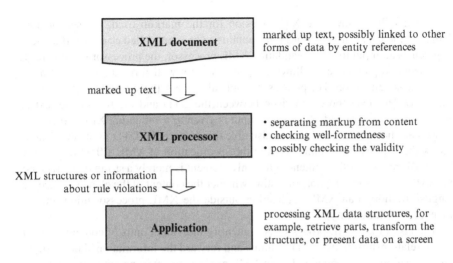

Fig. 2.1 The processing context of an XML document

rules are called *well-formed*. The checking is applied only to the marked up text, not the non-textual content linked to the marked up text by entity references nor the textual content indicated explicitly to be omitted from processing.

If an XML document has an associated DTD, then an XML processor may ensure not only that the document satisfies the well-formedness rules, but also that it satisfies the rules expressed in the DTD. An XML processor capable of performing this kind of testing is called *validating*, and the documents passing the tests are called *valid*. If an XML processor is only capable of testing the well-formedness of the input data, it is called *non-validating*.

Since an XML processor ensures that the input text follows defined syntactic rules, the processor is often called a *parser*. In computing environments, a parser is created for a particular language L, having particular grammar rules. The minimum functionality of the parser of any language is to inform the user (whether a human being or a software module) whether or not the input text belongs to the language L. Thus the parser in any XML processor tests whether the input belongs to the generic XML language. If the input is associated with a schema for a document type T, then the parser of a validating XML processor further tests whether the input belongs to the particular XML language called T.

Example 2.1 To give a more concrete idea about the tasks of an XML processor, we present a small example. Let the input be a file consisting of three text lines as follows:

```
<?xml version="1.0"?>
<!DOCTYPE plain_text [ <!ELEMENT plain_text (#PCDATA)> ]>
<plain_text>Today's weather is truly exceptional.</plain_text>
```

The first line shows the XML version for the markup used, the second line indicates the DTD, and the third line contains an element called plain_text. If the text is given as an input to a non-validating XML processor, the processor should check that the markup in the text follows the rules given for well-formed documents in the XML 1.0 specification. The processor should also check the syntactic correctness of the DTD. However, no comparison between the DTD and the rest of the text is made. On the other hand, if the same input is given to a validating XML processor, it does all the same tasks, but it is also able to compare the DTD to the element to check the validity constraints given in the specification of XML 1.0. However, for any XML processor the content of the only element is merely a string of characters; no XML processor is capable of testing whether the content of the element is proper English (although an XML application outside the XML processor might implement such functionality).

The task of an XML processor is to identify individual units of content, as well as the relationships between those units, and forward the information about them to an application. The application in an XML processing environment is any software module able to deal with XML data. Thus the application is the real consumer of XML data; the XML processor only checks the input and forwards the structural components to be handled by the application. For example, the application might connect to a database system to store the structural components into its internal structures. On the other hand, it might be capable of manipulating natural language text instead, and so it might be able to check that the content of the element in Example 2.1 is proper English.

Similarly to the parsers of programming languages, the XML processor informs its user (the application) about any violations of syntax rules in the text. The XML specifications define two kinds of violations of rules: *errors* and *fatal errors*. An XML processor may detect and report an error, and may recover from it, but not all XML processors need to detect errors. Fatal errors are kinds of violations that all conforming XML processors *must* detect and report to the application. Applications may be designed to handle data where the XML processor has found errors, but XML-conforming applications may not attempt to work normally when they are informed of fatal errors.[2] In the Web environment many authors of HTML documents are familiar with the flexibility of HTML browsers, which often represent documents that violate HTML rules in a manner in which the violations remain unnoticed. Typically, no information about the violations is given to the human reader of Web pages. This can also happen with XML documents for errors, but not for fatal errors. Thus an application's accommodation of XML data does not guarantee validity of a document, but well-formedness is assured.

The small example given above is intended to clarify the distribution of labor between an XML processor and application. In the following section we take a closer look at the components of XML documents.

---

[2] "Once a fatal error is detected, however, the processor *MUST NOT* continue normal processing (i.e., it *MUST NOT* continue to pass character data and information about the document's logical structure to the application in the normal way)." "This innocent-looking definition embodies one of the most important and unprecedented aspects of XML: 'Draconian' error-handling." [3]

2.3 XML Documents

Every XML document has a logical structure and a physical structure. Figure 2.1 shows an XML document as if it were stored in a single file. However, a document may consist of several physical files. In this section we first discuss the logical structure, then the physical structure, and finally the character encoding for XML documents.

2.3.1 Logical Structure

Effective communications among humans relies on organizing ideas into meaningful information structures. XML offers the means to present such communications in a form in which the structures and structural units are processable by software applications. The organization is expressed in the logical structure of documents, and the most important components of that structure are *elements*.

2.3.1.1 Elements and Nested Structures

Elements, like all other components of the logical structure, are indicated by explicit markup. As discussed in Chap. 1 and shown in our previous examples, elements in XML begin with a *start-tag* of the form < ... > and end with an *end-tag* of the form </... >. Both the start-tag and the end-tag include the name of the element.

XML does not set many restrictions for element names. They must start with a letter or an underscore (_) and can include arbitrarily many alphanumeric characters as well as periods, hyphens, underscores, diacritics, and various other typographic marks; most notably they cannot include white space characters. For example, if we want to label the string *1654* with the name *year*, we can present it as an XML element:

```
<year>1654</year>
```

The text between the tags is called the *content* of the element. Within a document, all elements having the same name belong to the same *element type*, and most applications are written such that all elements of one type are similarly processed. For example, a banking application could include processing code to handle all elements named deposit.

An element without content can be written without the end-tag, using a special kind of *empty-element tag* of the form < .../>. For example, the empty-element tag <br/> could be used to inform a printing application about the need for a carriage return. This is identical to the tagged string
</br> with no intervening characters.

An element's content can consist of plain character data, such as the year element above or the plain_text element in Example 2.1, or it can contain other elements as *child elements.* The child elements contained in a common *parent element* are called *sibling elements.* For example, an element showing a date could be written in the form

```
<date><day>11</day><month>12</month><year>1654</year></date>
```

This date element contains three child elements, named day, month and year, which are therefore siblings. The level of nesting is unlimited: any child element can itself have nested child elements. The following example shows three-level nesting of elements.

Example 2.2 The following XML document has two rhymes, one written in Finnish and the other in English. The outermost element is called rhymecollection (note that the name cannot include white space characters), and it contains two rhyme elements as its children. Each of the rhyme elements, in turn, consists of two line elements.

```
<?xml version="1.0"?>
<rhymecollection>
<rhyme>
<line>Ole aina iloinen</line>
<line>niin kuin pikku varpunen</line>
</rhyme>
<rhyme>
<line>See, see! What shall I see?</line>
<line>A horse's head where his tail should be</line>
</rhyme>
</rhymecollection>
```

An application showing tagged text to the user may highlight the nesting of elements through indentation. For example, if the text above is stored in a Microsoft environment as a file named with extension .xml, and the file is opened by Internet Explorer 6.0, the document is shown in the pretty-printed form:

```
<?xml version="1.0" ?>
- <rhymecollection>
  - <rhyme>
        <line>Ole aina iloinen</line>
        <line>niin kuin pikku varpunen</line>
    </rhyme>
  - <rhyme>
        <line>See, see! What shall I see?</line>
        <line>A horse's head where his tail should be</line>
    </rhyme>
  </rhymecollection>
```

The minus character (−) preceding a start-tag indicates that the element has child elements and the child elements are presented on the screen. By clicking the minus character, the child elements and the matching end-tag will be hidden and the minus character will be replaced by plus character (+). For example, after clicking the minus characters preceding the two rhyme elements, the document would be shown as

```
<?xml version="1.0" ?>
-<rhymecollection>
 +    <rhyme>
 +    <rhyme>
</rhymecollection>
```

All well-formed documents in XML have some restrictions on their nested structures, including the requirements for a single root element and proper nesting of elements. Thus, in the nested structure there is always exactly one outermost element, called the *root element* (or *document element*), and all non-root elements are fully contained in some other element. Thus, for example, in representing a collection of rhymes in an XML document, the rhymes have to be nested inside a common root element as was done in Example 2.2; there cannot be two elements at the outermost level of the nesting structure. *Proper nesting* means that if the start-tag of an element is part of the content of another element, the end-tag must also be part of the content of that same element. For example, markup such as

```
<date><day>11<month></day>12</month><year>1654</year><date>
```

is not correct in any XML document since elements day and month are not properly nested.

2.3.1.2 Unparsed Character Data

Text in XML documents consists of intermingled markup and character data. All text that is not defined as markup is character data. For cases where characters denoting markup should be included in the character data, a mechanism called a CDATA section is available. A CDATA section begins with markup <![CDATA[and ends with the markup]]>. All characters within these delimiters are regarded as character data, not markup. For example, to include the string

```
<lastname>Pirhonen</lastname>
```

as character data in some XML document, the following CDATA section would be used:

```
<![CDATA[<lastname>Pirhonen</lastname>]]>
```

This assures that none of the enclosed text is interpreted as markup.

2.3.1.3   Attributes

In the rhyme collection of Example 2.2, English and Finnish were the languages used in the rhymes. In this kind of situation, it might be useful to inform the application about the language in which a rhyme is written. This kind of extra information, or *metadata*, can be attached to elements by using *attribute specifications*. Attribute specifications can be added to the start-tag of an element, following some white space after the element name. An attribute specification gives the *name* of an attribute and a character string as the *value* of the attribute. For example, we can specify that a rhyme is in Finnish as follows:

```
<rhyme lang="FI"> ... </rhyme>
```

Notice that the end-tag does not repeat the attribute specification.

As a second example, assume the lastname elements in a document are used to give the current surname of a person. A former surname might be given by using the attribute earlier:

```
<lastname earlier="Rantanen">Korhonen</lastname>
```

The value of the attribute earlier for the element is Rantanen.

This example shows that there are two different techniques for providing a piece of data in XML elements: as element contents and as attribute values. In both cases a name can be attached to the datum. In the example above, the current surname of a person is expressed as the content of the lastname element and the former surname is given as the value of the attribute named earlier. It is also possible to give both names as child elements of the lastname element:

```
<lastname><current>Korhonen</current><earlier>Rantanen></earlier></lastname>
```

In this version, the current surname is given first in a child element named current and then the earlier name is given in a child element named earlier. The names could instead be given in the reverse order:

```
<lastname><earlier>Rantanen></earlier><current>Korhonen</current></lastname>
```

Yet another alternative is to give both names as attribute values of an empty element:

```
<lastname earlier="Rantanen" current="Korhonen"/>
```

or

```
<lastname current="Korhonen" earlier="Rantanen"/>
```

All of these alternatives provide information about the current and former surnames of a person. When the names are given as child elements of the same element, the XML processor informs the application about the order of the names. On the other hand, the order of attributes is insignificant. Therefore, from the point of view of an application, the last two alternatives are indistinguishable, whereas the others are all different.

2.3.1.4   Comments and Processing Instructions

As well as elements, which are the core components of the logical structure, other components of the structure are declarations, comments, and processing instructions. The XML declaration shown in Example 2.1 always starts an XML document. In XML version 1.0 the XML declaration is not mandatory, but it is in version 1.1. Nevertheless it is advisable to use it in all XML documents. Among the other declarations, the most essential are the markup declarations, which are described in Sect. 2.4.

Comments can be written to provide some extra information to the human reader of the marked up text. A comment begins with the character string '<!--' and ends with the string '-->', for example,

```
<!-- This is a comment -->
```

An XML processor may, but need not, make the text of the comment accessible to the application. Thus if comments are to be used by an application, it is important to ensure that the XML processor preserves them; however, to ensure robustness, applications are better designed if they treat comments as being completely optional.

Instead of using comments to pass information to an application, XML provides *processing instructions* to allow documents to contain instructions for applications. A processing instruction begins with the character pair '<?' and ends with the pair '?>'. The instruction is passed to the application and identified by a target name at the start of the instruction. The rest of the instruction is any character string meaningful to the application. The target name is intended to identify the application component to which it is directed. An example of the use of processing instructions is to provide information about an associated style sheet to some application rendering the document, as recommended by W3C [8]. For this purpose, the target name in the processing instructions is xml-stylesheet and additional information is provided by pseudo-attributes such as shown in the following example:

```
<?xml-stylesheet href="ownstyle.css" type="text/css"?>
```

The string after the target name xml-stylesheet looks like two attribute specifications, such as those that would be written inside the start-tag of an element. They are called pseudo-attributes because they are used to provide information to the application in the same way that attribute specifications are used, but they appear within a processing instruction rather as part of a start-tag. The example provides the application with information about an external CSS style sheet, in the same way as a style sheet association is given in HTML:

```
<LINK href="mystyle.css" rel="stylesheet" type="text/css">
```

2.3.1.5 Namespaces

A goal of the work at W3C is to support the reuse of XML structures once they are developed, especially if there is software available to support the processing of those structures. For example, structures relevant to banking (including withdrawals and deposits) may need to be handled by banking software and those relevant to mining (including the analysis of deposits and soil formations) may be handled by mining software. When reusing elements and attributes defined in previous environments, it is important that the XML processor can identify the context for each name and that document developers avoid name collisions. For example, element types named Title have been introduced in many different environments for different purposes. In one context the Title elements may be used for publication titles consisting of characters only, in another the Title elements may be used for property titles and contain child elements, and in a third Title elements may be used for titles of persons. If a developer wishes to use several or all of these element types in a single document, it is important that unintentionally duplicated names of elements or attributes can be distinguished.

As a more concrete example, let us consider the XHTML language, which describes the structures available in HTML, but is constrained so that XHTML documents are also XML documents. The structures and names defined in XHTML are widely known, and there is plenty of software able to process XHTML structures. It might be that some documents combine XHTML structures with structures from other XML-based languages, such as XQuery or MathML; in this situation, the processor should forward to the application information about the context within which to handle each structure. By following this approach, XHTML applications can manipulate the XHTML structures and ignore the others, if they wish to do so.

In order to support modularity of specifications and reuse of element definitions without name collisions, W3C has developed a method to associate an environment identifier with several element and attribute names so that the context can be recognized when they are used. Since the idea was developed after the original design of XML, the method is not described in the XML specification but in a separate *XML Names* specification [4].

A set of element and attribute names together with their identifier is called an *XML namespace*. The original method of identification was to use a *Uniform Resource Identifier (URI)* reference, which can be a URL (Uniform Resource Locator) that may be familiar from HTML links, or a URN (Uniform Resource Name). For example, the URI used to identify the elements and attributes defined in XHTML is http://www.w3.org/1999/xhtml, as indicated in the XHTML specification. In the new version of the XML Names specification, the identification mechanism was extended to *Internationalized Resource Identifier (IRI)* references [13]. Whereas a URI is a string of characters chosen from a subset of US-ASCII characters, an IRI extends URIs to a wider set of characters so that they can be used in the context of various natural languages.

A *namespace label*, which follows the rules for an element name, is bound to an IRI by a *namespace declaration* in the start-tag of the element where the namespace is introduced. For example, in the following element start-tag the label xhtml is associated with the IRI representing the XHTML namespace:

```
<report xmlns:xhtml = "http://www.w3.org/1999/xhtml">
```

Any names from this namespace are then referenced by using *qualified names* consisting of the label as a prefix and a name in the namespace, separated by a colon. Continuing with the example, after the namespace declaration introducing xhtml, any structural element or attribute from XHTML can be used within the element report by prefixing xhtml: to its name, producing qualified names such as, xhtml:meta or xhtml:h1. Thus, for example, within the report element, one might find

```
<xhtml:a xhtml:href = "example/figure">our results</xhtml:a>
```

Note that a namespace name can use any label, as long as it is distinct from other namespace labels. Therefore, instead of the label xhtml for the XHTML namespace we could define

```
<report xmlns:abba = "http://www.w3.org/1999/xhtml">
```

and then refer to the href attribute of the XHTML language as abba:href.

The XML Names specification does not constrain how the names within a namespace are defined. Often a namespace consists of all element and attribute names introduced in a document type definition or other kind of schema. However it is possible to specify the set of names included in a namespace by other means as well. In any case, to be able to refer to the names from a namespace requires the identification of the namespace by an IRI. Note that even if the namespace identifier is syntactically a URL, it does not refer to any location on the Web; rather it is simply a unique identifier. For example, if people in the sales department of MyCorp agree to use the URL http://sales.mycorp.com to identify a set of element and attribute names, this URL can be used for specifying the namespace, whether or not there is some data at that Web address.

2.3.2 Physical Structure

Each XML document has a physical structure as well as a logical one. The physical structure facilitates features not expressible by the logical structure alone. For example, the physical structure allows the inclusion of non-textual data in a document, even though the logical structure deals with marked up textual data only. Thus an XML document can also be a multimedia document. Building software to deal with the logical structure alone misses an important aspect of XML processing.

The physical structure of an XML document consists of units called *entities*. Each document includes a designated text entity called the *document entity* or *root entity*.

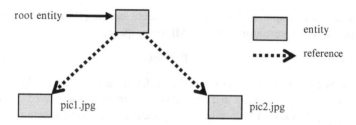

Fig. 2.2 A physical structure with three entities

All entities referred to directly or indirectly from the root entity are regarded as parts of the physical structure of the document. A common type of an entity is a non-textual file referenced from a text entity, and non-textual entities may include data in any format. Figure 2.2 shows the physical structure of a document with a root entity and two jpg images as non-textual entities.

2.3.2.1 Entity Types

Entities can be categorized according to three characteristics. The first indicates whether or not XML markup is to be interpreted: an entity is either *parsed* or *unparsed*. The second characteristic indicates where the content of an entity is given: an entity can be *internal*, in which case the content is given in the entity declaration, or *external* in which case the content is given as a separate physical object. The third characteristic indicates the use of entities: an entity is either a *general* entity, in which case it is used within the elements of the document, or a *parameter* entity used within the DTD. These three characteristics of entity types are further described as follows.

Parsed – unparsed. The content of a parsed entity consists of marked-up text intended to be analyzed by the XML processor. The root entity is always a parsed entity. An unparsed entity is a resource whose content may, or may not, be text; and if it is text, it may or not include XML markup. Regardless of content, however, an unparsed entity is not intended to be analyzed by the XML processor, and XML places no constraints on the content of unparsed entities. In Fig. 2.2 the document includes the tagged text of the document as a parsed (root) entity and the two figures as unparsed entities.

Each unparsed entity has an associated *notation*, identified by name. The notation informs the application of the data format of the entity so that the content can be managed appropriately.

The tagged text of a document need not be all stored at the root; it may be divided into two or more parsed entities. The ways text can be split into parsed entities is regulated by the rules defined for *well-formed parsed entities* in the XML specification, and in a well-formed document, all parsed entities must be well-formed. The well-formedness rules are defined so that the logical and physical structures in an XML document are properly nested. For example, both the start and end of an element must be within the same (physical) entity.

Example 2.3 In Example 2.2 a collection of rhymes was presented as an XML document stored in one entity. The rhyme collection can be divided into two or more parsed entities, but all of them have to be well-formed. For example, an entity with the following content is not acceptable because it contains the end-tag of the element rhymecollection but not its start-tag:

```
<rhyme>
<line>See, see! What shall I see?</line>
<line>A horse's head where his tail should be</line>
</rhyme>
</rhymecollection>
```

On the other hand, the text

```
<rhyme>
<line>See, see! What shall I see?</line>
<line>A horse's head where his tail should be</line>
</rhyme>
```

or the text

```
See, see! What shall I see?
```

or even

```
hat shall I se
```

could appear as the content of a well-formed entity.

External – internal. Memory units managed as separate files in XML processing environments represent external entities. An alternative type of an entity is an internal entity, a named piece of text contained within another entity and intended to be analyzed by an XML processor. The text piece is called the value of the entity. An internal entity is always a parsed entity. This kind of entity is used, for example, to avoid repetitive writing of long or otherwise complex pieces of text. For example, if we assign the name UJ to the string

```
University of Jyväskylä
```

we can include the longer text value in a document by referring to UJ. References to named, parsed entities are called *entity references*. In processing the XML document, the XML processor replaces the name by its value before transmitting data to the application. The syntax of entity references will be given below in Sect. 2.4.5.

Parameter – general. The separation of entities into general and parameter entities is based on the context of their use in a document. A parameter entity is for use within a DTD, whereas a general entity is for use within the element content of a document. A parameter entity is always a parsed entity.

Table 2.1 The five possible combinations of entity types

Parsed	Internal	Parameter
Parsed	Internal	General
Parsed	External	Parameter
Parsed	External	General
Unparsed	External	General

To conclude the characterization of entity types, let us consider the possible combinations of characteristics. Even though there are two possible settings for each of the three characteristics, all combinations are not possible. An unparsed entity cannot be internal, nor can it be a parameter entity. On the other hand, parsed entities can be either internal or external and either general or parameter entities. Therefore there are five possible combinations for characteristics of entity types, as summarized in Table 2.1.

2.3.2.2　Motivations for the Use of Entities

Casual authoring of XML documents can be done without knowing much about entities. In professional use of XML, however, entities play an important role.

There are several reasons why it is often important to divide an XML document physically into multiple pieces. We have already mentioned one: when *non-textual data* is to be included in XML documents, external unparsed (general) entities are needed. However, parsed entities can also provide support to document creators.

The possibility to name a piece of text and to refer to it by an entity reference, instead of writing it in full, is a valuable mechanism to ensure consistency when that text must be repeated many times. Just as the namespace mechanism facilitates reuse of element and attribute definitions originating from different sources, the entity mechanism facilitates reuse of text fragments, either in the element content or in the DTD. For example, a title appearing several times in a document can be defined as a general entity. Similarly a piece of a definition intended to be used in the DTD in several places can be defined as a parameter entity. In its simplest form, the repeated text is a single character, more particularly a special character not directly accessible from the keyboard. However, the entity can also be an arbitrarily large fragment of boilerplate.

Referring to a piece of text by its name, instead of using the text itself, often simplifies writing, but more importantly it supports *consistent* writing. This is especially important when boilerplate is required and in environments where several content authors coordinate in writing texts. For example, in a text about W3C technical specifications repeatedly mentioning the terms "W3C Recommendation", "W3C Proposed Recommendation", "W3C Candidate Recommendation", and "W3C Working Draft", and in the absence of controls, authors might easily write the terms in slightly different ways. If entity names, such as Rec, PRec, CRec, and WD, are used instead, then the terms for the various kinds of W3C technical specifications will appear in the final documents in a consistent form, in spite of sections being written by distinct content authors.

The naming facility is especially important for *modularity* and *maintainability*. For example, several schema designers may be involved in the design of a large DTD, which evolves through several versions. The work can be partitioned into modules by dividing the DTD into several entities where each of the designers focuses on his or her own module. If a designer makes changes to the definitions in one module, the other designers using the definitions by reference need not make any changes to their modules. Similarly if an organization's legal department updates the wording of a disclaimer, and that disclaimer is stored as the content of a parsed entity and referenced from each place it is required, the new wording will automatically be incorporated in all the organization's documents.

Entities can also be used to provide consistent *semantic information* aimed at human readers. For example, consider a situation where an attribute for a date is used in several element types. If the schema for the class of documents is defined by the DTD mechanism, the capabilities to constrain the attributes' values are very limited. However, the schema designer can provide information about the intended form of the dates by defining a parameter entity, say Date, that includes the following comment:

```
<!--a date given by eight digits in the form DDMMYYYY, for example, 24022005 -->
```

Such a comment might help document authors to write dates consistently. If consistent date forms are used, an application could be implemented to recognize the name Date as an attribute type and safely assume that the attribute values will be eight digit numbers representing DDMMYYYY.

2.3.3   Character Encoding

Text in XML documents is encoded using the Unicode character set. Unicode is intended to serve as a character set for representing textual data written in any natural language of the world; it is even independent of the writing direction of the language.

The set of characters available in Unicode is huge, and therefore mechanisms are needed to be able to express a particular character without the need to use a symbol representing that character in a particular natural language. For example, this is especially important in situations where a character is not directly accessible from the keyboard or other available input device. There are two ways to refer to single characters without using their symbols. First, as we mentioned in Sect. 2.3.2, the value of an entity may be merely a single character; how to reference such an entity will be described in Sect. 2.4.4. Secondly, a single character can be referred to by a *character reference*, without defining an entity for that character. A character reference provides a decimal or hexadecimal representation of a character's code point in Unicode. The reference begins with the characters &# and ends with a semicolon (;). The letter x after the characters &# signals the use of hexadecimal representation. For example, " or " refers to the quotation mark by specifying code point 34 (hexadecimal 22) in the Unicode character set.

One problem related to character coding is the continuous evolution of natural languages. Since languages evolve, Unicode must also evolve. This evolution was not realized in the specification of version 1.0 for XML, where the characters used in XML markup, like the element and attribute names, were defined to be characters from Unicode 2.0. This has caused limitations in the use of XML since Unicode has subsequently been extended to versions 3.0 and 4.0, and there will be later versions in the coming years. This problem related to Unicode versioning was one of the major reasons for developing the new version 1.1 for XML.

2.4   Declaring and Constraining Structures

Extensibility is an important feature of XML. Like its predecessor SGML, XML is a *metalanguage*, a language for describing other languages. The XML specification does not define the element or attribute names to be used in documents, nor the element structures to be used. The idea behind XML is to agree on a notation for developing special vocabularies and markup languages for particular purposes. Thus anyone can extend the rules provided in the XML specification with his or her own rules to constrain the documents for a particular application area.

2.4.1   DTD and Markup Declarations

Documents based on a common structure (or language) are said to be of the same *document type*, and the structure for a particular language is defined by markup declarations in a *Document Type Definition* (*DTD*). The declarations of a DTD define the accepted element types and attributes, as well as the logical structure of documents of the type. Along with the constraints for logical structure, declarations in the DTD are also used to introduce the entities available for inclusion in documents of the type. The markup declarations can be given either locally, in the root entity of the document in the *document type declaration*, or externally in a separate file, as a separate entity. In the latter case, the address of the file must be provided by the document type declaration. The terms *internal subset* and *external subset* refer to the locally and externally given markup declarations, respectively. The external subset is also an external entity.

In Example 2.1 a document was given with a local DTD:

```
<?xml version="1.0"?>
<!DOCTYPE plain_text [ <!ELEMENT plain_text (#PCDATA)> ]>
<plain_text> Today's weather is truly exceptional.</plain_text>
```

The document type *declaration* consists of the shadowed line, which contains the DTD (document type *definition*). If the DTD is specified externally, in a separate file, then the name of the file should be provided in the document type declaration in place of the DTD itself. Thus, an external DTD is attached to a document as follows:

```
<?xml version="1.0"?>
<!DOCTYPE plain_text SYSTEM "mytext.dtd">
<plain_text> Today's weather is truly exceptional.</plain_text>
```

In this example, the system identifier mytext.dtd specifies where to find the DTD for the document.

Four kinds of markup declarations are available for constraining XML documents: element type declarations and attribute list declarations to constrain the logical structure, and entity and notation declarations to constrain the physical structure. Before going into the particular types of declarations, we first give an introductory example to demonstrate how DTDs can be used to constrain documents.

Example 2.4 Example 2.2 above showed a document with two rhymes. The markup vocabulary and structure for the markup used in Example 2.2 can be defined by the following DTD:

```
<!DOCTYPE    rhymecollection [
<!ELEMENT    rhymecollection        (title?, rhyme+)>
<!ELEMENT    title        (#PCDATA)>
<!ELEMENT    rhyme        (line+)>
<!ATTLIST    rhyme
      xml:lang  (fi | en)   #IMPLIED
      author    CDATA       #IMPLIED >
<!ELEMENT    line        (#PCDATA)>        ]>
```

The definition consists of four *element* type declarations and one *attribute list* declaration (ATTLIST). The attribute list declaration introduces two attributes for elements of type rhyme. In the definition, the following constraints are defined for documents of type rhymecollection:

Element names. Only the element names rhymecollection, title, rhyme and line are allowed in the documents.

Attributes. Two attributes can be attached to the rhyme element: xml:lang and author. The data types of the attribute values are defined after the attribute names. In the example, the value of the attribute xml:lang is to be taken from an enumerated list (either the string "fi" or the string "en"), and the value of the attribute author is a character string (CDATA). The repeated keyword #IMPLIED indicates that either or both of the attributes can be given in the start-tag of a rhyme element, but neither of them is mandatory (and any application must infer a missing attribute's value from context).

Structure. The root element of the document is of type rhymecollection. The structural constraints concerning elements of the type are given by the content model (title?, rhyme+) using metasymbols ? and + from the EBNF notation introduced in

Sect. 2.1. It indicates that an element of the type rhymecollection contains one or more rhyme elements, possibly preceded by an element of type title. The content model (line+) defines a rhyme element as a structure consisting of one or more line elements. In the declarations of the element types title and line, the keyword (#PCDATA) indicates that the elements of these two types consist of character data devoid of markup characters.

Although it is well-formed, the tagged text describing two rhymes in Example 2.2 is not a *valid* document of any type, since there is no DTD attached to the text. However, the text meets the element type constraints defined in the DTD given in Example 2.4. Assume that the DTD is accessible at rhymes.dtd. The document of Example 2.2 would then be valid if it includes the following document type declaration after the XML declaration and before the root element:

```
<!DOCTYPE rhymecollection SYSTEM "rhymes.dtd">
```

2.4.2   Element Type Declarations

An element type declaration defines a name for a set of elements and constrains the content of those elements. In other words, it specifies what are acceptable element names and what is acceptable between the start-tag and end-tag in each element. The syntax for the element type declaration is given by production rules 45 and 46:

```
[45] elementdecl ::= '<!ELEMENT' S Name S Contentspec S? '>'
                                              [VC: Unique Element Type  Declaration]
[46] contentspec    ::= 'EMPTY' | 'ANY' | Mixed | Children
```

The validity constraint named Unique Element Type Declaration is attached to the element type declaration and specifies that an element name cannot appear in more than one type declaration.

Rule 46 gives four alternatives for constraining an element's content:

- The content must be empty (EMPTY),
- The content is completely unconstrained (ANY),
- The content may directly include child elements and character data (Mixed), or
- The content may directly include child elements only (Children).

If the element type specifies mixed content, then the elements of that type may contain character data optionally interspersed with child elements. Unlike the specification ANY, the types of the child elements may be constrained; unlike Children, the order and the number of occurrences of child elements cannot be constrained in mixed content.

Example 2.5 Suppose that the content of a paragraph should consist of character data interspersed with phrases intended to be rendered in italics or in bold. We could define an element type for such a paragraph where the rendering information is indicated by markup. The following types could be defined for this purpose:

```
<!ELEMENT    paragraph (#PCDATA | italics | bold)*>
<!ELEMENT    italics            (#PCDATA)>
<!ELEMENT    bold               (#PCDATA)>
```

All three element types are examples of mixed content definitions, but the content of the types italics and bold consists of character data only. A paragraph element may contain characters only, it may consist of arbitrarily many child elements of types italics or bold or both, or it may contain character data interspersed with such child elements, for example:

```
<paragraph>Viljo Revell is the architect of the Toronto City Hall</paragraph>
<paragraph>
  <bold>Viljo Revell</bold>is the architect of the<italics>Toronto City Hall</italics>
</paragraph>
<paragraph>
  <italics>Viljo Revell</italics> is the architect of the <italics>Toronto City Hall</italics>
</paragraph>
<paragraph>
  <bold>Viljo Revell is the architect of the Toronto City Hall</bold>
</paragraph>
```

Metasymbols |, *, (, and) are used in the mixed content definitions with the same semantics as in the XML syntax notation described in Sect. 2.1 above. The list of alternatives must start with #PCDATA, and the order of the child element types has no significance. Since the number of occurrences of child elements cannot be constrained, the symbol * always appears after the alternatives for child elements. An element type definition equivalent to the definition of type paragraph in Example 2.5 is

```
<!ELEMENT    paragraph    (#PCDATA | bold | italics)*>
```

but none of the following describe mixed content in a well-formed XML document:

```
<!ELEMENT        paragraph    (bold | italics | #PCDATA)*>
<!ELEMENT        paragraph    (#PCDATA |bold | italics)>
<!ELEMENT        paragraph    (bold | italics)*>
```

This is an example of the limitations included in the XML specification to simplify the building of XML processors. The incorrect forms of definition could make as much sense as the correct ones, but by constraining the forms allowed in element type definitions, the parsing of XML documents becomes easier and therefore building the software for parsing becomes more straightforward.

As these examples illustrate, the constraining capabilities of mixed content are limited. However, if the content is to include child elements only, without any interspersed character data, the element structure can be constrained by a *content model* where the metasymbols '+', '*', '|', '?', '(', and ')' are available to constrain the element structure. The semantics of the metasymbols is again the same as in the XML syntax notation (see Sect. 2.1). However, whereas no separate symbol is used to indicate concatenation in the XML syntax notation, in content models two successive content particles are separated by a comma (,).

Example 2.6 The following examples show four element type declarations:

```
<!ELEMENT      product        (mfg, model, description, clock?)>
<!ELEMENT      model          (#PCDATA)>
<!ELEMENT      description     (#PCDATA | feature)*>
<!ELEMENT      clock          EMPTY>
```

The first declaration defines an element content model, the second and third specify mixed content, and the fourth constrains the type to be empty. Elements of type product must always begin with an element of type mfg, then an element of type model, and after that an element of type description. At the end there may or may not be an element of type clock. Child elements of type model contain character data only, and description elements may contain character data interleaved with child elements of type feature. If there is a clock child, it will always be empty.

Example 2.7 Document type definition for a phone number:

```
<!DOCTYPE      phone [
<!ELEMENT      phone          (areacode, number)>
<!ELEMENT      areacode       (#PCDATA)>
<!ELEMENT      number         (#PCDATA)>            ]>
```

This grammar defines a language that includes each of the following three sentences:

- `<phone><areacode>0146119</areacode><number>2603031</number></phone>`

- `<phone><areacode>014</areacode><number>university</number></phone>`

- `<phone><areacode>#5 silly bits</areacode><number>2603031</number></phone>`

These examples demonstrate that even if a phone number in XML format is valid with respect to this DTD, it does not necessarily represent the correct form of a phone number as we normally understand it. The DTD mechanism is not always expressive enough to constrain elements' contents to values within the domain intended by the application designer. For this reason W3C has also defined the more powerful XML Schema facility, which is described briefly in Sect. 2.4.6.

2.4.3 Attribute List Declarations

Attributes are used to attach information to elements using name-value pairs. Attributes can be attached to elements in two ways, either explicitly by an attribute specification or by declaring a default value as part of the attribute in the document type definition. In the latter case, the XML processor associates the attribute name and value with the element. Explicit attribute specifications appear either in the start-tag of an element or in the empty-element tag. In a valid document all attributes written in tags must be declared.

An attribute list declaration defines the set of attributes pertaining to a given element type, establishes type constraints for the attributes, and provides default values and constraints on the presence of attributes. The syntax of an attribute list declaration is specified by productions 52 and 53:

```
[52] AttlistDecl ::= '<!ATTLIST' S Name Attdef* S? '>'
[53] AttDef    ::= S Name S AttType S DefaultDecl
```

The first rule states that an attribute list declaration includes a name and zero or more attribute definitions. The name given must refer to the name of an element type. In each of the attribute definitions, we find the name for an attribute, a data type for that attribute, and a default declaration. For example, in the following attribute list declaration an attribute called author is defined for the element type poem; the attribute must be a character string, denoted by the type CDATA:

```
<!ATTLIST      poem     author CDATA  #REQUIRED >
```

The default declaration in an attribute definition is used to provide information on whether the presence of the attribute is required, and if not, how an XML processor is to react if the declared attribute is not present in an element. The default declaration has four different forms:

- #REQUIRED   the attribute must always be explicitly provided
- #IMPLIED   the attribute may be provided; no default value is given
- AttValue   the attribute may be provided; AttValue (a quoted string) is the default value for the attribute if it is omitted
- #FIXED AttValue the attribute must always have the default value given by the quoted string AttValue

In the above example, the constraint #REQUIRED indicates that the attribute author must always be explicitly included in poem elements and no default value is given to the attribute. Thus in a valid document the start-tag <poem author="Murasaki Shikibu"> is correct but the stand-alone tag <poem> is not. On the other hand, if the attribute author is instead defined for the element type poem as follows

```
<!ATTLIST      poem     author CDATA  #IMPLIED >
```

then both of the start-tags <poem author="Murasaki Shikibu"> and <poem> are accepted
in a valid document. Similarly, both are valid if a default value is given, as in the
following declaration:

<!ATTLIST   poem   author CDATA "Ono no Takamura ">

In this case it is possible to provide the attribute explicitly in the element, as
above, but if it is not provided then the XML processor attaches the attribute to the
element with the default value. The symbol #FIXED should be specified in the declaration if the default must always be used as the value of the attribute.

While the character data in the content of elements cannot be constrained (#PCDATA
allows any characters to be included), attribute values can be constrained to be within
any of several data type families: a string type, several tokenized types, and enumerated
types. The *string type* is expressed in the declaration by the symbol CDATA as shown in
the above examples. *Tokenized types* are used in cases where the attribute value can be
constrained into a certain kind of token or list of tokens. There are seven different
tokenized types: ENTITY, ENTITIES, NMTOKEN, NMTOKENS, ID, IDREF, and IDREFS. The
plural forms refer to lists of tokens separated by white space.

The types ENTITY and ENTITIES are used to specify that the value of the attribute
must be a name of an unparsed entity or a list of such names, respectively.

The types NMTOKEN and NMTOKENS are used to specify values that are made up
of name characters only. For example, an attribute phase of type NMTOKEN could be
defined for an element type report as follows:

<!ATTLIST   report   phase NMTOKEN #IMPLIED >

The start-tag <report phase="draft"> would then be correct while the tag <report
phase="preliminary draft"> would not be accepted since a space is not accepted as a
name character. Both XML versions 1.0 and 1.1 define constraints for the first character accepted in a name. In version 1.0, only a letter, underscore (_), or colon (:) is
accepted as the first character of a name; version 1.1 is not as restrictive, but it also
does not accept any of the digits 0–9 at the start of a name.

Types ID, IDREF, and IDREFS allow users to associate unique names with elements in XML documents, and reference those names from other elements. The
values of type ID must be tokens accepted as names, and in a valid document every
ID value must be unique across all elements that bear any attribute of the type; that
is, a name must not appear as the value for an attribute of type ID more than once in
an XML document. For example, if attribute article_number has been defined to be of
type ID for the element type article and the value A123 appears as the value for article_
number on some article element, then it cannot appear as the value of *any* other ID
type attribute for another article nor for any other element type.

Each name appearing in the value of attribute types IDREF or IDREFS must appear
in the same document as the value of some ID type attribute. If attribute article_refer-
ence of type IDREF has been defined for the element type paragraph, the start-tag
<paragraph article_reference="A123"> can appear only if there is an ID type attribute
with the value A123 in the document. If the attribute article_reference is defined with
type IDREFS, the start-tag <paragraph article_reference="A123 A567"> can appear if

there is an ID type attribute with value A123 and another ID type attribute with value A567. A common practice is to give the name id to ID type attributes.

The attribute types ID and IDREF(S) offer a restricted tool for unique identification and cross-referencing. As just described, since each value of type ID must be unique within the document, the same value cannot be used for different element types nor for different attributes. Furthermore, in a valid XML document, the value associated with any attribute of type IDREF or included in a list of values for an attribute of type IDREFS must match the value associated with an attribute of type ID *within the same document*. Thus, the mechanism can be used only inside a single document, not across a set of documents.

In the attribute definition using an *enumerated type*, the attribute values to be accepted in valid documents are specified as part of the declaration. For example, if we would like to associate the root element of the document type report with an attribute phase to show the state of progress, the values could be given in the following way:

```
<!ATTLIST     report    phase    (draft | comments_requested | final)  #REQUIRED >
```

Instead of declaring the attribute to be mandatory, the declaration

```
<!ATTLIST     report    phase    (draft | comments_requested | final)  "draft" >
```

specifies that the value draft is the default value. In this case, if the attribute is not present in a report element, then the processor supplies the value draft.

Example 2.8 Two attributes are declared for the element type clock as follows:

```
<!ATTLIST     clock     setting  CDATA      #IMPLIED
                        alarm    (yes | no | dual) "yes"  >
```

The attribute setting is a string type attribute without any default value. Attribute alarm is of enumerated type with three valid values: yes, no and dual. Because of the specified default, if there is no attribute alarm explicitly included in the start-tag of a clock element, the XML processor must attach the attribute with value yes to the element. The following hypothetical product description provides an example of the use of these attributes:

```
<product >
   <mfg>Nokia</mfg><model>8890</model>
   <description> Intended for EGSM 900 and GSM 1900 networks.</description>
   <clock setting= "nist" alarm = "no"/>
</product>
```

The constraining mechanism provided by DTDs for attribute types is very limited. Nevertheless, if an application uses the DTD mechanism as the schema language, the existence of some limited facility for attribute typing and the lack of facilities for typing character data found in element content may be influential when deciding whether to use elements or attributes for some data.

In addition to application-defined attributes, there are two predefined attribute names, xml:space and xml:lang, available for use in XML documents. The prefix xml indicates that the names are reserved by the XML specification. Nevertheless, in valid documents these predefined attributes, like any other, must be declared if they are used. Attribute xml:space signals an intention that white space should be preserved by applications in the element, and its type must be an enumerated type with values default and preserve. The attribute xml:lang is used to specify the language of the contents and of other attribute values of an element. The values of the attribute must be a subset of the codes defined in the specification IETF RFC 1766, which uses abbreviations such as en, fr, fi, en-GB, and en-US to denote a language. For example, these attributes could be declared for the type poem as follows:

```
<!ATTLIST     poem     xml:space (default | preserve)    "preserve"
              xml:lang  (fi | en)    "fi"     >
```

Before an attribute's value is passed to an application or checked for validity, the XML processor normalizes it by applying the algorithm given in Sect. 3.3.3 of the XML specification. The normalization converts character and entity references and white space to a standard form in which references are replaced by their values. Character and entity references and their replacement are considered further in Sect. 2.4.5 below.

2.4.4   Entity and Notation Declarations

In a valid document, all entities must be declared before they are used. The declaration gives a name and, in the case of internal entities, a value for the entity. For external entities a reference to the external file must be provided. The value of the internal entity given in the declaration is called a *literal entity value*.

The declarations for parameter and general entities are distinguished by the presence or absence of one character: a parameter entity is introduced by a percent sign (%) before the name of the entity, whereas a general entity is not. As examples, consider first the following general entity declaration:

```
<!ENTITY xml-spec "Bray, T., Paoli, J., Sperberg-McQueen, C.M., & Maler, E. (Editors),
Extensible Markup Language (XML) 1.0 (Second Edition),
W3C Recommendation 6 October 2000">
```

The 156-character string starting with "Bray" and ending with "2000" is given the name xml-spec. Once declared as a general entity, it is usable as often as desired within the elements of a document, but not in the DTD. On the other hand, the character % in the following declaration shows that it is declaring a parameter entity:

```
<!ENTITY % chapter_attributes
         "author    NMTOKEN       #IMPLIED
          date      CDATA         #REQUIRED"    >
```

This entity is named chapter_attributes and is defined to represent two attribute definitions that may be needed repeatedly in the DTD. Unlike general entities, parameter entities are used in DTDs only and not elsewhere in documents.

Since parameter and general entities are recognized in different contexts, and they use different forms of reference, they also occupy different namespaces. This means that a general entity and a parsed entity with the same name are two distinct entities.

The literal value of internal entities is not necessarily the value by which the name of the entity is replaced at the place where it is used. As stated above, some processing of entity and character references in the literal may be needed before the replacement; this is further discussed in Sect. 2.4.5.

Example 2.9 The following examples of parameter entity declarations appear in the XHTML specification [20].

```
<!ENTITY % URI "CDATA">
    <!-- a Uniform Resource Identifier, see [RFC2396] -->
<!ENTITY % UriList "CDATA">
    <!-- a space separated list of Uniform Resource Identifiers -->
<!ENTITY % StyleSheet  "CDATA">
    <!--stylesheet data -->
<!ENTITY % Text "CDATA">
    <!--used for titles etc. -->
<!-- core attributes common to most elements
        id              document-wide unique id
        class           space separated list of classes
        style           associated style info
        title           advisory title/amplification
-->
<!ENTITY % coreattrs
        "id             ID                      #IMPLIED
        class           CDATA                   #IMPLIED
        style           %StyleSheet;            #IMPLIED
        title           %Text;                  #IMPLIED" >
<!ENTITY % heading  "h1 | h2 | h3 | h4 | h5 | h6">
<!ENTITY % list  "ul | ol | dl">
```

For external entities a *system identifier* is given to allow the XML processor or its client application to locate the entity. For example, an external entity section1 could be declared to be found at the location given:

```
<!ENTITY section1 SYSTEM "http://www.cs.jyu.fi/opetus/xml/section1.xml">
```

In this case the system literal is an absolute URI reference. It can also be a relative URI, to be converted to an absolute URI reference by the XML processor. The string given as a system literal may also contain characters intended to be escaped before a URI can be used to retrieve the referenced entity. The handling of relative URIs and escape characters is described in Sect. 4.2.2 of the XML specification. The system identifier is sometimes preceded by a public identifier, which is intended to provide a label generally understood by the applications. The XML processor may use any combination of the public identifier and system identifier, as well as some additional information, in attempting to retrieve the entity's content.

The previous example declared section1 to be an external parsed entity. The declaration of an *unparsed* entity requires the identification of the file format for the entity, which is specified by a notation name introduced by a *notation declaration*. The notation declaration provides an external identifier that allows the XML processor or its client application to locate a suitable application capable of processing data in the given format. Notation names are used not only in entity declarations to specify the format of unparsed entities, but can also appear in attribute-list declarations for enumerated attribute types. A notation for using pictures in gif format could be introduced by the following notation declaration:

```
<!NOTATION gif  PUBLIC
  "-//ISBN 0-7923-9432-1::Graphic Notation//NOTATION CompuServe Graphic
  Interchange Format//EN" >
```

The notation can then be used to declare an external unparsed entity as follows:

```
<!ENTITY picture1  SYSTEM "../pictures/scenery.gif" NDATA gif>
```

The presence of the token NDATA followed by the token gif declares that picture1 uses the notation gif, and together with the notation declaration notifies the XML processor that it should invoke an appropriate graphics handler.

Five general entities, amp, lt, gt, apos, and quot, are predefined in the XML specification and therefore need not, and must not, be declared in a DTD. These are used to escape the markup delimiters (ampersand (&), left angle bracket (<), right angle bracket (>), apostrophe ('), and quotation mark ("), respectively).[3]

2.4.5 *XML Processor Treatment of Entities and References*

A validating processor includes an entity in the physical structure of an XML document if it is the root entity, an external subset of the document type definition, or an entity referred to by its name in an entity included in the physical structure. A non-validating processor does not necessarily read external entities.

---

[3] By default, curly apostrophes and quotation marks are commonly used in place of straight ones in documents prepared by word processors. However, these marks are not accepted by XML processors and are a common cause of parsing errors when examples are copied for XML parsing.

Table 2.2 Contexts for referencing entities and characters

Referencing type	Contexts
Unparsed entity reference	• As attribute value in a start-tag or in an attribute definition
Parameter entity reference	• Document type definition
	• Entity value (for an entity used in a document type definition)
General entity reference	• Element content
	• Attribute value either in a start-tag or in an attribute definition
	• Entity value

Unparsed entities, which are always also external entities, are referenced by giving the name as an attribute value for some element. In a valid document the referencing attribute must have been declared as an entity type attribute (ENTITY or ENTITIES). Unparsed entities are not intended for processing by an XML processor. Instead, the processor merely passes the identifiers for each entity and the associated notation to the application.

On the other hand, parsed entities are processed by the XML processor, which replaces the entity name by the entity value, as described below. References to parsed entities, called *entity references*, may appear outside attributes. Parameter entity references always begin with a percent sign (%) and terminate with a semicolon(;), and the context of a parameter entity reference is always the document type definition. General entity references always start with an ampersand (&) and end with a semicolon. For example, &xml-spec; references the general entity xml-spec, and %chapter_attributes; designates the parameter entity chapter_attributes. Recall that a document may contain both a parameter entity and a general entity named title, for example; their uses are distinguished by the syntax of the references (%title; versus &title;) and whether they appear within a DTD or within the content of an element.

Table 2.2 summarizes the contexts in which invocations of unparsed entities and entity references might appear.[4]

To understand the processing of parsed entities and their references, it is important to distinguish between two kinds of entity content: the literal entity value and the replacement text. As mentioned in the previous section, the quoted string given in the declaration of an internal entity is called a literal entity value. The literal entity value may contain character, parameter entity, and general entity references. The *replacement text* for a parsed internal entity reference is derived by replacing character references by their character values and parameter entity references by their replacement texts.

---

[4] Character references are syntactically similar to general entity references and can appear in the same contexts. However, character references are not parsed as described in this section. See instead Sect. 2.3.3.

Example 2.10 Consider again some of the entity declarations from Example 2.9:

```
<!ENTITY % StyleSheet  "CDATA">
    <!—stylesheet data -->
<!ENTITY % Text  "CDATA">
    <!-- used for titles etc. -->
<!ENTITY % coreattrs
        "id        ID            #IMPLIED
        class      CDATA         #IMPLIED
        style      %StyleSheet;  #IMPLIED
        title      %Text;        #IMPLIED"  >
```

The literal entity value of the entity StyleSheet and of the entity Text is CDATA, which is also the replacement text for those entities. The literal entity value of the entity coreattrs is

```
id      ID                #IMPLIED
class   CDATA             #IMPLIED
style   %StyleSheet;      #IMPLIED
title   %Text;            #IMPLIED
```

whereas the replacement text is derived by replacing the parameter entity references by their replacement texts:

```
id      ID            #IMPLIED
class   CDATA         #IMPLIED
style   CDATA         #IMPLIED
title   CDATA         #IMPLIED
```

Any nested general entity references are left unexpanded when deriving such replacement text; instead expansion of general entity references, replacing each reference by the value of the entity referenced, takes place only when the entity reference is encountered in element contents and in attribute values.

For a parsed *external* entity, the literal entity value is the exact text contained in the entity (external file) and the replacement text is the content of the entity after stripping the text declaration, if there is one, but *without* any replacement of character or parameter entity references.

The *replacement* text for a parsed entity is regarded as an integral part of the document in place of its entity reference. The detailed way an XML processor treats an entity and its references depends on the type of references, their contexts, and the type of the processor. Non-validating processors need not deal with external entities, nor are they obligated to read and process entity declarations occurring within parameter entities. Hence a non-validating processor is not necessarily aware of all entity declarations. The details of the treatment of entities and references are described in Sect. 4.4 of the XML specification.

Example 2.11 The XHTML specification also contains the following entity declarations:

```
<!ENTITY % special.pre      "br | span | bdo | map ">
<!ENTITY %special           "%special.pre; | object | img ">
<!ENTITY % fontstyle        "tt | i | b | big | small ">
<!ENTITY % phrase
   "em | strong | dfn | code | q | samp | kbd | var | cite | abbr | acronym | sub | sup ">
<!ENTITY % inline.forms     "input | select | textarea | label | button">
<!ENTITY % misc.inline      "ins | del | script">
<!ENTITY % inline
   "a | %special; | %fontstyle; | %phrase; | %inline.forms;">
<!ENTITY % Inline"(#PCDATA | %inline; | %misc.inline;)*">
```

The literal value of the entity Inline is

(#PCDATA | %inline; | %misc.inline;)*

The replacement text is derived by replacing the references to parameter entities inline and misc.inline by their replacement texts. The literal value for the entity inline

a | %special; | %fontstyle; | %phrase; | %inline.forms;

must therefore be transformed to its replacement text, which requires examining its four referenced entities. When processing the literal value of the entity special

%special.pre; | object | img

the processor encounters a reference to the entity special.pre whose replacement text is

br | span | bdo | map

After expanding everything, the replacement text of the entity inline is found to be:

a | br | span | bdo | map | object | img | tt | i | b | big | small | em | strong | dfn | code | q | samp | kbd | var | cite | abbr | acronym | sub | sup | input | select | textarea | label | button

After also expanding the entity %misc.inline;, the replacement text of the entity Inline is found to be:

(#PCDATA | a | br | span | bdo | map | object | img | tt | i | b | big | small | em | strong | dfn | code | q | samp | kbd | var | cite | abbr | acronym | sub | sup | input | select | textarea | label | button | ins | del | script)*

2.4.6   XML Schema

The document type definition mechanism provided by DTDs is just one means to constrain XML data. Several other definition languages, called schema languages, have also been defined for XML. Software supporting each such language is able to check the validity of an XML document against the definitions of acceptable data types and structures declared by the document designers.

A language widely adopted for many applications is *XML Schema*, also known as *XSD*, developed by W3C and described in three parts: a primer summarizing the language and providing several examples [14], the specification for describing compound structures [21], and the specification for the 44 pre-defined atomic data types available in XSD [2]. This provides richer constraining mechanisms than those available through a DTD, and they can all be applied to both attribute values and element contents.

2.4.6.1   Overview

We begin by comparing some core features of XSD to those of DTDs, divided into the following areas:

- XML model
- Types
- Syntax
- Namespaces

Following that, we demonstrate how elements are declared and types defined, and then how attributes are declared.

XML model. As described in Sect. 2.3, the core concept of XML is a document with both physical structure and logical structure. The markup in an XML document provides information for both of these structures, and DTDs include definition capabilities for them both. A DTD is used by validating XML processors to assess the validity of XML documents with respect to element type declarations, attribute list declarations, entity declarations, and notation declarations.

As will be explained in Sect. 2.5.2 below, the nesting of elements in XML imposes a computational structure known as a *tree*. Based on this relationship, the XML Information Set (Infoset) model describes an XML document as an abstract tree structure consisting of 11 kinds of nodes called information items [12]. Unlike a DTD, an XSD instance is not intended to assess the validity of marked up XML documents but rather the validity of element and attribute information items as they are defined by the Infoset model. Thus even though both XSD and DTDs are languages that constrain the contents of XML documents, the target for XSD is different from that for DTDs.

Types. The most significant improvement of XSD over DTDs is the introduction of a rich typing system, allowing designers to declare restricted domains of values for each of the elements and attributes in their documents.

Consider first the following DTD declarations for a multilingual street name catalogue:

```
<!ELEMENT   streetCatalogue        (street+)>
<!ELEMENT   street                 (streetName+)>
<!ELEMENT   streetName             (#PCDATA)>
<!ATTLIST   streetName      lang   NMTOKEN   #REQUIRED>
```

This example includes declarations for three *element types* and one declaration associating an *attribute name* with an *attribute type*. For each street there may be several street names, and the language of each street name is provided using the lang attribute.

In a DTD, although the content of elements having children can be structurally constrained, elements without any child elements always contain arbitrary strings of character data (declared as #PCDATA). In the above example, the length of a street-Name cannot be constrained. In other situations where ages, monetary amounts, or dates are stored as element values, no constraints can be declared to ensure that valid integers or dates are actually stored. Attribute values can be constrained by the attribute type, but the choice of types is very limited, as described in Sect. 2.4.3 above.

In XSD the term *type* always refers to the set of values allowable for an element or attribute, never to its name. The typing system in XSD allows document designers to specify elements and attributes that include all the constraints available in DTDs, but many additional forms of constraint are also available. Types can be *simple* (such as integer, string, date, and time), which will be described in more detail in Sect. 5.1, or they can be structures with arbitrarily many sub-components (so-called *complex types*).

Elements and attributes are constrained by *schema components* in the form of definitions and declarations. *Definition* components specify *types* as sets of possible values, including both atomic and structured values. On the other hand, element, attribute, and notation *declarations* are used to enable elements, attributes, and notations with the specific names to appear in document instances and to constrain the contents of each appearance to conform to a defined type.

The declaration for an element or attribute may include a type definition directly or it may refer to the type by the type name. In the former case the type is *anonymous*. In the latter case the definition of the type with the given name may be included in the same schema, or the name can refer to a type defined in another schema or in the XSD specification itself. Note that the content specifications of element type declarations of DTDs correspond to XSD's anonymous type definitions.

Syntax. Whereas the syntax for DTDs is especially defined for markup declarations, XSD uses XML's element and attribute notation. For example, elements named element and attribute are used to declare elements and attributes, respectively, and elements named complexType and simpleType are used to define complex types and simple types (those without attributes and subelements), respectively. (Examples will be given in Sect. 2.4.6.2 below).

Schema instance files are usually named with the .xsd file extension when they are intended to be processed by XSD-aware software. However, XSD schema instances are also special cases of XML documents, and therefore they can be processed by general XML software. The extension .xml is used instead when the file is to be processed by general purpose XML software.

Namespaces. The element and attribute names in a DTD must appear in the same form as in the document validated against the DTD. Prefixed names denoting namespaces can be used in a DTD, but namespaces cannot be declared there since they can be declared only in the start-tags of elements. Therefore two documents that use identical namespaces but with different prefixes cannot be validated with a single DTD.

Parameter entities provide an alternative method to support reuse of declarations in DTDs. Reuse is also supported by modularization methods enabling the creation of schemas from well-defined sets of elements and attributes. Examples of these methods are presented by Eve Maler and Jeanne El Andaloussi in their extensive book on developing SGML DTDs [19] and in the descriptions of XHTML [1] and the Text Encoding Initiative (www.tei-c.org). These alternative methods, however, do not solve the problem of name collisions.

XSD supports the use of namespaces in several ways. The XSD syntax, being a subset of XML, allows the declaration of namespaces in the start-tag of any element. The vocabulary declared and defined in a schema forms a *target namespace*, which therefore includes the names declared for all elements and attributes, as well as of the names defined for types in the schema. For example, the following lines might start a schema:

```
<schema xmlns="http://www.w3.org/2001/XMLSchema"
        xmlns:school="http://www.example/schoolNames"
        targetNamespace="http://www.example/schoolNames">
    <element name="beginDate" type="date" />
```

The first line declares the XSD namespace as the default namespace for the schema itself. This allows the use of the names from the namespace http://www.w3.org/2001/XMLSchema without any prefix. The second line associates the prefix school with the namespace name http://www.example/schoolNames. The third line declares this particular namespace as the target namespace of the schema. As a result, that namespace is populated by the names declared for elements and attributes in the schema, as well as by the names defined for types in the schema. The last line declares the beginDate element to have the built-in type date. The name beginDate belongs to the target namespace, but the element names schema and element, the attribute names name and type, and the type name date are all taken from the namespace http://www.w3.org/2001/XMLSchema.

It is worth noticing that the namespace concept of XSD extends the XML Names specification [4] by including type names as well as names of elements and attributes. Thus the example above shows that the namespace http://www.w3.org/2001/XMLSchema includes the element names element and attribute and the attributes name and type, as well as the names of the built-in types such as date. Notice also that the names of types are not used as element or attribute names in schemas but instead as attribute values.

A schema defining a particular target namespace may be divided into several schema documents by using the include element to specify the location of the file from which schema components are included. In such a case, there is a single declared target namespace for all of the schema documents, and that target namespace is populated by the names declared and defined in all the documents.

The reuse of types is facilitated by the import element, which identifies the target namespace for the imported types. For example, the types defined in the target schema http://www.example/schoolNames could be reused by another schema by including the following schema element:

```
<import namespace="http://www.example/schoolNames"/>
```

2.4.6.2 Declaring Elements and Defining Types

Consider defining a schema for the following simple XML document:

```
<student>
    <name>Steve  Chung</name>
    <age>23</age>
    <phone>416-982-1111</phone>
</student>
```

The student element contains three subelements: name, age, and phone, each of which consists of character data. A possible DTD for the data might include four element type declarations as follows:

```
<!ELEMENT      student        (name, age, phone)>
<!ELEMENT      name           (#PCDATA)>
<!ELEMENT      age            (#PCDATA)>
<!ELEMENT      phone          (#PCDATA)>
```

An XSD definition for the same data is shown in Fig. 2.3, where the schema components are contained in the schema element. As in the example in the previous section, the XSD namespace http://www.w3.org/2001/XMLSchema is first declared as the default namespace, and then the prefix school is associated with the namespace http://www.example/schoolNames, which is also declared as the target namespace. The schema includes four element declarations, each specified in an element named element that associates a name, given with the attribute name, with a type.

Since name, age, and phone do not have any attributes or child elements, they can be declared to have a simple type. For example, the element

```
<element name="phone" type="string" />
```

```
<schema xmlns="http://www.w3.org/2001/XMLSchema"
        xmlns:school="http://www.example/schoolNames"
        targetNamespace="http://www.example/schoolNames">
    <element name="student">
        <complexType>
                        <sequence>
                            <element name="name" type="string" />
                            <element name="age" type="positiveInteger"/>
                            <element name="phone" type="string" />
                        </sequence>
        </complexType>
    </element>
</schema>
```

Fig. 2.3 A schema with an anonymous complex type definition

```
<schema xmlns="http://www.w3.org/2001/XMLSchema"
        xmlns:school="http://www.example/schoolNames"
        targetNamespace="http://www.example/schoolNames">
    <complexType name="PersonalData">
        <sequence>
            <element name="name" type="string" />
            <element name="age" type="positiveInteger"/>
            <element name="phone" type="string" />
        </sequence>
    </complexType>
    <element name="student" type="school:PersonalData"/>
</schema>
```

Fig. 2.4 A schema with a named complex type definition

declares the element name phone to have the built-in type string. Note, however, that unlike DTDs, XSD allows the age to be constrained to contain a string that represents a positive integer.

Unlike the other three elements, the student element has subelements, and it must therefore be declared as a complex type. In Fig. 2.3 the type is declared using an *anonymous type definition*: the elements complexType and sequence define a sequence structure consisting of the elements name, age, and phone.

Instead of using an anonymous type definition, an alternative is shown in Fig. 2.4, where a complex type named PersonalData has been defined separately from the student element declaration. The element declaration refers to this type by its name, prefixed by the name of the target namespace.

XSD allows document designers to declare new types that are derived from other atomic or complex types. For example, the type of the element phone in these examples was constrained to character strings, but any strings are allowed as element

```
<schema xmlns="http://www.w3.org/2001/XMLSchema"
        xmlns:school="http://www.example/schoolNames"
        targetNamespace="http://www.example/schoolNames">
    <element name="name" type="string" />
    <element name="phone" type="string" />
    <complexType name="PersonalData">
        <sequence>
            <element ref="school:name"/>
            <element name="age" type="positiveInteger"/>
            <element ref="school:phone" minOccurs="0" />
        </sequence>
    </complexType>
    <element name="student" type="school:PersonalData"/>
</schema>
```

Fig. 2.5 A schema with references to global elements

content. Instead, a designer can constrain the content to conform to a particular pattern by declaring a *restriction* of the type string as follows:

```
<element name="phone">
  <simpleType>
    <restriction base="string">
        <pattern value="\d{3}-\d{3}-\d{4}"/>
    </restriction>
  </simpleType>
</element>
```

The restriction is specified with a *facet* called a *pattern* from the *base type* string. The pattern "\d{3}-\d{3}-\d{4}" describes a string where three digits are followed by a hyphen, three digits, a hyphen, and four digits. With such a declaration for the element phone, an XSD-aware validator will reject phone elements having content that does not match the pattern.

Complex types can also be constrained. For example, a new type can be defined as a restriction of PersonalData specifying that the age be between 16 and 25. Alternatively, a new complex type can be defined as an *extension* of PersonalData that also includes an e-mail address.

Document designers may wish to use an element declaration in several places with in a schema or in several schemas. To refer to a declaration, it must be declared as global by placing it as a child of the schema element. For example, the student element is a *global* declaration in Figs. 2.3 and 2.4. On the other hand, the name, age, and phone elements in those schemas are *local* declarations because they appear inside complex type definitions.

A global element can be referenced from other declarations using the ref attribute. For example, the element declarations in the complex type definition in Fig. 2.5 use the attribute ref to refer to the global name and phone declarations, whereas age remains local. Notice that the type of the elements are not repeated when referring to a global declaration. In contrast to XSD, all elements in DTDs are global (their names can be used as references in other element type declarations); there is no corresponding mechanism to declare local elements.

In Fig. 2.5 the element referencing school:phone also includes a second attribute with the name minOccurs. With the value 0, this attribute constrains the number of occurrences of phone elements in the student element to be greater than equal to 0. Similarly, XSD provides the attribute maxOccurs to declare the maximum number of repetitions of an element. The value of the attributes minOccurs and maxOccurs may be any positive integer, or the term unbounded indicating that there is no maximum number of occurrences. The omission of either these attributes corresponds to including the attribute with a value of 1. Thus, in Fig. 2.5 school:name and age must occur exactly once (at least once and at most once), whereas school:phone may occur either 0 times or one time. In a DTD these constraints are expressed as

```
<!ELEMENT  student        (name, age, phone?)>
```

The attributes minOccurs and maxOccurs enable more precise constraints on the number of occurrences than allowed by a DTD's content model using the symbols ?, +, and *. For example, to allow at most five phone numbers, the element declaration would be written as follows:

```
<element ref="school:phone" minOccurs="0" maxOccurs= ="5" />
```

2.4.6.3   Declaring Attributes

Instead of encoding all data as element content, let us examine how attributes are declared in XSDs. Continuing with the earlier example, assume that the area code is given as attribute value, instead of including it as part of the whole phone number:

```
<student>
    <name> Steve Chung</name>
    <age>23</age>
    <phone area_code="416" >982-1111</phone>
</student>
```

In a DTD this change would require adding an attribute list declaration:

```
<!ELEMENT      student      (name, phone)>
<!ELEMENT      name         (#PCDATA)>
<!ELEMENT      age          (#PCDATA)>
<!ELEMENT      phone        (#PCDATA)>
<!ATTLIST      phone        area_code CDATA   #IMPLIED>
```

Note that in contrast to element declarations, all attributes in a DTD are declared local by associating them with an element name. In XSD it is possible to declare attributes to be global as well as local.

Using XSD, the phone element must have a complex type to enable it to have an attribute. Figure 2.6 shows how an appropriate complex type can be derived from a

```
<xsd:schema xmlns:xsd="http://www.w3.org/2001/XMLSchema">
  <xsd:simpleType name="phoneNumberType">
    <xsd:restriction base="xsd:string">
      <xsd:pattern value="\d{3}-\d{4}"/>
    </xsd:restriction>
  </xsd:simpleType>

  <xsd:simpleType name="areaCodeType">
    <xsd:restriction base="xsd:string">
      <xsd:pattern value="\d{3}"/>
    </xsd:restriction>
  </xsd:simpleType>

  <xsd:element name="student">
    <xsd:complexType>
      <xsd:sequence>

        <xsd:element name="name" type="xsd:string" />
        <xsd:element name="age" type="positiveInteger"/>
        <xsd:element name="phone">
          <xsd:complexType>
            <xsd:simpleContent>
              <xsd:extension base="phoneNumberType">
                <xsd:attribute name="area_code" type="areaCodeType"/>
              </xsd:extension>
            </xsd:simpleContent>
          </xsd:complexType>
        </xsd:element>

      </xsd:sequence>
    </xsd:complexType>
  </xsd:element>
</xsd:schema>
```

Fig. 2.6 A schema with an attribute declaration

simple type. (For variety, the schema has also been altered such that no target namespace has been declared – i.e., the default namespace is used for the target – and the namespace http://www.w3.org/2001/XMLSchema is explicitly associated with the prefix xsd).

In this example, two simple types have been defined to constrain the phone number and the area code respectively: the phoneNumberType restricts a string to the form where three digits are followed by a hyphen and four digits, and the areaCode-Type restricts a string to be three digits. The type of phone is an anonymous complex type. The element simpleContent indicates that the content of the element contains only character data, no sub-elements. The complex type is derived as an extension from the base type areaCodeType by adding an attribute with name area_code and type areaCodeType.

2.4.6.4   Extended XSD Example

Before concluding this section, we return to the earlier example of a rhyme to illustrate grouping, optionality, alternatives, and iteration in XML Schema. For simplicity, the example of alternative content shown here is via an enumerated type (for xml:lang); more general alternatives are defined using the element <xs:choice> in place of <xs:sequence>.

Example 2.12 XSD declarations for rhymes that parallel the DTD declarations in Example 2.4:

```
<xs:schema elementFormDefault="qualified" attributeFormDefault="unqualified"
           xmlns:xs="http://www.w3.org/2001/XMLSchema">
<xs:element name="line" type="xs:string" />
<xs:element name="rhyme">
   <xs:complexType mixed="false">
      <xs:sequence minOccurs="1" maxOccurs="1">
         <xs:complexType mixed="false">
            <xs:element ref="line" minOccurs="1"  maxOccurs="unbounded"/>
         </xs:complexType>
      </xs:sequence>
      <xs:attribute name="xml:lang" use="optional">
         <xs:simpleType>
            <xs:restriction base="xs:language">
               <xs:enumeration value="fi"/>
               <xs:enumeration value="en"/>
            </xs:restriction>
         </xs:simpleType>
      </xs:attribute>
      <xs:attribute name="author" type="xs:string" use="optional"/>
   </xs:complexType>
</xs:element>
<xs:element name="rhymecollection">
   <xs:complexType mixed="false">
      <xs:sequence minOccurs="1" maxOccurs="1">
         <xs:element name="title" type="xs:string" minOccurs="0" maxOccurs="1"/>
         <xs:element ref="rhyme" minOccurs="1"  maxOccurs="unbounded"/>
      </xs:sequence>
   </xs:complexType>
 </xs:element>
 </xs:schema>
```

In Example 2.12, a rhyme is specified as being a non-empty, unbounded sequence of lines with no interleaved text (mixed="false"). Each line is itself a simple string. A rhyme may optionally have attributes as follows: xml:lang is an enumerated type that restricts the built-in type xs:language, and author can take any string as its value.

A rhymecollection starts with an optional title and then has one or more elements of type rhyme, declared earlier.

In summary, XSD is more expressive than DTDs: it can be used to specify constraints that cannot be described using a DTD. The availability of many atomic types allows element content to be constrained rather than merely being declared generically as #PCDATA. In addition, minOccurs and maxOccurs can take any numeric values, not merely 0, 1, or unbounded. The items in a sequence are constrained to be in a fixed order (as in DTDs, where, for example, name, age, and phone number may all be required in that order), but by using <xs:all> instead of <xs:sequence> the component elements are allowed to appear in arbitrary order (name, age, and phone number must all be provided but any of the six possible orderings are acceptable). Elements of any type can be declared with the attribute nillable="true" to allow any instance of that element to have empty content when xsi:nil="true" is included among its attributes (assuming that somewhere in its enclosing context xmlns:xsi="http://www. w3.org/2001/XMLSchema-instance" has been declared); thus the fact that a value is missing, unknown or not applicable can be recorded for elements that must be present and otherwise could not be empty (such as integers, dates, or complex types with required sub-elements). Finally, any element can be declared to have a value that is unique with respect to all other elements in the same context; for example, employee id numbers can be declared to be non-repeating throughout the document, non-repeating within each organization listed in the document, or non-repeating within each division in each organization.

Finally, DTDs provide the attribute types ID, IDREF, and IDREFs to support links between elements within a document. XSD extends this to allow the definition of keys (similar to relational database keys, but with respect to a particular context within each document) and references (of type keyref) to those keys.

2.4.7 RELAX NG

A third data definition language is *RELAX NG*, developed by James Clark and Murata Makoto through OASIS and an ISO standard (ISO/IEC 19757–2) since December 2003 [10, 11]. RELAX NG is simpler than XML Schema, but it too includes a richer collection of data types than available in DTDs as well as support for namespaces.

As will be explained in Sect. 2.5.2 below, the nesting of elements in XML imposes a structure known in computer science as a *tree*. RELAX NG is designed to constrain the trees that are represented by XML documents rather than capabilities for constraining the document text directly. In RELAX NG, therefore, the content models for elements, as well as for the sets of valid values for attributes, are modeled as *tree-regular grammars*, a formalism similar to EBNF (as introduced in

Sect. 2.1) but describing trees rather than strings. RELAX NG is not able to describe all the constraints describable with XSD, but it is more expressive than XSD in specifying unordered and mixed content.

Grammars in RELAX NG can be expressed using XML structures (quite similar in style to that used in XSD), but a more compact syntax is also available, as illustrated in the following example:

Example 2.13 RELAX NG declarations for rhymes that parallel the DTD declarations in Example 2.4 and the XSD declarations in Example 2.12:

```
grammar {
        start = RhymeCollection
        RhymeCollection = element rhymeCollection { element title { text} ?, Rhyme+ }
        Rhyme = element rhyme {
                        attribute xml:lang { ("fi" | "en") },
                        attribute author {text},
                        Line+
        }
        Line = element line { text }
        }
```

2.5 Processing Models

As explained in Sect. 2.2, software that needs to read or modify data stored in an XML document accesses that data via an XML processor. The responsibility of the processor is to distinguish markup from content, to ensure that the document is well-formed, possibly to ensure that the document satisfies various validity constraints, to use the markup to identify individual units of content as well as the relationships between those units, and to identify suitable applications to handle non-textual components. This information is made available to the application software according to a pre-determined protocol that dictates the form of communication between the XML processor and the XML application. Such a protocol is typically embedded into an *application program interface*, or *API*, which is a set of functions that support the communication between the participating pieces of software.

There are two major protocols that are used by XML processors. In the first one, the XML document is viewed as a string of beads: a linear structure formed by interleaved markup and content. In the alternative protocol, the XML document is viewed as a bunch of grapes: a hierarchical structure matching the nested nature of the markup, with units of content situated at various points at the lowest levels of the hierarchy [22]. Managing text via these two models is discussed in the remainder of this section.

2.5.1 *Stream Processing*

Consider the XML element

```
<date><month>December</month><year>1654</year></date>
```

The simplest interpretation of the structure and content is to view this as a stream of tokens, where each token carries either a unit of markup or a unit of content:

Opening tag:	date
Opening tag:	month
String:	December
Closing tag:	month
Opening tag:	year
String:	1654
Closing tag:	year
Closing tag:	date

Tokens from this stream can be passed from the XML processor to the XML application in the order in which they appear, and it is up to the application software to handle the information conveyed by the tokens and their ordering in an appropriate manner to achieve its goals.

Applications that adopt this form of processing are typically based on SAX, the "Simple API for XML" [7]. With SAX, the XML processor signals the occurrence of each token in turn by calling an appropriate function, depending on the type of token. A suitable token handler must be written by the XML application programmer as the body of each designated function. For example, when a SAX parser encounters an opening tag, it calls the function startElement, passing parameters that contain the tag name, information to resolve the namespace, and the list of attribute-value pairs. Assuming that the software is written in the Java programming language, the XML application programmer must implement the function

```
public void startElement (String uri, String name, String qName, Attributes atts){ ... }
```

to handle a start-tag whenever it is encountered in the XML document. The following table lists the set of token types that may occur in a SAX stream:

Tokens from a DTD	
notationDecl	unparsedEntityDecl
Tokens from the body	
startDocument	endDocument
startElement	endElement
startPrefixMapping	endPrefixMapping
characters	ignorableWhitespace
processingInstruction	skippedEntity

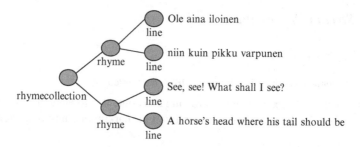

Fig. 2.7 XML document as a tree

2.5.2 Tree Processing

It is often important to consider the context of a fragment of an XML document in order to process it appropriately. In such circumstances, it is convenient to have easy access to the nesting structure implied by the markup. Thus, instead of viewing an XML document as a stream of tokens, some application programs are better served by viewing it as a hierarchical structure, and more specifically as an ordered, rooted tree. The document element is interpreted as the root of the tree, and each non-root element is interpreted as a child of the node corresponding to the element in which it is contained. An XML processor supporting the tree-based protocol for communicating the information about an XML document to an XML application must provide information about the order of sibling elements to that application.

Consider again the following XML document with two rhymes, one written in Finnish, another in English.

```
<rhymecollection>
    <rhyme>
    <line>Ole aina iloinen</line>
    <line>niin kuin pikku varpunen</line>
    </rhyme>
    <rhyme>
    <line>See, see! What shall I see?</line>
    <line>A horse's head where his tail should be</line>
    </rhyme>
</rhymecollection>
```

The corresponding tree structure can be depicted as shown in Fig. 2.7. In the tree the children of a node are ordered from top to bottom and reflect exactly the same order as they appear (left to right) in the corresponding elements in the tagged text.

Figure 2.7 shows only the element structure. Tree models for XML documents have been developed in four different specifications proposed through W3C: the XML Information Set (Infoset) model [12], the XML Path Language (XPath 1.0) data model

[9], the Document Object Model (DOM) [18], and the XQuery 1.0 and XPath 2.0 Data Model [15]. All four cover more than just the structure of elements. Each model defines a set of node types, including types for the root of a document as well as for elements, attributes, comments, and processing instructions. However there are some subtle differences between the models. For example, if a tree is created on the basis of the Infoset model, there is a distinct node for each character in the content of an element (thus resulting in 16 child nodes for the first line node in the above example), whereas the XQuery/XPath data model permits multiple-character strings in a content node and specifies that two adjacent sibling nodes may not both contain text (thus resulting in only one child node for each line node in the above example). Furthermore, although attributes are represented by nodes in all four models, there are some subtle differences in the way in which the four models account for the fact that there is no order defined among attributes of an element in the XML specification. The existence of competing tree models for XML data has caused some inconsistencies and incompatibilities in XML development.

The functionality available through XPath 1.0 provides an example of an application's access to an XML document using a tree-based protocol. An XPath expression is a sequence of steps in which each step is interpreted with respect to a starting node (the context node) and returns either a (possibly empty) set of nodes, a Boolean value (true or false), a number, or a character string. For example, starting from the root of the above tree, the expression rhyme/line yields a node set including all four line elements, rhyme[2]/line yields the last two line elements (i.e., the two English lines), and rhyme/line[contains(.,"niin")]/text() yields the contents of the second Finnish line, namely the string "niin kuin pikku varpunen".

More precisely, the steps are separated by slashes and each step includes an axis, a node test, and a predicate, defined as follows:

- Starting from a context node, an axis identifies a subset of nodes in the tree and imposes a linear ordering on that subset. For example, the child axis selects all element children of a node and orders them from first to last; the ancestor axis selects the parent of the node first, followed by the parent's parent, that node's parent, and so on until the root node is reached. XPath 1.0 defines 13 axes (ancestor, ancestor-or-self, attribute, child, descendant, descendant-or-self, following, following-sibling, namespace, parent, preceding, preceding-sibling, self), any of which can be specified in any step of an expression. For simplicity, an abbreviated form may be used wherein the child axis need not be specified, descendant-or-self is represented by omitting the step (thus effectively doubling the slash), parent is represented by a caret (^), and self is represented by a dot (.).
- Starting with the sequence of nodes designated by an axis, the node-test eliminates any node that does not match the specified element name or element type. For example, child::line selects only child nodes corresponding to elements named line and descendant::comment() yields all comment nodes within the subtree of the context node. When used as a node-test, an asterisk (*) matches all nodes designated by the axis.
- Starting from the sequence of nodes designated by an axis and passing the node-test, a predicate serves as an additional filter to select the subset of the nodes for

which it evaluates to *true*. As an abbreviation, if the predicate is a number, it selects the node from that position in the sequence, and if it is a path expression, it selects each node N for which that path expression evaluates to a non-empty set of nodes when N is used as the context node.

Finally, a path consisting of a sequence of steps is evaluated by determining the set of nodes from the first step, using each in turn as a context node to select nodes using the second step and forming the union of all returned node sets, and so forth. For example, starting from some context node, the XPath expression

chapter/section[2]//figure/^subsection

selects all child element nodes with name chapter, then selects all second sections that are children of those chapters, then all figures anywhere within those sections, and finally all subsections that immediately contain those figures.

2.5.3 Comparing Stream and Tree Processing

Processing an XML document as a stream of tokens allows an application to consider all components in the order that they appear in the document. Parsing a document for stream processing is straightforward and stream parsers are very efficient regardless of the size of a document. Stream processors are typically used for XML documents that are shipped from one application to another.

Tree processing requires the parser to build and maintain a nested representation of the document, usually within a computer's main memory. As a result, an application can navigate forward and backwards within the structure, climbing one branch of the tree and descending others that may have occurred before or after it in document order. The parser and the application interface are therefore somewhat more complicated, and typically document processing is restricted to documents, and their parses, that fit into main memory. Tree processors are therefore typically used for applications that require random access to sub-parts of a document, and they are more amenable to supporting XML validation, especially with respect to resolving attributes of type IDREF(S).

In spite of recognizing their advantages and disadvantages, however, it is important to remember that either type of processor is capable of preparing an XML document for use in any application.

References

1. Austin, D., Peruvemba, S., McCarron, S., Birbeck, M. (eds): XHTML™ Modularization 1.1 – Second Edition. W3C Recommendation (29 July 2010) http://www.w3.org/TR/xhtml-modularization/, Cited 10 March 2011.
2. Biron, P., Malhotra, A. (eds): XML Schema Part 2: Datatypes (Second Edition). W3C Re-commendation (28 Oct 2004) http://www.w3.org/TR/xmlschema-2/, Cited 10 March 2011.

3. Bray, T.: The Annotated XML Specification. http://www.xml.com/axml/testaxml.htm, Cited 10 March 2011.

4. Bray, T., Hollander, D., Layman, A., Tobin, R., Thompson, H.S. (eds): Namespaces in XML 1.0 (Third Edition). W3C Recommendation (8 December 2009) http://www.w3.org/TR/xml-names/, Cited 10 March 2011.

5. Bray, T., Paoli, J., Sperberg-McQueen, C.M. (eds): Extensible Markup Language (XML) 1.0. W3C Recommendation (10 February 1998) http://www.w3.org/TR/1998/REC-xml-19980210, Cited 10 March 2011.

6. Bray, T., Paoli, J., Sperberg-McQueen, C.M., Maler, E., Yergeau, F., Cowen, J. (eds): Ex-tensible Markup Language (XML) 1.1. W3C Recommendation (4 February 2004, edited in place 15 April 2004) http://www.w3.org/TR/2004/REC-xml11-20040204/, Cited 10 March 2011.

7. Brownell, D. (ed): SAX. http://www.saxproject.org/, Cited 10 March 2011.

8. Clark, J., Pieters, S., Thompson, H.S. (eds): Associating Stylesheets with XML documents 1.0 (Second Edition). W3C Recommendation (28 October 2010) http://www.w3.org/TR/xml-stylesheet, Cited 10 March 2011.

9. Clark, J., DeRose, S. (eds): XML Path Language (XPath) Version 1.0. W3C Recommendation (16 November 1999) http://www.w3.org/TR/xpath, Cited 10 March 2011.

10. Clark, J, Murata, M.: RELAX NG Specification, Committee Specification. OASIS (3 De-cember 2001) http://www.oasis-open.org/committees/relax-ng/spec-20011203.html, Cited 10 March 2011.

11. Clark, J, Murata, M.: RELAX NG Tutorial, OASIS Committee Specification (3 December 2001), http://www.relaxng.org/tutorial-20011203.html, Cited 10 March 2011.

12. Cowan, J., Tobin, R. (eds): XML Information Set (Second Edition). W3C Recommendation (4 February 2004) http://www.w3.org/TR/xml-infoset/, Cited 10 March 2011.

13. Duerst, M., Suignard, M.: Internationalized Resource Identifiers (IRIs). The Internet Society (January 2005) http://www.rfc-editor.org/rfc/rfc3987.txt, Cited 10 March 2011.

14. Fallside, D.C., Walmsley, P. (eds): XML Schema Part 0: Primer Second Edition. W3C Recommendation (28 October 2004) http://www.w3.org/TR/xmlschema-0/. Cited 10 March 2011.

15. Fernández, M., et al. (eds): XQuery 1.0 and XPath 2.0 Data Model (XDM). W3C Recom-mendation (23 January 2007) http://www.w3.org/TR/2007/REC-xpath-datamodel-20070123/, Cited 10 March 2011.

16. Goldfarb, C.F.: The SGML Handbook, edited by Y. Rubinsky. Oxford University Press, Oxford, UK (1990).

17. ISO/IEC JTC1/SC34 Web Server, Information Technology – Document Description and Processing Languages. International Organization for Standardization and the International Electrotechnical Commission. http://www.ornl.gov/sgml/, Cited 10 March 2011.

18. Le Hégaret, P., et al. (eds): Document Object Model (DOM). http://www.w3.org/DOM/, Cited 10 March 2011.

19. Maler, E., El Andaloussi, J.: Developing SGML DTDs. From Text to Model to Markup. Prentice Hall PTR, Upper Saddle River, NJ (1995). Available online at http://www.xmlgrrl.com/publications/DSDTD/, Cited 10 March 2011.

20. Pemberton, S., et al.: XHTML™ 1.0 The Extensible HyperText Markup Language (Second Edition): A Reformulation of HTML 4 in XML 1.0. W3C Recommendation (26 January 2000. revised 1 August 2002) http://www.w3.org/TR/xhtml1/, Cited 10 March 2011.

21. Thompson, H.S., Bech, D., Maloney, M., Mendelsohn, N. (eds): XML Schema Part 1: Structures Second Edition. W3C Recommendation (28 October 2004) http://www.w3.org/TR/xmlschema-1/. Cited 10 March 2011.

22. Tompa, F.W.: What is (tagged) text? In: Dictionaries in the Electronic Age, Proceedings of the Fifth Annual Conference of UW Centre for the New Oxford English Dictionary and Text Research, pp. 81–93. Waterloo, Ont.: University of Waterloo (1989). Available online at http://citeseerx.ist.psu.edu/viewdoc/download?doi=10.1.1.40.5411&rep=rep1&type=pdf, Cited 10 March 2011.

23. W3C, All Standards and Drafts. http://www.w3.org/TR/, Cited 10 March 2011.

Chapter 3
Why Use XML?

Abstract Since its inception a decade ago, XML has become a standard technology for software engineers, all Web browsers are able to parse and show XML documents, and huge XML data resources are available from the Internet. Many of the documents are in XHTML, but other XML applications are quite common as well. XML has also become a format that is increasingly common in the files of local disks. This success would not have been possible without collaborative efforts throughout the Web community. Such world-wide collaborative development has included standards, software applications, and case implementations that can serve as models when developing new solutions. In this chapter we consider what kinds of benefits might be expected when adopting XML in organizations.

Keywords Business applications • Interoperability • Open data • Standardization • W3C • Web enabling • XML accessories • XML applications • XML family of languages • XML transducers

XML has been widely adopted as the standard format for data in various application areas and in numerous organizations. Converting to use XML in place of some legacy technology may be a major effort and may take significant resources in an organization or organizational network. In considering and discussing such a change, there is a need to weigh the benefits against the challenges related to the transfer. In this chapter we discuss the benefits of adopting XML in an organizational context. First we consider the benefits available during the migration to XML: support of collaborative standardization and the XML family of languages. In the remaining sections we consider the benefits gained once XML-based solutions have been adopted: the variety of software available, application independence of data assets, the ability to access data from the Web, and interoperability. Some of the accompanying challenges are introduced in the context of these benefits and examined in more detail in Chap. 8.

3.1   Collaborative Standardization

In order for information technology to support communication, it must be based on standards.[1] The success of the adoption of the Internet and the World Wide Web has resulted from finding common agreement about how to present information and exchange information between software applications, between various communication networks, and among many communities. Finding common agreement requires collaboration of many parties, and in the context of the Internet, standardization requires systematic, organized, continuous effort.

When the adoption of XML is considered in a specific organizational environment, there is a need to develop the rules governing how XML will be used for particular kinds of data in that context, and how the adoption of the rules is implemented in the environment. One of the benefits of adopting XML is that the development work rarely needs to be started from scratch. XML is at the core of extensive standardization work where specifications for different needs are developed by collaborative efforts involving many people, organizations and companies. The practices for a particular organizational environment can and should be based on rules developed in anticipation of the organization's needs.

Three major inter-related levels of standardization can be identified: universal, sectoral, and local standardization (see Fig. 3.1). Universal standardization is

Local
- rules and practices for the adoption and implementation of XML in a particular organization or group of organizations
- development by the organization

Sectoral
- rules for the adoption of XML for the purposes of a specific sector or application domain, e.g. electronic commerce, health care, finance
- development by industry organizations, such as OASIS, XBRL International, HL7, or by public sector organizations, such as Great Britain's Office of Pulic Sector Information

Universal
- rules for wide use across diverse sectors and domains
- development by national and international standards and specifications organizations, such as ANSI, W3C, IETF, ISO, Unicode Consortium, IANA
- examples: URI, Unicode, XML, XML Names, XML Schema, XQuery

Fig. 3.1 Levels of XML standardization

---

[1] We use the terms *standards* and *standardization* to reflect agreements for practice that are broadly accepted among organizations, whether or not these agreements are formally endorsed by a nationally or internationally recognized standardization body such as ANSI or ISO. In particular, many of the W3C accepted practices have not been considered for sanction by national and international standardization organizations, but they nevertheless serve as *de facto* standards that strongly influence practice and have wide-ranging support among producers and consumers of information technology.

Fig. 3.2 The idealized recommendation process at W3C

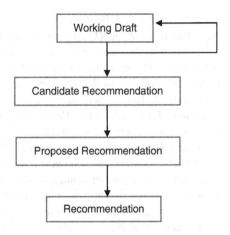

managed by broadly-based bodies such as the World Wide Web Consortium (W3C), Internet Engineering Task Force (IETF), International Organization for Standardization (ISO), Unicode Consortium, and Internet Assigned Numbers Authority (IANA). Universal standards serve as a basis for sectoral standardization, which addresses the needs of a particular segment of business or industry. Such standardization has been actively going on in several sectors, including electronic commerce, health care, and the public sector. Finally, standardization within an individual organization is based on standards for the associated industrial sector as well as on universal standards.

Since most of the universal standardization activities for XML take place in the W3C working committees, we consider the efforts at W3C more closely. In Sect. 3.1.2 we discuss sectoral standardization within some industries and the public sector.

3.1.1   Standardization at W3C

The World Wide Web Consortium (W3C) [24] was founded in 1994 to coordinate and support international, open development of technologies related to the Web. W3C membership is open to all organizations, and individuals can join W3C as Affiliate Members.

W3C publishes technical reports called *W3C Recommendations*, which serve the role of approved (albeit *de facto*) standards. A technical report goes through four maturity levels when advancing towards W3C Recommendation: *Working Draft*, *Candidate Recommendation*, *Proposed Recommendation*, and *Recommendation*. Figure 3.2 shows the default flow through which the maturity of a technical report proceeds. A Working Draft is usually versioned several times, after which progress through the remaining phases is more stable. For example, before reaching the Candidate Recommendation phase in November 2005, the technical report for specifying the query language XQuery for XML went through 14 Working Draft versions, published between February 2001 and September 2005. The W3C Recommendation for XQuery was finally published in January 2007.

Importantly, however, work on a technical report at any maturity level may cease at any time. Alternatively, it may continue within some other development work, or it may be divided into the development of several technical reports. Occasionally, the Candidate Recommendation phase is skipped, the Candidate Recommendation is versioned, or a Candidate Recommendation may return to the level of Working Draft for more extensive reconsideration.

After a Recommendation has been published, it might remain a Recommendation indefinitely. In some cases, however, modifications might be started or W3C might rescind the entire Recommendation. Rescinding may take place, for example, if the Recommendation becomes so outdated that further modification is not considered useful, in which case W3C publishes a technical report labeled as *Rescinded Recommendation*. So far, no Rescinded Recommendations have been published.

Modifications to a Recommendation are distinguished according to the type of change needed. If new features are planned, then the full process of advancing the technical report to a Recommendation is re-started from a new Working Draft. If there are no new features, but the modifications are more than minor corrections and they affect the conformance of implementations of the solutions described in the report, the modification process may involve a technical report at the maturity level *Proposed Edited Recommendation*. During this stage, the working group responsible for the Recommendation seeks confirmation for the proposed modifications from other W3C working groups and from the public before the modified version can achieve the status of Recommendation.

3.1.2   Sectoral Standardization

Rules for the purposes of a specific sector or application domain are defined at the sectoral level. Such rules supplement the universal rules and serve as the basis for tailoring further specifications at the local standardization level. The developer of sectoral specifications is often a consortium of organizations within a specific sector, but it may also be an individual or a single organization, such as a software company. We consider sectoral standardization within the electronic commerce community in the case study at the end of this chapter.

In the public sector, XML-related standardization is advancing on both the international and national levels. The European Parliament has established the EU Interoperability Forum for developing XML-based rules for the administration of the European Union. National XML standardization efforts in many countries include special recommendations and e-government services. In Finland, for example, the Ministry of Finance has developed recommendations for the use of XML in the public sector. In Denmark, an XML Committee established to support XML standardization published a handbook for standardization and many XML schemas. In the United Kingdom, several recommendations and XML schemas have been published at the Govtalk Web site at http://www.cabinetoffice.gov.uk/govtalk/. Among the UK standards, there are, for example, 11 XML schemas available for presenting address and personal information, 6 schemas for archives and records management, and 6 schemas for education. XML standardization in the Finnish public domain is further discussed in the case study in Chap. 8.

3.2   XML Family of Languages

A rich collection of languages related to XML has evolved to serve the needs of Web communication and the management of data (particularly on the Internet). The discussion in this subsection is restricted to the XML-related languages developed at W3C, which we call the XML family of languages. We introduce a classification of the languages and briefly describe the languages that have reached the W3C Recommendation phase (see Fig. 3.3).[2] In our discussion, we omit some languages having their own specifications but defined solely for the needs of some other language.

XML Transducers	XML Applications			
	Web Publishing	Semantic Web	Web Communication	Non-textual Data
CSS	XHTML	RDF	P3P	SMIL
DOM	XML Events	RDF Schema	XML Signature	MathML
XSLT	XForms	OWL	XML Encryption	SMIL Animation
XSL		WebCGM XFC	SOAP	SVG
Canonical XML		GRDDL	CC/PP	RubyAnnotation
XInclude		SPARQL	XKMS	VoiceXML
XQuery		POWDER	WSDL	SSML
XProc			SML	EMMA
				TTML
XML Accessories				
XPath, XML Names, XML Stylesheet, XML Schema,				
XLink, XML Base, XPointer, xml:id, ITS				
XML				

Fig. 3.3   XML family of languages

---

[2] Rather than relying on explicit references to each recommendation individually, readers should consult the W3C site [25] to access any of the specifications mentioned in this chapter.

3.2.1   Classification of the XML Languages

The XML-related languages developed at W3C can be divided into four main categories based on their purpose. The first category includes all versions of XML itself. They create the basis for the other three categories: XML accessories, XML transducers, and XML applications.

XML accessories are languages that are intended for wide use to extend the capabilities specified in XML. Examples of XML accessories are the XML Schema language, extending the definition capability of XML DTDs, and XML Names, extending the naming mechanism of XML to allow element and attribute names in a single XML document that are defined for and used by multiple software modules. These have both been introduced in Chap. 2. Specifications of the languages in this group are typically used as (normative) references in other specifications of the XML family, and also widely in specifications of XML-based languages developed outside W3C. Consequently, together with XML itself, the XML accessories class creates the basis for the other two classes: XML transducers and XML applications.

XML transducers are languages that are intended for converting some input XML data into some output form. A transducer language is associated with a processing model that defines the way output is derived from input. Examples of XML transducers are the style sheet languages CSS and XSL, intended to produce external presentations from XML data, and XSLT and XQuery for transforming XML documents into other XML documents or into data in another form.

XML applications are languages that define constraints for a class of XML data that is to be used in some special application area. The constraints are expressed by means of a schema for a whole document type or for some special elements and attributes, where the defined set of element and attribute names is usually identified by a namespace URI. Examples of XML applications are MathML, defined for mathematical data, and RDF, intended for metadata. XML applications always have an XML syntax (possibly with other syntaxes as well), whereas XML accessories and XML transducers may not have any XML syntax. The languages in the XML applications category can be further divided into four subcategories according to the application area:

- Web publishing
- Metadata and Semantic Web
- Web communication and services
- Non-textual forms of data

The following subsections briefly introduce the languages of the XML family, excluding XML itself. Each table in these subsections lists the languages included in a class or a subclass and, for each language, its purpose and the year(s) it achieved W3C Recommendation status. The languages in each table are listed chronologically. The tables are compact forms of tables found in the Web portal *XML Family of Languages* [17], which also includes languages that have not yet reached the Recommendation level as well as W3C reports closely related to the languages, such as requirements and use case documents. The portal also provides links to the official W3C reports.

Table 3.1 XML accessories

Language	Purpose	Recommendation
XML Names	Qualifying element and attribute names	1999, 2004, 2006, 2009
XML Stylesheet	Associating style sheets with an XML document	1999, 2010
XPath	Addressing parts of XML documents	1999, 2007, 2010
XML Schema	Constraining a class of XML documents	2001, 2004
XLink	Creating and describing links	2001, 2010
XML Base	A base URI service	2001, 2010
XPointer	Fragment identifiers especially for URI references	2003
xml:id	Attribute xml:id in XML documents	2005
ITS	Mechanism to support internationalization and localization of content	2007

3.2.2 XML Accessories

XML accessories are languages that are intended for wide use to extend the capabilities specified in XML. Table 3.1 lists the XML accessories that have matured to Recommendation status, in chronological order of their first Recommendation.

The accessory languages can be divided into two groups. XML Names and XML Schema provide important means for developing XML applications for particular sectors and for particular organizations. The rest of the languages are typically needed for the development of technological implementations. Understanding the capabilities of the languages in the first group is important to people participating in schema development, especially for those having expertise of a particular domain but not necessarily much technical knowledge in IT. We introduced these languages in Chap. 2.

As also described in Chap. 2, *XPath* defines how to address parts of XML documents. It is intended to be embedded in other languages, such as XSLT and XQuery (see Sect. 3.2.3 below).

XML Stylesheet in Table 3.1 refers to the specification for associating style sheets with XML documents, providing a means to specify how documents should be rendered or transformed. The association is declared in the prolog of a document by means of a specific processing instruction. Transducer languages to define the style sheets for rendering and transformation are described in the Sect. 3.2.3.

XLink, XML Base, and XPointer are closely related languages facilitating identification and linking of resources. *XLink* is intended for description and creation of links between Web resources. It is defined using XML syntax and can therefore be regarded as a special XML application for hypermedia. Links can be simple and unidirectional, similar to hyperlinks found in HTML, but XLink can also be used to define relationships among more than two resources. Links can be embedded in documents, or alternatively they can reside in a location separate from the linked resources. Links can also be associated with metadata.

Uniform Resource Identifiers (URIs) are used in XML documents to refer to Web resources. URI references can be absolute or relative, and they may include a fragment identifier to refer to a part of a document or point inside a resource.

Table 3.2 XML transducers

Language	Purpose	Recommendation
CSS	Rendering	(1996), 1998, 2008
DOM	Parsing	1998, 2000, 2004
XSLT	Transformation	1999, 2007
Canonical XML	Canonicalization	2001, 2002, 2008
XSL	Rendering	2001, 2006
XInclude	Merging	2004, 2006
XQuery	Querying	2007, 2010
XProc	Pipelining a sequence of operations	2010

XML Base provides a service to resolve relative URIs. It defines a special attribute xml:base for this purpose. *XPointer* defines fragment identifiers for URI references pointing to whole nodes, ranges, or points inside XML resources.

As described in Sect. 2.2.3, XML provides a special attribute type ID for attaching unique identifiers to elements. The second last entry in Table 3.1 refers to a specification defining a special attribute xml:id of the type ID. The purpose is to encourage authors of XML documents to name their ID attributes xml:id to increase interoperability on the Web. Finally, *ITS* refers to Internationalization Tag Set, which introduces a set of elements and attributes that are intended to be used for the internationalization and localization of schemas and documents. An implementation is provided for three schema languages: XML DTD, XML Schema, and RELAX NG.

3.2.3   XML Transducers

The XML transducers are intended for converting XML data into some other form. Table 3.2 lists the XML transducers, which include languages for parsing (DOM), rendering (CSS and XSL), transformation (XSLT), canonicalization (Canonical XML), merging (XInclude), querying (XQuery), and pipelining (XProc).

The Document Object Model (DOM) specifies a set of interfaces for treating the components of the logical structure of an XML document as a collection of objects. This provides the basis for implementing an XML application that processes a document as if it were a tree, as described in Sect. 2.5.2. DOM Level 1 provides interfaces for manipulating XML and HTML documents through Java or ECMAScript programs. DOM Level 2 adds interfaces for views, events, style sheets, document traversal, and ranges within documents; DOM Level 3 introduces additional interfaces for loading and saving documents and for updating them while ensuring they remain (or become) valid.

There are two style sheet languages available for specifying how XML documents are rendered for human perception. *CSS* is a language for specifying style sheets for any structured documents. *CSS1* published as a Recommendation in 1996 was developed especially for HTML documents. Subsequently, the XML notation was explicitly accommodated in developing *CSS2*. The resulting level 2 CSS was accepted as a

Recommendation in 1998, and active development of level 3 CSS started a few years later. The goal in *CSS3* is to create a modularized CSS specification.

On the other hand, *XSL* is a style sheet language especially designed for XML documents. In contrast to CSS, it uses XML syntax for style sheets. XSL contains the transformation language *XSLT* as one of its components. Because XSLT is a major development tool that can be used independently of XSL, it was formalized in a separate recommendation. XSLT will be described more extensively in Sect. 4.2.

The XML specification does not define when two XML documents should be regarded as equivalent. Therefore small changes to a document may or may not affect an application's behavior. This has caused problems, especially in security critical applications, for example, those dependent on using digital signatures. *Canonical XML* defines a process to create a specific physical representation, a canonical form, for an XML document or a document subset. Canonical XML defines the syntax for the result of canonicalization, and it is thus not a language for specifying an application-specific transduction as are the rendering, transformation, and query languages.

XInclude is a language for describing how to merge a set of XML documents. The language is specified by defining a namespace with two special elements: include and fallback. The attributes of an include element specify the resource to be included and the way the resource is processed. The fallback element is used inside the include element to recover missing resources.

XQuery is intended to provide flexible facilities to retrieve data from persistent XML data resources and from virtual XML resources, whether they are local resources or resources elsewhere on the World Wide Web. The language is a superset of XPath and is defined in terms of the *XQuery 1.0 and XPath 2.0 Data Model*. The semantics of XQuery expressions are described informally in the *XQuery 1.0* specification document and formally in the *XQuery 1.0 and XPath 2.0 Formal Semantics* document. There is also XML syntax, called *XQueryX*, defined for the queries. XQuery will be further introduced in Sect. 4.5.

The latest of the XML transducers is *XProc*, a pipeline language that enables description of a sequence of operations to be performed on a collection of XML input documents.

3.2.4 XML Applications

Many of the languages introduced above can or must be expressed using the XML syntax and therefore could also be included in the category of XML applications. Here we introduce those XML applications developed at W3C that are not included in the previous classes.

An extensive list of XML applications has been collected by Robin Cover [6], but the list is no longer regularly updated. Nevertheless, the list shows the rich variety of XML applications developed by many organizations and individuals to embrace XML technology.

We divide the applications developed at W3C into four subcategories. The first subcategory consists of the languages intended for Web publishing, to replace HTML. The second subcategory includes languages important for building the Semantic Web. The third subcategory consists of applications related to Web communication and services. Finally, the fourth subcategory includes languages intended for non-textual forms of data.

3.2.4.1 Web Publishing

HTML has been a huge success as a language for publishing content on the Internet, and for many organizations a significant fraction of their information resources are in HTML format. As mentioned in Sect. 1.3, HTML is an SGML application that has a less constrained syntax than XML. For example, HTML does not require full tagging. Therefore most HTML resources cannot be processed by XML software. While XML is adopted in organizations for other purposes and the variety of XML software available is expanding, HTML resources still require their own software. This problem can be avoided by changing from the use of HTML to the use of XHTML that defines identical constructs to those of HTML but follows XML rules.

HTML is a content language aimed at many kinds of devices in addition to laptops and workstations. These devices include TV screens of various sizes, handheld computers, portable phones, etc. In some environments, a change from HTML to XHTML may require only a change to obey the XML rules in HTML markup. However, the markup planned for a traditional computer screen does not function well, for example, on very small portable devices having the need to print onto lowcost printers. Therefore it is important that there are several well-defined variants of the XHTML markup. There is also a need to embed other markup within XHTML if users wish to display non-textual marked-up data. Some browsers are already available for supporting the use of markup beyond XHTML. For example, the W3C's Amaya browser allows combining XHTML, mathematical formulae described by MathML, and vector graphics described by SVG markup.

Thus XHTML supports flexibility beyond what is available in HTML. XHTML is actually a family of languages (see Table 3.3). This family facilitates the use of XHTML modules, i.e., sets of elements and attributes, in various combinations for various platforms, embedding other markup languages within XHTML, embedding XHTML modules within other markup languages, and extending XHTML for future emerging platforms.

3.2.4.2 Metadata and Semantic Web

Metadata and metadata standards are necessary to manage the data on the Web. Special efforts have been made at W3C to create rules for adding semantic metadata in a form understandable by computers.

XML provides syntactic rules for organizing and presenting data from any application domain in structured documents. These rules define customized vocabulary chosen

Table 3.3 XML applications for Web publishing

Language	Purpose	Recommendation
XHTML	Reformulation of HTML 4.0 in XML specified by three document types: Strict, Transitional, Frameset	1999, 2000, 2002, 2010
XHTML Basic	The minimal core of XHTML	2000, 2010
XHTML Modularization	Definition of XHTML elements and attributes in a set of modules	2001, 2010
XML Events	Representation for asynchronous occurrences, such as mouse clicks, in XHTML or in other XML markup	2003
XForms	Definition of Web forms allowing online interaction between human users and software, to be used in XHTML or in other XML markup	2003, 2006, 2009
XHTML-Print	Simple XHTML suitable for printing from mobile devices as well as for display	2006, 2010

specifically for the type of data and its anticipated applications. The names in the vocabulary and their hierarchic relationships in the markup are intended to be understood by people developing the language, content authors, and people retrieving information from the content. Typically the semantics expressed in the markup is understood within the intended community. For example, consider the following document:

```
<rhyme author="tellervo" title="Oma loru">
        <line>Talven jälkeen</line>
        <line>tulee kesä</line>
</rhyme>
```

Readers understanding both Finnish and English can easily understand that the attribute title does not refer to an honorific title of the author but rather to the title of the rhyme, that this is a kind of poem, and that tellervo is the person who has written the poem. Such reasoning is easy for a human who knows the natural language meanings of the words. Human users can also be informed about the meaning of markup by means of comments added to the schema.

For computers, reasoning like this is not so simple, especially if the resources are written using multiple kinds of markup. For example, on the Internet there are many resources related to poems, a great deal of them represented as marked up text. Some of the markup vocabularies are based on TEI [22], others are based on DocBook [23], and most of them are simply HTML documents. All of these different markup languages have important benefits in the communities where they have been adopted. Combining data from these sources, and reasoning about the collection, however, requires human intermediaries. To build a portal to retrieve information from the poem-related resources requires some middleware between the portal and the resources.

To facilitate more effective use of the resources available on the Web, W3C started the development of technologies and languages to support the evolution of the current Web into the Semantic Web. The goal in building the new Web is not to

Table 3.4 XML applications for metadata and Semantic Web

Language	Purpose	Recommendation
RDF (Resource Description Framework)	Model and XML-based language for metadata describing Web resources	1999, 2004
RDF Schema	Mechanism to define RDF vocabularies	2004
OWL (Web Ontology Language)	Language for publishing and sharing ontologies	2004, 2009
WebCGM XCF	Metadata for WebCGM pictures	2007, 2010
GRDDL	Definition of markup for declaring that an XML document includes RDF compatible data	2007
SPARQL	Query language for RDF	2008
POWDER	Metadata to describe a group of Web resources	2009

restrict heterogeneity of Web content. Instead, the goal is to facilitate building meta-data resources on top of the heterogeneous resources to describe properties of those resources in a standardized way. At this metadata level the resources and properties are identified by unique identifiers. Like the identification of namespaces, the URI mechanism has been chosen as the syntax for the identifiers. A benefit of using the same identification mechanism is that if there are well-defined concepts in a pre-defined namespace, we can adopt those names for our metadata description. For example, if we want to describe the title and author of a poem by widely understood properties, we might identify the properties by the URIs

> http://purl.org/dc/elements/1.1/title
> http://purl.org/dc/elements/1.1/creator

In these URIs, http://purl.org/dc/elements/1.1/ identifies the namespace for the Dublin Core elements, version 1.1 [7]. In that namespace, title is defined as "a name given to the resource" and creator is defined as "an entity primarily responsible for making the resource." Through the use of such unique identifiers, these meanings can be shared by various pieces of software.

Table 3.4 summarizes the XML applications that provide standards for various kinds of metadata on the Web and especially for the Semantic Web. Two of the specifications are intended for any metadata. *XCF* (XML Companion File) is designed for the externalization of any non-graphical metadata related to Web graphics. The associated graphics metadata is described using WebCGM. *POWDER* (Protocol for Web Description Resources) is intended for organizations and indi-viduals to publish machine-readable metadata that describes a group of Web resources. The other languages are described below.

RDF provides a general model and XML syntax for metadata describing Web resources. Unlike XML, the model is not based on the hierarchic containment struc-ture of documents. Instead RDF allows users to specify various characteristics of things. These things may be accessible on the Web, but they need not be. Anything that can be identified by a URI is regarded in RDF as a Web resource and can be described by RDF. Web resources can include, for example, digital documents, soft-ware, or services accessible on the World Wide Web, or they can be organizations, buildings, or individuals identified by a URI.

RDF descriptions can be created, for example, by content authors, content publishers, or brokers who provide metadata for content published by various parties. Since there are many alternative ways to describe resources using RDF, it is important to have a schema language to force consistency among the descriptions within a community, and thus provide better means for computers to process them. *RDF Schema* has been developed for this purpose. It allows the definition of RDF vocabularies and some relationships between concepts and properties in the vocabularies.

Furthermore, by using *OWL*, more complicated relationships can be defined. For example, with OWL we might define properties Contains and Contained for things called Publication and specify that both of the properties are transitive properties and inverses of each other. Using that information OWL compliant software would be able to reason about containment relationships of publications.

If RDF data is written using XML syntax then any XML query language can be used to query the data. However, *SPARQL* is the W3C query language defined especially for querying RDF data. The use of RDF is also supported by a mechanism called *GRDDL* (Gleaning Resource Descriptions from Dialects of Languages). It introduces markup for declaring that an XML document includes data compatible with RDF and for linking to algorithms to extract this data from the document.

Suppose the definitions mentioned in the previous paragraphs are included in an ontology used by publishers as part of the RDF descriptions of their publications. Such an ontology would include properties such as Creator, Contributor, Title, Type, and so forth from the Dublin Core element set, in addition to the properties Contains and Contained. If the RDF descriptions were available on the Web, there might also be a special-purpose browser available that can retrieve online publications and find answers to queries such as: Who is the author of the short story entitled *The Overcoat*? Is the English translation of *The Overcoat* contained in some collection? What are the collections written in Finnish containing *The Overcoat* along with short stories of other Russian writers from the same time period? The browser could allow users to change the language of the user interface so that they can refer to authors, publications, stories, and so on, in their own language.

RDF, RDF Schema, and OWL descriptions are XML documents. Therefore they can be processed by XML tools. For example, the publication browser described above could be implemented by an XQuery engine. Because the queries written in XQueryX or SPARQL have XML syntax themselves, they could be stored in a user profile. These queries could later be combined or manipulated in other ways by using XML tools. The result is a very powerful facility for supporting computer-based and computer-driven access to Web-based resources. These ideas are explored further in Chap. 6.

3.2.4.3 Web Communication and Services

The more there are resources and services available on the Internet, the greater the need to define clear rules governing how data and services are exchanged between software agents in a secure manner. This has become especially important with the growth of electronic commerce. Software applications developed on various operating systems

Table 3.5 XML applications for Web communication and services

Language	Purpose	Recom-mendation
P3P (Platform for Privacy Preferences)	To enable Web sites to express their practices to collect and use data collected from users of sites	2002
XML-Signature	Associating digital objects by digital signatures in XML format	2002
XML Encryption	Encrypting data and representing the result in XML	2002
SOAP (Simple Object Access Protocol)	Rules to exchange structured and typed information between peers in a decentralized, distributed environment	2003, 2007
CC/PP (Composite Capabilities/Preference Profiles)	A format for how a client device tells an origin server about its user agent profile	2004
XKMS (XML Key Management Specification)	Protocol for distributing and registering public keys	2005
WSDL	To describe Web services	2007
SML	Service modeling	2009

and platforms must be able to communicate with each other about business matters in spite of corporate firewalls. The messages sent between applications may travel through several servers located in various countries and on various host systems.

For example, in the case of business transactions or in exchanging patient records, it is essential that the receiving application has a means to make sure that the digital objects sent have not been changed, destroyed, or lost in an unauthorized or accidental manner. In many situations whole documents or parts of them have to be exchanged in encrypted form and decryption keys are required to recover the content. Software applications providing services to consumers often collect significant amounts of data from the users, including, for example, personal data, financial data, and data about their communication devices and software. Therefore there is a need to create and exchange rules related to the collection and use of data. W3C has developed XML-based languages for all these purposes (see Table 3.5).

During the last several years there has been widespread interest in developing Web service technology to support automation in building and using Web services in business processes. Many scenarios have been presented, some of them combining Semantic Web technologies and Web service technologies. In these scenarios software agents support business needs to find suitable business partners, to make agreements about inter-organizational business procedures, to perform services using these procedures, and to negotiate possible changes needed after making an agreement. Work in this area has been realized in service registries such as *Universal Description, Discovery and Integration* (UDDI) and languages describing business processes and services. Several competitive standards have evolved. The language developed at W3C to describe Web services is called *WSDL* (Web Services Description Language). It is intended to facilitate definition of service interfaces and functionalities so that services needed for a particular situation can be automatically accessed and connected to other services.

Table 3.6 XML applications for non-textual data

Language	Purpose	Recom-mendation
SMIL (Synchronized Multimedia Integration Language)	To integrate a set of independent multimedia objects into a synchronized multimedia presentation	1998, 2001, 2005, 2008
MathML (Mathematical Markup Language)	To support mathematical notation, especially for encoding mathematical material for the Web	1999, 2001, 2003, 2010
Ruby Annotation	To define markup for ruby, short annotations alongside the base text typically used in East Asian documents	2001
SMIL Animation	To provide animation functionality in XML documents	2001
SVG	To describe two-dimensional vector and mixed vector/raster graphic	2001, 2003
VoiceXML (Voice Extensible Markup Language)	To describe audio dialogs and thus support interactive voice response applications on the Web	2004, 2007
SSML (Speech Synthesis Markup Language)	To assist generation of synthetic speech in Web and other applications	2004, 2010
EMMA (Extensible Multimodal Annotation Markup Language)	To enable access to the Web using multimodal interfaces	2009
TTML (Timed Text Markup Language)	Textual information that is associated with timing information	2010

The W3C standards listed in Table 3.5 provide a toolbox to implement the components needed to build secure Web Services. *SOAP* is a general mechanism for exchanging service requests and responses, and *CC/PP* provides a facility for describing client behavior. *XML-Signature*, *XML Encryption*, and *XKMS* provide secure services for communication, *P3P* provides mechanisms to document privacy policies, and *WSDL* facilitates the description of the messages sent and received in a service, to describe what kinds of functionality the service provides, and where and how to access the service. Finally, *SML* enables the modeling of complex services and systems.

3.2.4.4   Non-textual Data

XML was designed to enrich text consisting of Unicode characters by adding markup. In Sect. 1.5.2 we briefly discussed the ways non-textual data can be included in XML documents. Typically this data is intended to be represented for human perception in some form other than conventional, linear text, for example, using voice, image, or multimedia presentations.

Basically there are two distinct ways to include non-textual data in XML documents: either as external entities or as descriptions of that data using marked up text. Table 3.6 shows the markup language standards of W3C for non-textual forms of data. The latest of the standards in this class are the Extensible MultiModal Annotation language *EMMA* and the Timed Text Markup Language *TTML*. EMMA is intended to enable the access to the Web using multimodal interfaces. It is used for describing the interpretation of user input, for example, transcription of raw signals derived from speech or pen input into words. TTML is intended to be used as an interchange format for timed text information among heterogeneous authoring systems. Some of the languages for non-textual data will be described further in Chap. 5.

3.3 Variety of Software

A major benefit of XML markup is its text form: documents can be created by human authors using any simple text editor or automatically by means of software in any platform. This applies equally well to schemas and style sheets. However, an XML parser is needed to check the well-formedness or the validity of documents. Furthermore, to use XML reliably as part of an information system, more advanced software is needed. The rapid development of a rich variety of software has been supported not only by the text format, but also by other factors:

SGML inheritance. XML is a restricted form of SGML, and there was a remarkable selection of software available for SGML document management before the introduction of XML. Much of the software intended for XML document management is adapted from SGML software. This software includes editors for DTDs and document instances, parsers, formatting and publishing software, database software, query engines, and conversion software.

Open standards. Open standards for XML and other languages of the XML family facilitate the design of commercial software for many platforms and by various vendors, as well as the development of open source software by individuals and organizations. For example, a long list of software for using XML with databases is given at the Web site maintained by Ronald Bourret [3]. The list includes both commercial and open source software. W3C distributes its own open source software at http://www.w3.org/Status, including, for example, validators for several languages of the XML family (XHTML, SVG, MathML, CSS, XML Schema, and RDF), the Amaya Web Editor/Browser integrating several W3C technologies (XML, XHTML family, MathML, and SVG), and the DTD2Schema conversion tool to transform DTDs to schemas in XML Schema. A guide to free XML software is published by Lars Marius Garshold at http://www.garshol.priv.no/download/xmltools/.

Strong support for programming. Public-domain and commercial XML processors have been available for use with a variety of programming languages since 1998. Programming interfaces are generally, although not exclusively, made available using either SAX or DOM.

SAX [2], briefly introduced in Sect. 2.5.1, is an application programming interface (API) that provides the basis for a processor to scan XML text as a stream of tokens and receive notification of important *events* (such as the start of the document, the start of an element, the end of an element) as they are encountered. Originally,

SAX was defined for Java, and several Java-based processors for XML have been developed, but it has since also become available for other languages, including C++, Perl, Python, and C#.

As an alternative, the Document Object Model (DOM) was developed by W3C to provide a tree-based interface to HTML and XML documents, as described in Sect. 3.2.3 above. XML processors incorporating DOM provide applications with facilities to traverse the nodes in a document tree and to update the tree as needed. W3C describes language bindings for Java and ECMAScript, but other languages (including C++, Perl, Python, and C#) have also incorporated DOM interfaces.

Collaborative development. The Internet and the World Wide Web have facilitated strong collaboration of individuals and organizations around the world. Software companies participate actively in the standardization work at W3C, as well as in some other standard development organizations such as OASIS (see Sect. 3.7). Thus the needs and experiences of commercial software vendors influence standards development. In return, participating companies can test their implementation of the standards during their early development phases.

Modular standard development. Section 3.2 showed that the standardization work at W3C has been strongly modular, resulting in the family of languages shown in Fig. 3.3. Software applications can be built to implement individual languages or various combinations of them. W3C working groups maintain lists of implementations. For example, the XML Query Working Group has published a list of over 50 XQuery implementations.

3.4   Application-Independent Data Assets

Data assets for most organizations are often stored in application-dependent formats, such as proprietary file formats controlled by document authoring systems. This causes problems for data integration and for long-term accessibility of information in data repositories. Furthermore the owners of data may become overly dependent on particular software vendors for providing access to their own valuable assets.

The capability to store data produced in organizational processes in open standard formats gives the benefit that the data can be accessed and processed by software from various vendors. Furthermore, when XML is used as the format, the information can be organized in schemas, documents, and style sheets so that all of them are accessible using the same tools, processable by diverse but standard software, and also readable by human individuals.

The public sectors in many countries have been especially concerned about application dependency for their digital data assets and long-term accessibility of information. Much of the data assets in the public sector are documents created by office systems. OASIS has developed and maintains the XML-based file format called *OpenDocument Format for Office Applications* (*OpenDocument* or *ODF*). Version 1.0 was approved as an OASIS standard in 2005 and as an ISO and IEC (International Electrotechnical Commission) standard in 2006 [11]. Version 1.1 was approved as an OASIS standard at the start of 2007. The schemas for OpenDocument have been defined using the RELAX NG schema language [5]. OpenDocument XML.org, an online community, maintains a site hosted by OASIS at http://open-document.xml.org/ to support the adoption of OpenDocument and to distribute related open source software. The site is sponsored by three major companies: Google, IBM, and Sun Microsystems (now part of Oracle).

Microsoft, the dominant supplier of office applications, is not among the sponsors of OpenDocument XML.org and has not participated in the development work of OpenDocument. Instead, in partnership with several other organizations, Microsoft developed alternative XML-based formats for office documents called *Office Open XML File Formats* [15]. These formats are also called OOXML or OpenXML and are available as part of the 2007 Microsoft Office software. The formats were accepted as ECMA[3] standards [8] in 2006, submitted to an ISO/IEC committee for adoption as an international standard under the "fast track" procedure, and adopted by ISO and IEC in 2008 [12]. Thus, in spite of extensive international controversy, both formats are now ISO/IEC standards.

Competing standards are not rare in information technology, and they may be seen to promote competition and innovation. However, for governments and private enterprises which develop standardization policies on electronic document formats, the existence of two competing standards for the same purpose causes extra efforts in the decision process. Several technical comparisons have been published, including one by Becta, a British agency overseeing the national policy in taking advantage of information technology in education [1]. A well-documented example of the difficulties in making a decision is the multi-year study conducted by the state of Massachusetts [19], which is further examined in Sect. 8.3.2.

3.5   Web-Enabled Access

The World Wide Web, where published material is available as Web pages organized into Web sites, is the dominant single publication channel today. Human readers access the content of the sites by using Web browsers such as Mozilla Firefox, Safari, Opera, or Internet Explorer. The language of Web pages is HTML or XHTML. Special Web browsers and special markup languages are used in small mobile devices including mobile phones. Only some of the pages accessible on the Web are stored on the sites as static Web pages in the format used for displaying the content to the readers. The rest of the Web pages, known as the *Deep Web*, are created dynamically at the time of access from data stored in databases or other data repositories.

When XML is used as the format of data in repositories, its users gain the benefit that the information content of the repositories can be made accessible through Web

---

[3]ECMA International (European association for standardizing information and communication systems, http://www.ecma-international.org) is an industry association dedicated to the standardization of information and communication technologies and consumer electronics.

browsers using standard transformation tools such as XSLT. Using the same tools, the content can be distributed for various browsers and devices. In Sect. 4.2 we will give an example of a transformation from XML to XHTML.

Recently many governments and other organizations have been active in making their datasets publicly available for examination or download through Web browsers and for reuse in software applications. This *open data* is often provided in XML format, or in a format that can be transformed into XML with standard tools. For example, at the Data.gov site, many U.S. Federal Executive Branch datasets can be accessed. (As of May 2011, nearly 200 of the datasets include the search term XML, and all these are available in XML format. Alternatively, the open data search http:// opendatasearch.org/?spatial=USA+Federal+Government returns 260 US Federal Government files in XML format).

3.6 Interoperability

The need for interoperability is probably the most important reason for the adoption of XML in many environments and for the central role of XML in the standardization policies published by various government agencies. Interoperability refers to the ability to work together. At a narrow technical level the term refers to the ability of software applications to exchange information. At a broader level the term refers to the ability to exchange information in an efficient and uniform manner across systems, organizations, or business processes. The use of open standards, and XML in particular, is an important facilitator of integration in many domains. For example, the impact of XML on biomedical information interoperability has been described in an article by Shabo et al. [18] in the special issue of the *IBM Systems Journal* celebrating 10 years of XML [9].

XML is mentioned as a core standard in all Government Interoperability Frameworks (or GIFs) developed for the public domain during the last several years. In practice, the interoperability frameworks are essentially catalogues of standards. Examples of the frameworks are listed in Table 3.7. In the interoperability framework published by the European Commission, three kinds of interoperability are considered: organizational, semantic, and technical. Semantic interoperability refers to the ability to exchange information between applications so that data received from another application can be processed in a meaningful manner. XML is

Table 3.7 Government interoperability frameworks

Country	Title and Reference
European Union	European Interoperability Framework for Pan-European eGovernment Services, Version 1.0 [10]
United Kingdom	e-Government Interoperability Framework Version 6.1 [4]
New Zealand	New Zealand Interoperability Framework (NZ e-GIF), Version 3.3 [20]
Australia	Australian Government Interoperability Framework, Version 2 [21]
Hong Kong	The HKSARG Interoperability Framework, Version 6.0 [14]

recommended to be used as a means to create common semantics. The use of XML-based standards is recommended also for technical level interoperability, supporting the connection of computer systems and services.

3.7   Case Study: Business Applications

An important motivation for the development of XML and XML-related technologies came from the needs of business. In the middle of the 1990s the new business opportunities of the World Wide Web were realized, but a major barrier was the lack of a common data format and business rules in a form in which various software applications could be flexibly connected to each other and process business data. Therefore, following the publication of XML many development activities evolved with expectations to enable a shift to a new kind of network economy by defining vocabularies, protocols, frameworks, schemas, registries, repositories, and methods for business needs in general, and for particular business sectors with common interests.

Organizing collaborative development work has clearly been challenging in many sectors. Partly the problems have been related to the turbulence of the global economy. For example, over a decade ago there was a proposal to build a Common Business Library for XML components for use in electronic commerce applications [13]. Both the company that initiated the proposal and the industry association that planned to charter the development have since ceased. This doomed the development of the Common Business Library.

The major organizational coordinator and supporter of the development work for business needs has been OASIS. It was originally formed in 1993 as SGML Open to develop guidelines for interoperability among products that support SGML. The name OASIS (the Organization for the Advancement of Structured Information Standards) was adopted in 1998 to reflect the expanded scope of the development activities, especially to include XML-related work. OASIS has more than 5,000 members and 75 sponsoring organizations including major information technology companies such as Google, Hewlett-Packard, IBM, Microsoft, Nokia, Novell, Oracle, SAP, and Sun and several technology user organizations such as the US Department of Defense, the World Bank, and Visa International. More than 300 organizations worldwide participate as contributors to the OASIS technical work, including companies from a variety of sectors, public sector organizations, and research institutes.

In 1999, together with the United Nations Centre for Trade Facilitation and Electronic Business (UN/CEFACT), OASIS established a joint initiative called ebXML (Electronic Business using XML) to develop a modular set of specifications to enable enterprises to conduct business over the Internet. The goal was to help enterprises to complement and extend their existing business solutions, for example, to use their old Electronic Data Interchange (EDI) formats for business documents within the new ebXML framework. ISO has approved five specifications under the common name "Electronic business eXtensible Markup Language (ebXML)":

Part 1: Collaboration-protocol profile and agreement specification (ebCPP), ISO/ TS 15000-1:2004 defines how a business partner may describe its message exchange capabilities in a Collaboration Protocol Profile (CPP), and how two partners may express their mutual agreement about conducting business as the intersection of two CPPs in a Collaborative Protocol Agreement (CPA). A DTD and equivalent XML Schema for CPP and CPA are provided.

Part 2: *Message service specification (ebMS), ISO/TS 15000-2:2004* defines XML-based enveloping constructs to exchange electronic business messages. It permits the messages themselves to contain data in any traditional business message syntax such as UN/EDIFACT or ASC X12. The specification uses the W3C's SOAP protocol (see Sect. 3.2.4.3) and defines a set of elements to be used in SOAP messages. A schema for the elements is given by the XML Schema language. The specification also defines how to use W3C's XML Signature (see Sect. 3.2.4.3) to sign messages. The specification includes links as defined in XLink (see Sect. 3.2.2) to reference other documents.

Part 3: *Registry information model specification (ebRIM), ISO/TS 15000-3:2004* defines how organizations can store documents related to Business-to-Business partnerships in a persistent registry. The registry is intended to facilitate ebXML-based partnerships and transactions. The information model for a registry is described using the Unified Modeling Language (UML), and it includes what types of objects are stored in a registry and how they are organized. The model may be implemented in the form of a relational schema, among other representations. The data types are defined as XML Schema data types.

Part 4: *Registry services specification (ebRS), ISO/TS 15000-4:2004* defines the services that provide access to an ebXML registry. The Query Management Service allows a client of an ebXML registry to search for various sorts of registry objects. The Life Cycle Manager Service is used by a client to manage the life cycle of repository items. A Query Management Service supports "filter queries" that are expressed in XML and provide query capabilities for any ebXML registry implementation. An optional SQL Query mechanism is defined, and future versions of the specification will consider the use of XQuery.

Part 5: *ebXML Core Components Technical Specification, Version 2.01(ebCCTS), ISO/TS 15000-5:2005* describes a methodology for developing a common set of building blocks for general types of business data. It is aimed at defining data models and standards for communication parties to support information interoperability. The development work has been done at UN/CEFACT. The results of employing the methodology should be maintained in a freely accessible Core Component Library. The specification uses UML to describe the meta-models and rules for describing the structure and contents of data models, process models, and information exchange models. The specification does not require the use of UML in its implementation.

In addition to these ISO approved specifications, the ebXML consortium has published the ebXML Business Process Specification Schema, which describes how to specify business processes by means of either XML or UML and a specification for the ebXML technical architecture. For business documents an OASIS committee has developed a library of schemas under the name Universal Business

Language (UBL), which includes schemas for business documents such as purchase orders and invoices in XML format.

In addition to OASIS and UN/CEFACT, an important consortium is RosettaNet, founded in 1998 to develop standards for global supply chains for the needs of the information technology and electronics industry. The core idea is to standardize business processes between supply chain partners by defining Partner Interface Processes (PIPs) to define the business logic, message flow, and message content between the partners [16]. RosettaNet consortium has schemas for XML messaging for over 100 PIPs. The associated models describe the roles of partners in messaging and the flow of communication between the partners.

An important business application is XBRL (eXtensible Business Reporting Language [26]), a language for the electronic communication of business and financial data. The language was developed through a non-profit consortium comprising approximately 550 companies and agencies worldwide. XBRL is used by the banking and financial sector worldwide. XBRL case studies have been published at http://www.xbrl.org/CaseStudies/.

In conclusion we see that the adoption of XML has contributed to widespread deployment of tools and services that augment existing business applications or provide new models for conducting business over the Web. This has been achieved primarily because of the open standards, wide variety of software, and general interoperability that results from managing data assets encoded using XML.

References

1. Becta Report: Microsoft Vista and Office 2007. Final report with recommendations on adoption, deployment and interoperability (January 2008) http://webarchive.nationalarchives .gov. uk/20101102103654/publications.becta.org.uk//download.cfm?resID=35275, Cited 10 March 2011.
2. Brownell, D. (ed.): SAX. http://www.saxproject.org/, Cited 10 March 2011.
3. Bourret, R.: XML Database Products (Last update June 20, 2010) http://www.rpbourret.com/xml/XMLDatabaseProds.htm, Cited 10 March 2011.
4. Cabinet Office: e-Government Interoperability Framework Version 6.1 (18 March 2005) e-Government Unit. http://interim.cabinetoffice.gov.uk/media/253452/eGIF%20v6_1(1).pdf, Cited 10 March 2011.
5. Clark, J, Murata, M. (eds): RELAX NG Specification, Committee Specification. OASIS (3 December 2001) http://www.oasis-open.org/committees/relax-ng/spec-20011203.html, Cited 10 March 2011.
6. Cover, R. (ed): Cover Pages. XML: Proposed Applications and Industry Initiatives. http://xml.coverpages.org/xml.html, Cited 10 March 2011.
7. Dublin Core Metadata Element Set, Version 1.1 (Jan 14, 2008). Dublin Core Metadata Initiative. http://dublincore.org/documents/dces/, Cited 10 March 2011.
8. ECMA, Standard ECMA-376. Office Open XML File Formats, second edition (December 2008) http://www.ecma-international.org/publications/standards/Ecma-376.htm, Cited 10 March 2011.
9. Horn, P., Mills, S. (eds): Special Issue on XML. IBM Systems Journal **45**, 2 (2006).
10. IDABC, European Interoperability Framework for Pan-European eGovernment Services. Version 1.0. IDABC. Luxembourg: Office for Official Publications of the European Communities (2004). http://ec.europa.eu/idabc/en/document/3782/5584.html, Cited 10 March 2011.

11. ISO/IEC 26300:2006. Information technology – Open Document Format for Office Applications (OpenDocument) v1.0.

12. ISO/IEC 29500-1:2008. Information technology – Document description and processing languages – Office Open XML File Formats – Part 1: Fundamentals and Markup Language Reference (2008).

13. Meltzer, B., Glushko, R.: XML and electronic commerce: Enabling the network economy. SIGMOD Record **27**, 4, 21–24 (1998).

14. Office of the Government Chief Information Officer: The HKSARG Interoperability Framework [S18] Version: 8.0. The Government of the Hong Kong Special Administrative Region. (December 2009) http://www.ogcio.gov.hk/eng/infra/download/s18.pdf, Cited 10 March 2011.

15. Rice, F.: How to: Manipulate Office Open XML Formats Documents. Office 2007 (December 2006) http://msdn.microsoft.com/en-us/library/aa982683(office.12).aspx, Cited 10 March 2011.

16. RosettaNet PIPs. http://www.rosettanet.org/Standards/RosettaNetStandards/PIPs/tabid/475/Default.aspx, Cited 10 March 2011.

17. Salminen, A.: XML family of languages. Overview and classification of W3C specifications (2000–2010) http://users.jyu.fi/~airi/xmlfamily.html, Cited 10 March 2011.

18. Shabo, A., Rabinovici-Cohen, S., Vortman, P.: Revolutionary impact of XML on biomedical information interoperability. IBM Systems Journal **45**, 2, 361–372 (2006).

19. Shah, R., Kesan, J., Kennis, A.: Implementing open standards: a case study of the Massachusetts open formats policy. Proceedings of the 9th Annual International Digital Government Research Conference, pp. 262–271. Digital Government Society of North America (2008) Available at the ACM Digital Library, doi = 1367832.1367877.

20. State Services Commission: New Zealand Interoperability Framework (NZ e-GIF), Version 3.3 (February 2008) http://www.e.govt.nz/standards/e-gif, Cited 10 March 2011.

21. Stewart, A. (ed): Australian Government Technical Interoperability Framework (July 2005) http://www.finance.gov.au/publications/australian-government-technical-interoperability-framework/, Cited 10 March 2011.

22. TEI Consortium (eds.): TEI P5: Guidelines for Electronic Text Encoding and Interchange. 1.3.0. February 1, 2009. TEI Consortium. http://www.tei-c.org/P5/. Cited 10 March 2011.

23. Walsh, N.: DocBook 5: The Definitive Guide (Hamilton, R. L., ed.), O'Reilly Media, April 2010, 560 pp.

24. W3C Home Page. http://www.w3.org, Cited 10 March 2011.

25. W3C Technical Reports and Publications. http://www.w3.org/TR/, Cited 10 March 2011.

26. XBRL Internal Home Page, http://www.xbrl.org/, Cited 10 March 2011.

Chapter 4
Document Management

Abstract In this chapter the methods and techniques for managing structured documents, particularly documents in XML format, are summarized. Unlike database systems, document management systems emphasize operations that transform documents from one representation to another, including functions to render them for reading through various media and to isolate passages that are of particular interest to a reader. XSLT is an XML standard that has been recommended by W3C for expressing document transformations. The chapter concludes with a case study that examines dictionaries as prototypical structured documents.

Keywords CSS • Dictionary encodings • Indexing • Information retrieval • Querying • Rendering • Structured documents • Transformations • XSL • XSLT

Documents have traditionally been the predominant medium for aggregating and storing information to be used for communication. An author creates, organizes, presents, and stores the content, intended to be understood by readers as information pertaining to a topic. Software is needed for authoring, storing, accessing, and reading of digital documents. Although typically both the authors and the readers have been humans, for a digital document an author or a reader may instead be computer software.

In addition to supporting the functions of authoring and reading, digital documents can be processed by computer software in many different ways. The term *document management* refers to the methods and techniques needed to create, organize, store, process, access, and use documents. Often the term is used in contrast to the more general term *data management*, in order to emphasize the management of documents for human communication.

In this chapter we first introduce the main characteristics of structured documents and contrast structured document management to traditional text management. Although structured document management is akin to database management, one primary characteristic differs: whereas querying is the most important operation in database management, structured document management instead relies primarily

A. Salminen and F. Tompa, *Communicating with XML*,
DOI 10.1007/978-1-4614-0992-2_4, © Springer Science+Business Media, LLC 2011

on various kinds of transformation. In Sect. 4.2 we describe transformation as the characteristic operation on structured documents and XSLT as the language developed for XML transformations. Rendering and querying, both of which can also be regarded as special kinds of transformations, are then considered in Sects. 4.3 and 4.4, respectively. In the last section we introduce a case study where dictionaries are presented as structured documents.

4.1 Structured Documents

The term *structured document* refers to documents in which the author (or designer) has specified and named various parts such that applications can identify, retrieve, and process those parts. Of course, the structuring is often indicated using XML.

4.1.1 Structure Versus Content Versus Layout

As introduced in Chap. 1, the structure, content, and layout of a document can be separated from each other (Fig. 4.1), and each of the three components can be processed separately. Such separation of the facets brings modularity to the management of structured documents, since the planning and definition of structures for document classes within an application area can concentrate on one facet at a time. Furthermore, such separation makes it possible to define the architecture and potential external presentations for a particular class of documents, before there are any document instances. When the separation conforms to open standards, many kinds of software applications can be implemented to process structured documents or their components.

To accommodate the separation of the facets, a repository of structured documents consists of three kinds of resources: schema resources, instance resources, and layout resources. There is a need for versioning and evolution in all three kinds of resources. The management of these different versions and their relationship to each other are major challenges in a structured document management environment.

Even though a structured document is conceptually considered to comprise all three facets, in practice there is not necessarily either a separate structure description

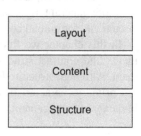

Fig. 4.1 The three facets of a
structured document

or a separate layout definition. In using XML as a notation for structured documents, various schema languages, including DTD and XML Schema, are available for defining the structure; the content consists of the marked up, nested document element together with any external entities referred to in the element; and the layout can be described by a style sheet. However, neither the schema nor the style sheet is mandatory. If there is no schema attached, a default structure definition can be extracted from the structure of the content. If the content is intended for a software application only, and not for human readers, then there is no need for specifying layout at all.

4.1.2 Characteristics of Structured Document Management

Managing structured documents differs essentially from managing traditional word processor files and is often more similar to managing databases. The structure definitions serve as schemas corresponding to database schemas, and the collections of document instances correspond to database instances. The following features are important in structured document management:

Design. Adopting the approach of structured document management in an environment requires careful planning *before* the creation of documents. This contrasts with the authoring of traditional documents by means of word processors, which is often initiated without any separate planning phase. Even in some organizational environments where document templates may be designed, those templates are used to control the document layout rather than its structure.

The schema design for a particular organization participating in inter-organizational business processes may be a tedious and complicated task. The design may be closely connected to the standardization activities of other parties. The schema should be based on the standards developed for a particular sector and standards developed for the Web. The standardization activities at different levels and in different communities may not be fully synchronized.

However requiring schema design has a benefit: like in database environments, schema design forces document designers to analyze the needs of the environment and plan systematic solutions. Whereas database design consists of schema and view design, in structured document management schema and layout design are important. Even though layout can be separated from the structure of documents, it may be important to plan the layout, at least to some extent, alongside the schema design. This was realized, for example, when the Finnish Parliament was adopting the structured document approach [12].

Content production. Database content is usually created gradually using the update facilities of the database system, and the validity of input is checked during such update. In contrast, in structured document environments document instances may be created using various types of software applications. When using syntax-directed content production, checking the validity of document instances against the schema takes place at the time of content production. When using alternative content production environments, validity is checked in a separate parsing phase, typically initiated when a document is uploaded to a document repository.

Evolution. Schema versioning is a well-known problem in database management. An important goal in schema versioning is backward compatibility: the old database instances should conform to the new schema. In his article, Sedlar compares the schema versioning challenges in relational databases and XML data repositories and points out some capabilities provided in XML technologies useful for the management of schema evolution [14]. Unlike in relational databases, however, in structured document management versioning needs must also accommodate layout specifications. Furthermore, it is common that in addition to temporal versioning, there is a need to manage multiple co-existing variants.

Operations. In database management environments querying is the most important database operation. Even though queries are also used in structured document management, the most typical operation in a structured document environment is some kind of transformation. (In fact, processing a query and applying a style sheet can also be regarded as special forms of transformation).

W3C has developed several languages that are intended to define a conversion from XML data to some other form, possibly still described by XML. In the classification of W3C languages in Sect. 3.2, we called those languages *XML transducers*, which include the style sheet languages CSS and XSL, the transformation language XSLT, the canonicalization language Canonical XML, XInclude for merging a set of documents, and XQuery for querying. We examine some of these languages in the following sections.

Correctness. Whereas a database usually serves as a repository to be accessed exclusively through a single database management system, structured documents typically are accessible directly through multiple independent software systems. Thus there is no single management software that ensures data consistency, security, and availability. Instead, these properties are achieved by requiring that each software component operates through standard protocols. It is therefore incumbent on each component to validate its input data, not merely for compliance to XML standards but also compliance to any additional assumptions being made by the application.

4.2 Transformations and XSLT

One of the promises of descriptive markup is that document contents can be re-used for multiple purposes. For example, product descriptions can be used in inventory systems, catalogs, and requests for tenders; catalogs can be printed in pamphlets, displayed on the Web, and spoken over a telephone. The content and the markup need to be presented in different forms for each of these purposes, and thus documents need to be transformed.

Document transformations can be characterized according to the scope of changes that are applied:

Grammar-preserving modifications include changes to the content without any alteration to the markup, as well as insertions, deletions, and rearrangements of repeatable elements and insertions and deletions of optional attributes. For example, changing the name of a product or inserting and deleting corporate locations from a list of branch offices are the simplest forms of transformation.

Local structural modifications include other insertions and deletions, as well as rearrangements of elements within their parent elements. Examples from this category are deleting the director element from each branch office element, inserting a count element to show the number of items in a product line, or reversing the order of presentation for each supplier's name and address.

Global rearrangements include all transformations that span multiple elements within a document. This might involve moving information from one element to another one, or it could involve a systematic inversion of the data. An example of the former is moving a list of corporate officers from the list of contacts to a corporate overview, and the latter is illustrated by changing a list of products per supplier into a list of suppliers for each product.

Multi-document segmentation and integration may split one document into several documents or combine parts of several documents into a single result. For example, a union catalog can be segmented into several documents each reflecting the parts available from a branch office, or sections of a draft annual report might be created by extracting parts from several press releases.

W3C has developed the XML Stylesheet Language (XSL) for rendering XML documents (see Sect. 4.3), from which the XSL Transformation language (XSLT) evolved [9]. XSLT is a functional language that is used to describe a conversion of a source tree representing the input document into a result tree representing the output document. An XSLT program, known as a *style sheet*, consists of a set of templates that include pattern-matching phrases (expressed as XPath expressions) and directives to *push* tree fragments from the source tree to the result tree or *pull* tree fragments into the result tree from wherever they are in the source tree.

To understand the behavior of an XSLT program, it is important to observe that the result tree is created in a strictly top-down, left-to-right order; there are no capabilities to revise or delete pieces of the output tree already produced or to insert additional fragments anywhere other than at the rightmost fringe of a partially-built output tree.

Consider the style sheet fragment in Fig. 4.2. The template is to be applied whenever a node n is encountered in the source tree and starting from node n there is some other node that matches the XPath expression class/student. The actions to be executed with respect to the node n are:

1. For each of the child nodes of n, considered one by one in left-to-right order, apply whatever template is applicable to that node. These applications may or may not cause some structures to be appended to the output tree.

```
<xsl:template match="class/student">
  <xsl:apply-templates/>
  <newNode>
    <xsl:value-of select="instructor/firstName"/>
  </newNode>
</xsl:template>
```

Fig. 4.2 Example XSLT template

2. Append a new rightmost child element, named newNode, to the current node in the output tree and copy over as children of that node all elements that match the pattern instructor/firstname using the context node *n* in the source tree.

   Various actions are available in XSLT, some of which are summarized here:

   • Pattern matching is to be applied to the *current* source node if the specified pattern is matched and the processing state is in the specified mode. Any such template can also be assigned a name. The priority helps to determine which template to use if several ones meet all the applicability constraints.

```
<xsl:template match=pattern name=qname priority=number mode=qname>
 ... possibly including call/apply with other templates ...
</xsl:template>
```

   • Child elements or other source nodes specified by select are to be considered in turn as *current*, but only templates matching the mode (if specified) are applicable.

```
<xsl:apply-templates select=sequence-expression mode=qname>
 ... provide sorting criteria or parameters if applicable ...
</xsl:apply-templates>
```

   • Apply the rules specified by the named template.

```
<xsl:call-template name=qname>
 ... provide template parameters if applicable ...
</xsl:call-template>
```

   • Copy into the output tree the substructures matched by the select pattern.

```
<xsl:value-of select=sequence-expression />
```

   • Source nodes specified by select are to be considered in turn as *current*.

```
<xsl:for-each select=sequence-expression>
 ... provide sorting criteria if applicable ...
</xsl:for-each>
```

   • Assign the value of the expression to the variable having the given name.

```
<xsl:variable name=qname select=expression />
```

- Apply the statements only if the expression evaluates to true.

```
<xsl:if test=expression>
  ...
</xsl:if>
```

- Apply the statements that occur within the first block for which the test expression evaluates to true, or if none of the expressions are true, apply the statements in the otherwise block.

```
<xsl:choose>
<xsl:when test=expression>
  ...
</xsl:when>
  ...
<xsl:when test=expression>
  ...
</xsl:when>
<xsl:otherwise>
  ...
</xsl:otherwise>
</xsl:choose>
```

Much of the power of XSLT results from the existence of precedence rules for choosing which of several matching templates to apply and from the existence of default rules, as well as defaults for any omitted attributes template rules:

- By default, process a node by doing the appropriate actions for each of the node's children.

```
<xsl:template match ="*|/" mode="#all">
  <xsl:apply-templates/>
</xsl:template>
```

- By default, copy text elements and attributes from the source tree to the output tree.

```
<xsl:template match="text()|@*" mode="#all">
  <xsl:value-of select="."/>
</xsl:template>
```

- By default, omit processing instructions and comments.

```
<xsl:template match="processing-instruction()|comment()" mode="#all"/>
```

Figure 4.3 contains a complete XSLT program that extracts all course elements from the input and, for each course, inserts a list of all other course numbers for courses that meet at any of the same times. Note that the default rules copy text content only, and thus the third template is required to copy complete elements instead.

```xml
<?xml version="1.0" encoding="utf-8" ?>
<xsl:stylesheet version="2.0"
    xmlns:xsl="http://www.w3.org/1999/XSL/Transform">

<xsl:template match="/">
    <course-catalog>
        <xsl:apply-templates select="//course" />
    </course-catalog>
</xsl:template>

<xsl:template match="course">
    <course>
        <xsl:apply-templates />
        <xsl:variable name="my-cnum" select="cnum/text()" />
        <xsl:variable name="my-time" select="time/text()" />
        <conflicts>
            <xsl:for-each select="//course">
                <xsl:if test="not($my-cnum= cnum/text())">
                    <xsl:if test="$my-time = time/text()">
                        <xsl:apply-templates select="cnum" />
                    </xsl:if>
                </xsl:if>
            </xsl:for-each>
        </conflicts>
    </course>
</xsl:template>

<xsl:template match="@*|node()">
    <xsl:copy>
        <xsl:apply-templates select="@*|node()"/>
    </xsl:copy>
</xsl:template>

</xsl:stylesheet>
```

Fig. 4.3 Example XSLT program

4.3 Rendering

The content of an XML document is by definition readable by XML software. If it is intended for humans to perceive and understand as information, then a corresponding human perceivable *external representation* must be defined. For example, the two rhymes are readable from the XML document shown in Example 2.2, but this form is not intended for people interested in content only. XML markup should not appear in a printed book of rhymes, even if the rhymes are stored as an XML document.

The XML specification does not regulate how to define the external representation of an XML document. There are various ways to inform an application about the way it should present the content of a document on a screen or through some other medium. One widely used means to render content is to re-express it in HTML format and let a Web browser interpret the HTML tags to create an external presentation on the screen. Competing browsers render text in slightly different ways, but much of the representation semantics is defined in the HTML specification.

```
<?xml version="1.0" encoding="UTF-8"?>
<!DOCTYPE html PUBLIC "-//W3C//DTD XHTML 1.0 Strict//EN"
          "DTD/xhtml1-strict.dtd">
<html xmlns="http://www.w3.org/1999/xhtml" xml:lang="en" lang="en"
      xml:lang="fi" lang="fi">
<head><title>An Example: Two Rhymes</title></head>
<body>
    <p xml:lang="fi" lang="fi"><i>Ole aina iloinen<br/>
                    niin kuin pikku varpunen</i></p>
    <p xml:lang="en" lang="en">See, see! What shall I see?<br/>
                    A horse's head where his tail should be</p>
</body>
</html>
```

Fig. 4.4 The rhymes from Example 2.2 as an XHTML document

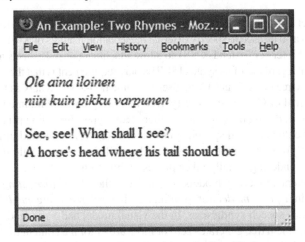

Fig. 4.5 Screen dump of the document from Fig. 4.4 rendered by Firefox

For example, the two rhymes, one in Finnish and the other in English, contained in the XML document of the Example 2.2 could be presented as the XHTML document shown in Fig. 4.4. The rendering semantics of the markup <p>, </p>, and <br/> have been utilized to display some space between the rhymes and force the line break between the two lines of a rhyme. Furthermore, the Finnish rhyme has been surrounded by the markup <i> and </i> to inform the browser to make a separation of the Finnish rhymes from the English ones by displaying the former in italics. The language of a rhyme is indicated by the attributes xml:lang and lang to help search engines and other applications classify pages by language. The former attribute is the one recommended for denoting the language in XML, and the latter is recommended for HTML. The document may be rendered by the Mozilla browser as shown in Fig. 4.5. The actual visualization, however, depends on the size of the window: if the user shrinks the window then the browser splits each long line into multiple lines.

Often the external representation of an XML document is defined by a *style sheet* associated with the document. Like referring to DTDs, there are two ways to attach style sheets to documents. One way is to embed one or more style sheets in a document instance; another is to define style sheets for particular structure classes and to refer to the style sheets from within document instances. Style sheets can also be attached to an HTML document, to provide additional rendering information beyond the information included in the markup, or to overrule the HTML markup semantics.

The rendering of a structured document may be regarded as a process in which a structured source document, parsed into a form of a structure tree, is transduced into a form where the styling information is understood by a formatting and presentation application. In this section, we first look at CSS as a language for rendering, and then we summarize how XSLT can be used as a component of the XSL family of languages in the context of rendering. The reader is encouraged to find additional examples and tutorials on the Web.

4.3.1 Rendering with CSS

The style sheet language CSS (Cascading Style Sheets) was originally developed for HTML but can also be used to specify external presentation features of XML documents. CSS2, the level 2 version, extends CSS1 to allow attachment of style sheets to any structured document regardless of its syntax [5]. The only requirement is that the structure can be parsed into a tree of elements. CSS2 uses the same non-XML syntax as CSS1.

The main goal of CSS is to simplify Web authoring and site maintenance, but it also facilitates rendering the content on other media types, including print, handheld devices, Braille devices, and speech synthesizers. Regardless of medium, the space where the CSS formatted content is rendered is called a *canvas*. Although the canvas is infinite, rendering usually takes places within a finite region.

Three different rendering models are defined: the *visual formatting model* for screen rendering, *page model* for printing, and *aural rendering model* for audio devices such as a speech synthesizer. In the visual model and page model, each element in the document tree generates zero or more *boxes* for the content of the element. In the aural rendering model the canvas consists of a three-dimensional physical space and a temporal space. A good example of specifying the rendering of the same document for several media types can be found in the CSS specification [5], where the sample style sheet for HTML/XHTML documents describes the typical formatting of HTML/XHTML documents on screen, on print media, and on speech media.

A CSS style sheet consists of style rules that are applied to the elements of a document tree. A *selector* in a style rule determines to which elements the rule is applied, and a *declaration* in the rule determines what is done to the element. The declaration consists of a *property* and a *value*. For example, in the following CSS rule

```
line {text-indent: 3em; }
```

the selector ('line') is followed by a property ('text-indent') and a value ('3em'). This simple rule by itself may be a complete style sheet, and as such it causes the indentation of all elements having the name line in the document tree.

In the example above the selector was simply an element name. More generally a selector is a pattern that is matched against the elements of the tree. If the conditions for the pattern are true, the rule is applied to the element. A style sheet can also be used to add some content that is not in the document tree.

```
<?xml version="1.0"?>
<?xml-stylesheet type="text/css" href="rhymes.css"?>
<rhymecollection>
      <rhyme xml:lang="fi">
            <line>Ole aina iloinen</line>
            <line>niin kuin pikku varpunen</line>
      </rhyme>
      <rhyme xml:lang="en">
            <line>See, see! What shall I see?</line>
            <line>A horse's head where his tail should be</line>
      </rhyme>
</rhymecollection>
```

Fig. 4.6 An XML document with a reference to a CSS style sheet

```
line    {display: block;   font-family: Veranda, Arial, Helvetica;   font-size: 13px}
rhyme   {display: block;   margin-bottom: 10pt;}
rhyme[lang="fi"]   {font-style: italic}
rhyme::before   {content:"Rhyme:";   font-weight: bold}
```

Fig. 4.7 The rhymes.css style sheet

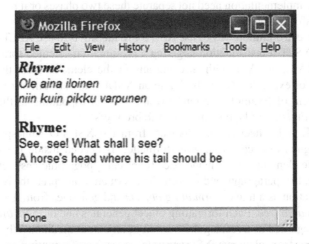

Fig. 4.8 The document from Fig. 4.6 as shown by Firefox using the style sheet in Fig. 4.7

Suppose we would like to use CSS to render the two rhymes, displayed in Fig. 4.5 via an encoding in HTML, directly from an XML source. In Fig. 4.6 a style sheet file named rhymes.css has been attached to the XML document, and the content of a corresponding style sheet is shown in Fig. 4.7.

The display property value block is defined to display each rhyme and each line as a block level element, thus forcing line brakes between the elements. Each box is surrounded by margins, and the bottom margin of a rhyme box is specified to be ten points in order to separate the rhymes from each other. The third rule uses an *attribute selector*: only rhymes for which the lang attribute has the value fi match this rule; thus only Finnish rhymes are set in italics. Finally, the fourth rule includes the *pseudo-element* :before to insert text before each rhyme; note that all rules for rhymes also apply to the inserted text. The result is shown in Fig. 4.8.

4.3.2 Rendering with XSL

XSLT is an alternative system for specifying the transduction needed to render a document. This extends the discussion begun in the previous section, where we considered the use of XSLT primarily from the point of view of transforming an XML document into another XML document.

XSL differs from CSS in that it was developed specifically for XML documents, and it is expressed using XML syntax. XSL also provides more powerful specification capabilities; within an XSL style sheet there are three different languages available to define the rules to specify rendering: XPath to refer to parts in an XML document, XSLT to define tree transformations, and XSL-FO (XSL Formatting Objects) to specify the formatting. The XSL specification [3] explains the general model for using XSL style sheets and specifies the formatting language XSL-FO. XPath and XSLT have their own separate specification documents.

XSL processing as a whole consists conceptually of two phases: first an arbitrarily complex tree transformation by means of XSLT, and then the production of a tangible form perceivable by a reader or a listener by formatting the result tree using XSL-FO. An implementation need not separate these two phases or it might support only the transformation or only the formatting phase.

For example, a common way to use XSL for rendering is to use XSLT and XPath to define an XSLT transformation targeting a presentation-oriented format such as HTML, XHTML, or SVG, without using any of the elements from the XSL-FO namespace. For example, we might define an XSLT transformation to convert the XML document of Example 2.2 into a result tree corresponding to the XHTML document of Fig. 4.4, to be rendered by Web browsers.

If the XSL style sheet adopts elements from the XSL-FO namespace, then a rendering engine, also called an XSL formatter, is needed inside the style sheet processor. The elements of the namespace represent typographic abstractions, such as page, table, list, paragraph, and so forth. The formatter interprets the result tree of the transformation as a tree of *formatting objects* and generates from it a data structure called an *area tree*. Each formatting object generates one or more *areas*, where each area is regarded as a rectangular portion of an output medium. Whereas CSS2 generates boxes from elements, XSL generates areas from formatting objects.

The specification of a formatting object class in the XSL specification defines several *properties* to control the objects of the class. Some of the properties are taken directly from CSS2 properties. However, XSL provides more powerful capabilities for designers to control features needed in pagination and to provide from the same content output suitable for browsing on the Web.

4.4 Information Retrieval

When users search for information, they use a combination of querying (selecting the subset of documents that match given criteria) and browsing (moving from one document to the next). This corresponds to users in a library finding a set of books with the help of a card catalog vs. looking along a library shelf to find (other)

Fig. 4.9 Interactive information retrieval environment

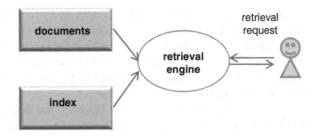

books of interest. Any relationship among documents can be followed when browsing, for example, it can involve following a chain of citations from one article to the next, retrieving articles one after another from a list of recommendations, or accessing several books by the same author.

Information retrieval systems accept users' requests and attempt to match the criteria expressed in those requests against the characteristics of available documents. Those documents (or document fragments) that best match a user's perceived needs are returned in decreasing order of the expected goodness of the match.

4.4.1 Indexing

An important method for finding documents is indexing, which has been used long before the existence of digital documents. For example, it is common at the end of a printed book to include an index listing terms and page numbers locating their occurrences in the text of the book. A reader uses the index to find where in the book a particular subject is discussed.

Digital document repositories are often very large and often have limited browsing facilities. Thus the role of indexes is even more crucial than in printed books. Figure 4.9 depicts an interactive information retrieval environment where the application used by the end-user contains an index-supported retrieval engine. The *index* includes a list of *index terms*, usually words or phrases, and for each term provides a *posting list* of references to their counterparts, which are called *index elements*, occurring in the documents. The counterparts of an index term can be exactly the same words or phrases or other textual items matching the index term. For example, a document repository containing this book with this chapter might offer an index where the index term "render" could be used to refer to the occurrences of the index elements "render", "rendering", and "rendered" in this section.

Given a retrieval request from the end-user, the engine identifies the terms in the request. It is expected that the user is interested in the documents or document parts where these terms occur. If several terms are specified in a query, documents that contain all the terms are preferred to documents that contain only some. Users can specify their requests more precisely by including Boolean connectors

(Jaguars or Mustangs) and not (animals or wildlife)

or proximity connectors

(economics or finances) near "H1N1 influenza"

The engine does not, however, look for the query terms in the documents directly, but rather it finds the index terms matching the terms in the user request. For each matching index term, the engine then extracts the posting list giving the locations of the corresponding index elements, and combines those lists to form one list representing the matches to the user's query. Finally the engine returns the resulting list of locations of index elements to the user.

The index therefore affects search behavior and determines what the user can easily find. Creating an index, possibly consisting of several sub-indexes, is called *indexing*. Indexing may be manual, automated, or semi-automated, and there are many methods for automated indexing. In manual indexing a human indexer chooses index terms, or keywords, to characterize a document, and the user must use those terms in requesting documents. In automated, full-text indexing the index is created by selecting words or phrases that appear in the text to serve as index terms.

Indexing methods often omit the most common words occurring in a natural language, referring to the excluded words as *stop words*. For example, articles ("a", "an", "the"), common verbs ("is", "are", "do", "make"), prepositions ("of", "by", "from"), pronouns ("she", "who", "them"), and other often used words ("if", "therefore", "many", etc.) are typically not regarded as index elements in English text. Stop word lists have been developed for many natural languages.

Indexing also often applies normalization rules to index elements to combine postings lists. For example, the lists for "rendering" and "rendered" will typically be combined with the list for "render" rather than being stored separately. Techniques to derive index terms from index elements can be based on natural language morphology but are more commonly simple lexical rules known as *stemming*. Whatever normalization is used to create the index must also be applied to each information request, so that query terms can be properly matched to index terms.

Readers interested in learning about the various techniques for index storage, index construction, and query evaluation should refer to the tutorial of Justin Zobel and Alistair Moffat [17]. The article compares text indexing with database indexing and talks about the special features and challenges in text indexing. The article does not, however, cover methods developed for structured documents.

In search engines designed for structured documents, the indexing algorithms incorporate structural information. Indexing can be restricted to some chosen parts, or different types of parts may be indexed in different ways. Web search engines maintain huge indexes containing references to documents stored on the Web [10]. Many of the documents are structured by means of HTML markup. Indexing algorithms may choose to index, for example, only the content of the title and meta elements. Most indexes store information about element and attribute names, about their occurrences in the text, and the hierarchic relationships among elements. Further details are provided in Sect. 4.4.3 below. Pioneering solutions for structured text indexing and retrieval were included in the PAT system, designed and implemented at the University of Waterloo in the 1980s [8, 13].

When documents contain primarily natural language text, the effects of structural indexing on retrieval must be considered at the time of creating markup solutions [7]. Texts may embed very rich markup to add linguistic, historical, and semantic information. The search environment may be able to utilize the markup effectively, for example to distinguish "mace" as money from "mace" as a club or a spice, but the markup can also interfere with full text retrieval. For example, someone might suggest the following markup:

> In the illustration above, we see an <animal>alligator</animal>
> <stem>snap</stem>ping at a <animal>turtle</animal>.

Dividing the word "snapping" into two pieces could be problematic for a naïve indexing algorithm, where "ping" might be misleadingly recognized as a separate word. (A naïve text formatter might also add a space between "snap" and "ping" and thus show a different sentence than intended.) Similar problems can arise when phrases or sentences are interrupted by markup.

4.4.2 Retrieval Effectiveness and Ranking

Unlike users of database systems, users seeking information from text typically specify only vague criteria for retrieving documents. In fact, often users specify one or two query terms only and expect the system to infer which documents best meet the users' implied needs. Therefore, when an information retrieval system identifies documents that match a user's input terms, it must also rank those documents to present the ones more likely to meet the user's needs before others that might also be of interest.

The effectiveness of an information retrieval system can be evaluated by measuring how well it ranks documents returned for various classes of query. To this end, given a specific query, documents in a collection are classified into four groups: they may or may not be relevant to the user's needs and they may or may not be returned to the user by the system. Ideally, documents are returned to the user if, and only if, they are relevant; however, given the vagueness of users' requests and the complexity of natural language, this ideal is impossible to meet. Therefore, systems are measured in terms of their *precision P* and *recall R* as follows:

$$P = \frac{A}{A+B} \quad \text{and} \quad R = \frac{A}{A+C}$$

where A represents the number of relevant documents returned by the system, B is the number of irrelevant documents returned, and C is the number of relevant documents that are not returned to the user. The ideal performance would have precision and recall both equal to 1 for all possible queries. In practice, however, there is usually a trade-off between increasing precision and increasing recall: at the extremes, if no documents are returned, the precision is 1 and the recall 0; if all documents in the collection are returned, the recall is 1 but the precision is very low.

In many environments, it is infeasible to return a large collection of documents in response to a user's request. Instead, documents are ranked by the system's guess at relevance and then returned in decreasing order by presumed relevance. Therefore, rather than being assessed based on precision and recall, such systems are evaluated using a combined measure known as *precision at k*, which measures the precision of the first *k* documents returned. This measure then reflects the fraction of the top *k* documents that are relevant to the user's query. One special case of this measure is *precision at 1*, which evaluates the effectiveness of the system in identifying a single relevant document for each query evaluated. If the system returns results in batches of ten (as do many Web search engines by default), then *precision at 10* reflects how many entries on the first page of results are relevant to a search request.

4.4.3 Querying XML Data

When a document collection includes structured text, three additional considerations are important: the placement of content within the structure might be indicative of a document's relevance, users' needs can be expressed in terms of text structure as well as text content, and elements from within a document can be returned rather than returning complete documents only.

As mentioned in Sect. 4.4.1, the structure of a document might influence the indexing of various terms: for example terms appearing within a figure, a footnote, or an appendix could be omitted from the index altogether. As a less extreme measure, varying weights could be assigned to identical terms in distinct contexts in determining how closely a document matches the user's request. For example, terms appearing in headings might be given higher weight than terms appearing in the body's paragraphs, which in turn might be weighted higher than terms appearing in footnotes or figure captions. To support such variable weighting of terms, each posting list must include an indication of the context for each index element. This context could be as simple as the enclosing element name, or it could include the names of additional ancestors or other positional information reflecting sibling order.

A second way to benefit from the structural information present in XML documents is to allow users to specify structural constraints as part of their queries. That is, rather than limiting queries to key words and phrases, possibly connected by Boolean and proximity conditions, an XML retrieval system will also allow users to limit matching index elements to occur within specific contexts or to restrict them from appearing in other contexts. For example, W3C has proposed search facilities incorporating some information retrieval facilities in XQuery and XPath [6]. Thus queries can include both structural and content conditions:

    //book [title ftcontains "garden party"]

or

    //article[//paragraph[1] ftcontains "scientific discovery"] [. ftcontains ftnot "miracle cure"]

Alternatively, more conventional retrieval languages can be augmented to allow XPath-like expressions to be used in place of simple index terms.

The third way to incorporate XML structure into information retrieval systems is to allow document fragments to be returned to users. The simplest approach is to allow a user to specify the element type(s) to be returned by a query. For example, the W3C specification for full-text querying uses standard XQuery and XPath syntax to describe the fragments to be retrieved (e.g., book elements or article elements in the two examples just given). Alternatively, when the type of element to be returned is not specified, the system can determine which elements are the best matches to each query, so-called *focused retrieval* [11]. Rather than evaluating whole documents for similarity to a query, individual elements can be matched and ranked as if they were complete documents. Usually this involves finding the locations of all index elements matching terms in the query, identifying the smallest XML elements including those occurrences, and then finding the lowest common ancestor element that spans elements including each of the terms. For example, if sibling elements include matches for query terms one and two, respectively, then the parent of those elements may be a good match for the two terms considered together.

Finding the best elements to return is more complex than assessing independent documents because of the overlapping content inherent in nested elements. For example, is it better to return a subsection of an article that includes many occurrences of two of the three given index terms specified by a user or to return the whole article if the third term is mentioned once in some remote subsection? Only careful evaluation of user satisfaction can resolve this problem.

4.5 Case Study: Storing and Accessing Dictionaries

Dictionaries and other reference books are complex texts that have benefited from being managed as structured documents. In fact, the Text Encoding Initiative (TEI) [15], created to help humanists and social scientists recognize best practices for encoding various texts, includes a chapter on "human-oriented monolingual and multilingual dictionaries, glossaries, and similar documents." Machine-readable printed dictionaries were analyzed as sources of computational lexical information before 1980 [1] and were first viewed as databases of lexical terms when the Oxford University Press embarked on its ambitious project to computerize the *Oxford English Dictionary* (*OED*) in 1984 [16]. Other dictionaries, both large and small, have since adopted this viewpoint.

The *OED* is a historical dictionary, showing the development of words and word senses from approximately 1500 to the present day [2]. A prototypical *OED* entry includes a headword (the word being defined), pronunciation, part of speech, etymology, and a nested set of word senses; each word sense includes a definition and a sequence of illustrative quotations cited from published works. An individual sense or a complete entry may be tagged with one or more usage labels (indicating a subject such as *Chemistry*, a region such as *Australia*, a grammatical form such as *collective*, a level of formality such as *slang*, or a situation such as *figurative* in which it might be used) or with an indication that it is obsolete or a word that is not yet fully naturalized. The quotations are arranged chronologically with citations giving the date, author, title, and detailed location (e.g., page or line number) for the quoted text.

```
<entry>
    <form>
        <orth>grade</orth>
        <pron>greId</pron>
    </form>
    <gramGrp>
        <pos>n</pos>
    </gramGrp>
    <sense level="1" n="1">
        <def>an incline</def>
    </sense>
    <sense level="1" n="2">
        <sense level="2" n="a">
          <def>a standard</def>
          <quote>Can he make the grade?</quote>
        </sense>
        <sense level="2" n="b">
          <def>a level in school</def>
          <quote>She was promoted to grade 5.</quote>
          <cit>
              <usg type="geo">U.S.</usg>
              <quote>The third grade class went on a field trip.</quote>
          </cit>
        </sense>
        <sense level="2" n="c">
          <def>a mark in a class</def>
          <quote>His grade in history was B+.</quote>
        </sense>
    </sense>
</entry>
```

Fig. 4.10 Encoding for a hypothetical dictionary entry

grade /greId/ *n* **1** an incline. **2a** a standard: *Can it make the grade?* **b** a level in
school: *She was promoted to grade 5.* Chiefly U.S.: *The third grade class
went on a field trip.* **c** a mark in a class: *His grade in history was B+.*

Fig. 4.11 Rendering of a hypothetical dictionary entry

An XML encoding of a dictionary includes elements capturing each dictionary
component. Figure 4.10 shows a hypothetical dictionary entry encoded using the
TEI recommendations from which the more familiar form shown in Fig. 4.11 can be
rendered. The dictionary can be searched using the W3C recommendations or a
region-based query language such as PAT:

orth within (docs entry incl ("abstract painting" within docs def))

or

/entry[//orth = "cat"]//sense[. ftcontains "jungle" ftand "lion" distance at most 9 words]//quote

The reasons for using XML for dictionaries are similar to the reasons for adopting XML for other structured texts. Dictionary creators who adopt XML can lever-
age the widespread availability of XML tools for maintaining their works and
publishing them on various print and electronic media. Transformation tools can be

used to create derivative dictionaries [4]. Dictionary users can search and browse entries through familiar Web interfaces. Applications can embed standard interfaces to read and manipulate dictionary data from a variety of sources, and therefore benefit from state-of-the-art computational lexicology.

References

1. Amsler, R. A.: Machine-readable dictionaries. Annual Review of Information Science and Technology **19**, 161–209 (1984).
2. anon.: About the Oxford English Dictionary. Oxford University Press (2010). http://www.oed.com/public/about, Cited 19 Apr 2011.
3. Berglund., A. (ed): Extensible Stylesheet Language (XSL) Version 1.1. W3C Recommendation (5 December 2006) http://www.w3.org/TR/xsl/, Cited 19 Apr 2011.
4. Blake, G.E., Bray, T., Tompa, F.W.: Shortening the OED: Experience with a Grammar-Defined Database. ACM Trans. Inf. Syst. **10**, 3, 213–232 (1992).
5. Bos, B., Lie H.W., Lilley, C., Jacobs, I. (eds): Cascading Stylesheets, level 2. CSS2 Specification. W3C Recommendation (12 May 1998, revised 11 April 2008) http://www.w3.org/TR/2008/REC-CSS2-20080411/, Cited 19 Apr 2011.
6. Case, P., et al. (eds): XQuery and XPath Full Text 1.0. W3C Recommendation (17 March 2011) http://www.w3.org/TR/xpath-full-text-10/, Cited 19 Apr 2011.
7. Fawcett, H. J.: Adopting SGML: The Implications for Writers. Tech. Rept. OED-89-03, UW Centre for the New OED and Text Search, University of Waterloo (1989).
8. Gonnet, G.H.: Examples of PAT applied to the Oxford English Dictionary. Tech. Report OED-87-02, UW Centre for the New OED and Text Search, University of Waterloo (1987).
9. Kay, M. (ed): XSL Transformations (XSLT) Version 2.0. W3C Recommendation (23 January 2007) http://www.w3.org/TR/xslt20/, Cited 19 Apr 2011.
10. Levene, M.: An Introduction to Search Engines and Web Navigation, Second Edition. Hoboken, NJ: Wiley (2010).
11. Pehcevski, J., Thom, J.A.: Evaluating focused retrieval tasks. Proceedings of the SIGIR 2007 Workshop on Focused Retrieval, pp. 33–40. New York: ACM Press (2007).
12. Salminen, A., Lyytikäinen, V., Tiitinen, P., Mustajärvi, O.: Implementing digital government in the Finnish Parliament. In: Huang, W., Siau, K., Wei, K.K. (eds), Electronic Government Strategies and Implementation, pp. 242–259. Hersley, PA: IDEA Group Publishing (2004).
13. Salminen, A., Tompa, F.: PAT expressions: an algebra for text search. Acta Linguistica Hungarica **41**, 1–4, 277–306 (1993).
14. Sedlar, E.: Managing structure in bits & pieces: the killer use case for XML. Proceedings of SIGMOD 2005, pp. 818–821. New York: ACM Press (2005).
15. TEI Consortium. TEI P5: Guidelines for Electronic Text Encoding and Interchange. 1.3.0 (February 1, 2009. TEI Consortium.) http://www.tei-c.org/, Cited 19 Apr 2011.
16. Weiner, E. S. C.: Computerizing the Oxford English Dictionary, Scholarly Publishing **16**, 3, 239–253 (1985).
17. Zobel, J., Moffat, A.: Inverted files for text search engines. ACM Computing Surveys **38**, 2, 1–56 (2006).

Chapter 5
Data-Centric and Multimedia Components

Abstract The content of XML documents is often primarily plain text, interspersed with various headers and perhaps some lists and tables. However, there are many applications for which the content of documents is not primarily narrative in nature, but instead includes (portions of) data records that are subject to storage and computational manipulation. The latter documents are sometimes referred to as *data-centric* or *record-like*, and they rely extensively on precise descriptions of the forms of data that can appear. In this chapter we first introduce the data type definition capabilities in XML Schema. We then consider the types of data very common in traditional databases: numeric data, dates, and time, after which we introduce examples of more complex data types often found in XML documents: graphics and multimedia data, as well as data for science, the humanities, and social sciences.

Keywords Data types • Electronic books • Graphics • Multimedia • Numeric data • Scientific data • Text Encoding Initiative

SGML was developed for data intended for human reading in the form of narrative documents. Encoding such documents was also an original focus for XML, but supporting the interchange of data of all kinds was an equally important goal. XML has therefore been used for representing financial data, business transactions, mathematical and chemical formulas, engineering drawings, and many other forms of data that are quite unlike narrative text.

Computer processing of XML-encoded data includes application of the techniques described in the previous chapter. Transformations, rendering as text, and information retrieval remain important, and therefore the use of standardized textual markup remains beneficial. However, additional, data-specific processing is also often required.

For example, music can be rendered as sounds by audio technology so that it can be heard or by printing the notes and lyrics so that it can be read. The music data itself might dominate a document, or it could be isolated to small fragments of a document that is primarily devoted to narrative performance information, theoretical

A. Salminen and F. Tompa, *Communicating with XML*,
DOI 10.1007/978-1-4614-0992-2_5, © Springer Science+Business Media, LLC 2011

information, or historical information. Developers who adopt a standard format can build music software that is able to manipulate extensive and shared collections of data effectively. If this standard format is based on XML, music information can be embedded with other kinds of XML data, and any general XML software can be applied even though the software is not able to interpret the music-specific data included in the markup.

In Sect. 3.2.4.4 we briefly introduced the languages developed at W3C for non-textual data. Today this class of languages includes W3C Recommendations for the Mathematical Markup Language (MathML), Synchronized Multimedia Integration Language (SMIL), SMIL Animation, Scalable Vector Graphics (SVG), Voice Extensible Markup Language (VoiceXML), Ruby Annotation, Speech Synthesis Markup Language (SSML), Extensible MultiModal Annotation markup language (EMMA), and Timed Text Markup Language (TTML). In this chapter, some of these languages will be examined in more detail as examples of the markup used for various specific forms of data. Before that, however, we first consider the data types found in XML Schema.

5.1   Data Types in XML Schema

The capability to define, use, and reuse types that constrain the character string content of elements and attribute values is an important property for effective use of XML in many domains. The constraint mechanisms available in DTDs are not sufficient for many applications in which the correctness of the data is critical for success as, for example, in healthcare records [16]. The need for more refined mechanisms for constraining the character string content within XML documents prompted the development of the XML Schema language (XSD) and its type system. XSD provides mechanisms for defining *simple* types (those that constrain the values of attributes and the text-only content of elements) which can then be combined to define *complex* types, as was illustrated in Sect. 2.4.6. In this section we take a closer look at XSD's type system and how it applies to simple types.

The specification of the type system is divided into two normative parts that together comprise the XML Schema specification. Part 1 [41] describes the type definition hierarchy, provides an XSD abstract data model, and describes the semantics and XML syntax of the components of the abstract model. Part 2 [7] describes the type system for data types.[1]

As mentioned in Sect. 2.4.6.1, the term *data type* in XSD refers to the collection of possible values that are encompassed by a type definition. Each data type has a *value space* and a *lexical space*. A simple data type's value space can be defined in one of the four ways: *primitive* types are defined axiomatically (that is, by describing computational rules) or by explicit enumeration; *derived* types are defined by restricting a value space of an existing data type or by combining values from one or more other value spaces (as a *list* to define sequences of values or a *union* to

---

[1] Although the W3C recommendation uses the single word *datatype*, we prefer the more commonly accepted spelling as two words.

Primitive built-in types
    string
    decimal, float, double
    duration, dateTime, time, date, gYearMonth, gYear, gMonthDay, gDay, gMonth
    hexBinary, base64Binary
    anyURI, QName, NOTATION, boolean
Derived built-in types
    integer, nonPositiveInteger, nonNegativeInteger, positiveInteger, negativeInteger, long, int, short, byte,
        unsignedLong, unsignedInt, unsignedShort, unsignedByte
    normalizedString, token, language, Name, NCName, NMTOKEN, ENTITY, ID, IDREF
    NMTOKENS, ENTITIES, IDREFS

Fig. 5.1 The built-in XSD data types

merge value spaces). Often an informal reference to generally understood concepts is also included to help a reader. For example, definition by enumeration is used for the data type Boolean:

> boolean has the value space required to support the mathematical concept of binary-valued logic: {true, false}. [7]

Each value of a value space corresponds to one or more representations in the lexical space: the valid textual literals for the data type. Every literal in the lexical space, however, denotes only one value in the value space. If there are multiple lexical representations for a single value, the specification may define a subset of the lexical space and a one-to-one mapping between the value space and the subset. The resulting *canonical lexical representation* for the data type includes exactly one lexical representation for each value. For example, the lexical space defined for the data type boolean consists of the set {true, false, 1, 0}, providing two valid lexical representations for each of the two boolean values; the canonical representation for boolean is the restricted set of literals {true, false}.

Many commonly used data types are defined as part of the XSD specification. These are referred to as *built-in* data types, and they are available for use in all schemas. In addition, users can define their own simple types (as well as complex types), and these are referred to as *user-derived* data types. Examples of both will be illustrated in the remainder of this section.

5.1.1   Classification of Data Types

Data types are categorized along various dimensions. As mentioned above, the specification distinguishes between *primitive* and *derived* data types and defines 19 primitive types[2] and 25 derived types (in total, 44 built-in types) that are available for use in all schemas. The primitive and derived built-in data types are listed in Fig. 5.1. The type string corresponds to character data found in most XML documents. The second line of primitive data types shows those with numeric values, and the

---

[2]An additional primitive data type (precisionDecimal) and three additional derived data types (yearMonthDuration, dayTimeDuration, and dateTimeStamp) are proposed in the working draft for XML Schema 1.1 [8].

third line lists the time-related data types. The two types on the fourth line are for binary data, and the last line lists the primitive types for URIs, qualified names, notations, and Boolean values. The first (extended) line of the derived built-in types shows numeric data types derived directly or indirectly from the primitive data type decimal. The data types of the remaining lines are derived directly or indirectly from the primitive data type string; those on the middle line are defined by restriction and those on the last line by forming lists.

All primitive data types are said to be *atomic*. The values of an atomic data type are elementary values that cannot be further decomposed using the capabilities defined in the specification. For example, even though a value of type string may consist of ten characters and an application might enable access to substrings or individual characters within the string, it is said to be atomic because XML Schema does not provide any means for such decomposition. Data types that are derived from atomic data types by restriction are also said to be atomic.

As described in the previous section, instead of restricting value spaces, simple data types can also be derived by combining value spaces, producing either a *list* or a *union* data type. The value space of a list data type is a finite sequence of values of an atomic data type (or of a union of atomic data types), which is called the *item type* for the list. Each literal in the lexical space of a list type is a space-separated sequence of literals of that same atomic (or union) data type. Built-in list data types in XSD correspond to attribute types IDREFS, NMTOKENS, and ENTITIES, as found in DTDs. For example, if the attribute value for the start-tag

```
<line refs="r11 r20">
```

in an XML document is declared to be of type IDREFS, it is considered during validation as a list of two strings (r11 and r20) and not as a single string. In contrast to DTDs, however, XSD list types can also be used to constrain elements, not only attributes.

Additional list types, such as lists of integers, can be defined as user-derived types. For example, after defining the phoneNumberType (as we did in Fig. 2.6), it can serve as the item type for a list type listOfPhoneNumbersType:

```
<xsd:simpleType name="phoneNumberType">
    <xsd:restriction base="xsd:string">
      <xsd:pattern value="\d{3}-\d{4}"/>
    </xsd:restriction>
</xsd:simpleType>
<xsd:simpleType name="listOfPhoneNumbersType">
    <xsd:list itemType="phoneNumberType"/>
</xsd:simpleType>
```

Thereafter, if the element phones were declared to have the data type listOfPhoneNumbersType, then <phones>123-4567 987-6543 555-5555</phones> would be valid.

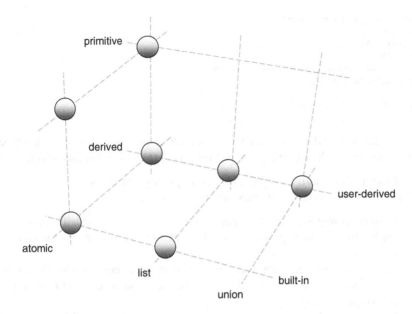

Fig. 5.2 Possible combinations of classes of simple data types

A *union data type* is derived from two or more other data types, and the participating types are called *member types* of the union data type. The value space and the lexical space of a union data type comprise the value spaces and lexical spaces of the member types. A user-derived union data type is defined by a simple type definition using the union element of the XML Schema namespace. The member types are provided either by using the attribute named memberTypes and a value equal to a list of the names of the member types, or by defining the member types as subelements of the union element. In the following example switchType is defined as a union derived from the built-in type boolean and user-derived type OnOffType:

```
<xsd:simpleType name="switchType">
    <xsd:union memberTypes="xsd:boolean OnOffType"/ >
</xsd:simpleType>
```

Figure 5.2 shows the possible combinations of the data type categories. Thus, atomic data types can be either primitive or derived and either built-in or user-derived, list types are not primitive, and union types are neither primitive nor built-in.

5.1.2   Facets

The properties of *identity* (i.e., two values are indistinguishable) and *equality* (i.e., two values, A and B, cause the relation $A = B$ to return *true*) are defined over the

```
length, minLength, maxLength
pattern
enumeration
whiteSpace
maxInclusive, maxExclusive, minInclusive, minExclusive
totalDigits, fractionDigits
```

Fig. 5.3 Constraining facets

value spaces of each data type. In addition, the value space of each simple data type is characterized by the following abstract properties, known as *fundamental facets*:

- A data type is *numeric* if its values are conceptually quantities.
- If a data type is *ordered*, the order can be *total* or *partial*.

  – Total order requires that every pair of values can be compared. This property applies to the built-in primitive type decimal and to all types derived from it by restriction.
  – Partial order applies when some, but not all, pairs are comparable. This property applies to the numeric primitive types float and double, and to all time-related primitive types.
  – No ordering relationship is defined for the data type string, nor for any other of the remaining built-in types.

- A data type's *cardinality* must be either *finite* or *countably infinite*.
- A data type is *bounded* if it is both finite and numeric.

In addition to these fundamental facets, *constraining facets* for a data type reflect properties that can be used to restrict the values from the value space, and thus they can be used to derive a new data type by *restriction* based on an existing data type. The *base type*, from which another type is derived, can itself be either primitive or derived. In the definition of phoneNumberType above, we showed how a new data type is derived by using the pattern facet. The list of available constraining facets is shown in Fig. 5.3.

The facets length, minLength, and maxLength constrain the number of units of length, where the unit of length depends on the base type. For example, for data type string and all types derived from it, the length is the number of characters, and for list data types, the length is the number of list items.

The pattern facet restricts the values of the lexical space to conform to a given pattern, which is expressed as a regular expression. This is illustrated by the definition of phoneNumberType.

The enumeration facet constrains the value space to the set of specified values. For example, we might define the type OnOffType as follows:

```
<xsd:simpleType name="OnOffType">
    <xsd:restriction base="xsd:NMTOKEN">
        <xsd:enumeration value="ON"/>
        <xsd:enumeration value="OFF"/>
    </xsd:restriction>
</xsd:simpleType>
```

anySimpleType

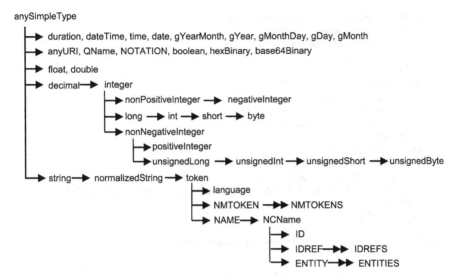

Fig. 5.4 Type hierarchy for the built-in data types

Similarly the values for attribute xml:lang were restricted to being either fi or en in Example 2.12.

The whiteSpace facet can be set to preserve, replace, or collapse to constrain the white space normalization rules in data types derived from string.

Finally, the facets maxInclusive, maxExclusive, minInclusive, and minExclusive can be used to constrain the upper and lower bounds of values when deriving from ordered base types, and the facets totalDigits and fractionDigits can be used to constrain the values of data types derived from decimal.

5.1.3 Type Hierarchy

Types of XML Schema are in hierarchic relationships to each other. In the hierarchy there are two distinguished built-in types: the complex type called anyType and the simple type called anySimpleType. The former serves as the root of the type hierarchy, and the latter is one of its children and the root of the subtree that contains all simple types. All other types are derived directly or indirectly from these, i.e., their value spaces are subsets of these value spaces. Every complex type is outside the subtree rooted by anySimpleType, and, other than anyType, is either a restriction of a complex base type or an extension of a simple or complex base type. An extension allows element or attribute content in addition to that of the base type. All values for a data type defined by restriction must conform to the constraints of the base type, but the restricted type can impose additional constraints on the value space as well.

The type hierarchy for built-in data types is shown in Fig. 5.4. In this figure, single-headed arrows denote subtypes in the hierarchy that are restricted from the

```
<xsd:simpleType name="PopulatedStringType">
    <xsd:restriction base="xsd:string">
        <xsd:minLength value="1" />
    </xsd:restriction>
 </xsd:simpleType>
<xsd:simpleType name="YesNoType">
    <xsd:restriction base="xsd:string">
        <xsd:enumeration value="yes" />
        <xsd:enumeration value="no" />
    </xsd:restriction>
</xsd:simpleType>
<xsd:simpleType name="EmailAddressType">
    <xsd:restriction base="xsd:string">
        <xsd:pattern value="[0-9A-Za-z'\.\-_]{1,127}@[0-9A-Za-z'\.\-_]{1,127}" />
    </xsd:restriction>
</xsd:simpleType>
```

Fig. 5.5   Type definitions from http://www.govtalk.gov.uk/core

data type depicted at the start of the arrow. For convenience, when several types are separated by commas, they are each derived from the same base type. For example, the data types duration, dateTime, …, gMonth, anyURL, …, base64Binary, float, double, decimal, and string are all derived from anySimpleType. Similarly, ID, IDREF, and ENTITY are each derived from NCName, which is derived from NAME. A double-headed arrow indicates derivation by list, as shown for the types NMTOKENS, IDREFS, and ENTITIES. These three types, however, are nevertheless also restrictions of the data type anySimpleType.

Each user-defined simple type extends the hierarchy of Fig. 5.4. If the new type is derived by list or by union, the new type is a restriction of anySimpleType, otherwise the new type is a restriction of either anySimpleType or some other simple type. Understanding the type hierarchy is important to be able to determine the inherited facets, such as equality and ordering.

5.1.4   Example: Data Type Definitions for the UK Government

XML Schema design is an important part of the standardization efforts that are undertaken by government organizations to facilitate interoperability between public domain software systems. For example, the schema library provided by the British Cabinet Office at the GovTalk site (www.govtalk.gov.uk) contains 106 schemas for 16 subject areas, including address and personal details, archives and records management, geographical data, health, and transport. The core definitions are identified by the namespace http://www.govtalk.gov.uk/core, and they consist of the data types needed in many schemas.[3] These core definitions include the restrictions of the built-in type string, as shown in Fig. 5.5. The type PopulatedStringType constrains its values to have at

---

[3] The schema for the core definitions is available at http://www.esd.org.uk/standards/ XmlSchemas/ CommonSimpleTypes-v1-3.xsd.

least one character, the type YesNoType is restricted to either of two accepted values, and the type EmailAddressType requires its values to conform to a specific pattern.

5.2 Numeric Data

Most Web data communicated between human users consists of text, videos, photos, and audio. Nevertheless, numeric data is important for many application domains, such as business transactions and online banking.

Numeric data is defined in a variety of ways in various contexts. Programming languages support several types of numeric data, such as the C language's integer, short integer, long integer, unsigned integer, unsigned short integer, unsigned long integer, arguably character and unsigned character, floating point, double precision floating point, and extended double precision floating point. Similarly, various numeric data types are available in database systems, such as smallint, int, bigint, decimal, decfloat, real and double in DB2. There are also numeric data standards such as the *IEEE Standard for Floating Point Arithmetic* (*IEEE 754*), widely used for representing real numbers in hardware and software. In Figs. 5.1 and 5.4 we included the numeric data types found as built-in types in XML Schema.

If the schema lacks information about the character data content of an element that is intended to be numeric, then the validator is not able to check its correctness. For example, the prices and quantities for the following take-out restaurant order are intended to be given by numbers:

```
<order>
    <item><product>pizza</product>
            <type>vegetarian</type>
            <size>large</size>
            <price>3000</price>
            <quantity3</quantity>
    </item>
    <item><product>coffee</product>
            <type>espresso</type>
            <size>single</size>
            <price>1.50</price>
            <quantity>U4</quantity>
    </item>
</order>
```

The price 3000 and the quantity U4 are certainly erroneous. By using the XML Schema built-in types, the price could be constrained by the data type decimal and the quantity by the data type positiveInteger. By using user-derived types, further constraints could be provided by specifying values for the facets minInclusive and maxInclusive. With these constraints, blatant errors such as those in the example could be avoided. Furthermore, if the data type used for the two elements is numeric, arithmetic operations could be safely applied, for example, to calculate the total price for the order.

5.3   Dates and Time

Like numbers, date and time values also appear in many documents. In a restricted community, communication about date and time may be simple and unproblematic. There are long traditions for presenting the data, but these are dependent on culture, language, and time. Therefore, in the global Web, variances in date and time formats easily cause interoperability problems between software systems and confusion among the human communicators.

For example, during history there have been several calendars, the most common today being the Gregorian calendar. Within that calendar, however, some cultures place the month before the day, some place the day before the month, and some prefer the year to precede both. Furthermore, the current time is dependent on the time zone and also on local practices for observing daylight savings. To complicate matters further, the precision needed for the time differs greatly. In precise scientific communication it may be significant that the length of the day is subject to small variations, but in ordinary communication the variation is insignificant.

The time system used in many Internet standards is called Coordinated Universal Time, abbreviated UTC. Universal time is based on a 24 h clock, and zero hours UTC is midnight in Greenwich, England (or 1 a.m. when Greenwich is on British Summer Time). The International Organization for Standardization has defined the standard ISO 8601 for presenting date and time, and this is used in many computer systems. This standard defines representation for calendar dates, week dates, time of day, UTC, local time with offset to UTC, date and time, time intervals, and recurring time intervals. The Internet Society's RFC 3339 (www.ietf.org/rfc/rfc3339.txt) further defines a profile of ISO 8601 for use in Internet protocols, and especially in timestamps to indicate particular events. RFC 3339 is more limited than ISO 8601, assuming all dates being somewhere between 0000 and 9999 AD, all times having a stated relationship to UTC, and date and time expressions indicating an instant in time; there is no standard representation for time intervals.

Both RFC 3339 and ISO 8601 have been used or adapted as the format for date/time in various XML-based languages. For example, the date values of the Atom Syndication Format (tools.ietf.org/html/rfc4287#section-3.3) must conform to the RFC 3339 standard. Thus, in an Atom feed the element

```
<updated>2009-09-09T22:56:50Z</updated>
```

indicates that the feed was modified 56 min and 50 s after the 22 h of September 9th, 2009, UTC.

The XML Schema data types for dates and time were listed in Figs. 5.1 and 5.4, and these types can be used to constrain the values of elements and attributes. There are also application domains, especially in humanities, where time-related information is included in natural language text such as

> This is a glorious day in early September in 2009, when the lake is glimmering behind the trees dressed in their fall colors.

If this piece of text is marked up with TEI encoding [40] to be included in a collection of texts from different historical periods, the encoder might choose to indicate the time as follows:

> This is a glorious day in <date calendar="Gregorian" value="2009-09" certainty ="approx"> early September 2009</date>, when the lake is glimmering behind the trees dressed in their fall colors.

In the TEI encoding, date tags are used to indicate that there is date information in the text. The calendar, date in the ISO 8601 format YYYY-MM, and the degree of precision are given by means of attributes. TEI mark up capabilities will be further described in Sect. 5.6.2.

5.4 Graphics and Multimedia Data

Marked up text is used to communicate information to both the computer software processing the document and the humans perceiving its external presentation. Typically the external presentation consists of the text included as character data within elements, possibly augmented with unparsed entities representing figures and pieces of video. The way the text and external entities are rendered can be described in an associated style sheet or through additional markup.

In the markup languages developed for graphics and multimedia, the textual format with markup is used to provide information about graphical objects such as lines, curves, rectangles, animated graphics, various regions with colors, and complex combinations of media objects containing audio, video, animation, images, and additional text. In this section we present an overview of two languages developed by W3C for graphics and multimedia: SVG [3] and SMIL [9]. We introduce the basic concepts and characteristics of the languages, describe some of their application areas, and give examples of the software applications developed for the languages.

5.4.1 Scalable Vector Graphics

Graphics formats can be divided into two major categories: raster formats present images as bitmaps, and vector formats describe the geometric shapes in images using some description language. An image in vector format can also include parts in raster format. Examples of raster formats are JPEG (Joint Photographic Experts Group) and TIFF (Tagged Image File Format). PNG (Portable Network Graphics) is the raster format published jointly as a W3C Recommendation and ISO standard (www.w3.org/TR/PNG). Vector graphics formats, however, provide more flexible and scalable rendering of images than raster formats, thus supporting many displays and paper sizes.

For the Web communication the most important vector format is Scalable Vector Graphics (SVG). It was created to describe two-dimensional graphic images that can be stored and shared on the Web. In addition to enabling the description of static two-dimensional images with various forms and colors, it can also be used to describe animations as time-based modifications of document elements. Furthermore, a document using SVG can mix raster graphics with vector graphics and provide interactivity. For example, a user can initiate an animation by pressing a button on a pointing device, initiate a hyperlink by a mouse click, or zoom in or out on an image.

5.4.1.1   Fundamentals of the SVG Language

An SVG description is stored in an svg element, which is called an *SVG document fragment*. In a stand-alone *SVG document*, an svg element is the root of the XML document. SVG document fragments can also be nested within other elements; they can therefore form parts of XML documents or be nested within other SVG document fragments. A simple SVG document fragment describing a red rectangle with orange filling follows:

```
<svg width="12cm" height="4cm">
    <rect x="400" y="100" width="400" height="200"
          fill="orange" stroke="red"  stroke-width="10" />
</svg>
```

The rectangle is defined as an empty element where the attributes describe the characteristics of the rectangle. The attributes width and height define the intrinsic size of the SVG document fragment, and stroke-width defines the thickness of the outline.

A reader familiar with style sheet languages will recognize that the rendering of the rectangle is defined in a manner similar to the rendering of text, by attaching properties to elements in the tree structure. In fact, SVG has adopted many of the *styling properties* from CSS and XSL. The styling properties can be attached to SVG elements by using presentation attributes, like in the example above. Another way to define the rendering is to attach the styling properties with a style sheet language like CSS or XSL.

When using SVG, *graphics elements* are placed on a *canvas*, the space where the SVG content is rendered. Graphics elements are divided into three types: shapes, text, and images.

A *shape* consists of straight lines and curves. There are six element types for predefined *basic shapes*: rect, circle, ellipse, line, polyline, and polygon. A seventh element type, called path, enables drawing on the canvas by moving a virtual pen from one point to another, either in a straight line or curve.

The graphics element *text* is defined by the element type text and combines the characteristics of graphics and text on the Web. Text is rendered like other graphics elements, and the properties available for shapes are also available for text. For example, both shapes and text can be filled and stroked. A text element can be rendered in a straight line or along the trajectory of a path element. SVG supports both horizontal and vertical orientation of text as well as supporting languages such as Hebrew and Arabic, which intermix right-to-left and left-to-right writing. Since XML character data is used in the content of text elements, the text data is available for searching, selecting, and copying.

Whereas the XML elements for shapes carry all information about each shape in the element type name and attributes, the elements of type text are more complex. The *glyphs* to be rendered from a text element are defined using attributes, XML character data in the content of the element, and possible child elements. Often there is one-to-one-correspondence between glyphs and Unicode characters to be drawn, but multiple glyphs can be used to render a single character or a single glyph can be used to render multiple characters. The information needed to map characters in the text element content to glyphs is provided in glyph tables.

The graphics element *image* is represented by the element type image. The element refers to a file that can be a raster image. The content of the file is rendered into a given rectangle area as in the following example:

```
<svg width="20cm" height="15cm" version="1.1"
     xmlns="http://www.w3.org/2000/svg" xmlns:xlink="http://www.w3.org/1999/xlink">
        <image x="50" y="100" width="600px" height="300px"
                       xlink:href="terassikuva.jpg">
        </image>
</svg>
```

5.4.1.2   Characteristics of the SVG Language

Without going into more detail of the extensive language, we list some of the most important characteristics of SVG.

Scalability. SVG is intended to be used in a variety of applications on the Web, encompassing various hardware and user environments. Hence it scales flexibly to reflect an increase or decrease in resolution, size of image, number of files, and number of users. Scalability with respect to authoring is supported by allowing an SVG document fragment to include other SVG document fragments and references to external graphics. Complex illustrations can be designed by several people in a modular fashion.

Painters model. The SVG rendering is based on the "painters model." Each successive operation paints over some area on the output device, and the new paint can
partially or completely obscure the old. Elements in an SVG document fragment are
painted in the order they appear. Filter effects can be applied to fragments, for
example, to blur an image or to fatten or thin the lines or text in an image. Since
filter effects affect what can be seen underneath, an element is first rendered on a
temporary canvas and then the possible filter effects are applied to create a new
canvas. SVG implementations need not to implement the model as described here,
but the result should match the result achieved by following this model.

Animation. Vector graphics within SVG can be defined to change over time and thus
produce animation. This can be achieved in two alternative ways: by scripting or
through declarative definitions using animation elements. The animation elements
were designed in collaboration with the developers of the Synchronized Multimedia
Integration Language (SMIL), and a subset of the animation elements are SMIL
Animation elements, while others are extensions to SMIL Animation elements.
(See Sect. 5.4.2 below for further information about SMIL.)

Grouping. SVG includes special element types for grouping related graphics elements. A name can be given to a group using the id attribute. Named groups are
needed, for example, in animations and for re-using the related elements as a single
graphic object.

DOM interfaces and scripting. The SVG specification defines interfaces to the SVG
structural components so that they can be accessed and manipulated using the
Document Object Model (DOM) and ECMAScript or other scripting languages.
Similarly to the facilities available in HTML, a script element can be embedded in
SVG content to include code for interactivity and animation. The default scripting
language for an SVG document fragment is provided as an attribute of the svg element, but each script element can specify which scripting language is used for the
particular script. Under program control, users can cause scripts to execute by pre-
cipitating events such as pressing a button on a mouse.

Styling. In HTML the most effective presentational effects, optionally including
interactivity and animation, can be achieved by the combination of HTML, DOM,
scripting, and a style sheet language. As explained in Chap. 4, CSS2, the level 2
version of CSS, and XSL are the style sheet languages used with XML documents,
and many of the styling properties from CSS and XSL can be used as styling attributes for SVG.

Extensible. SVG permits the use of elements and attributes from external namespaces
within SVG data, and it also allows graphic objects created by non-SVG software to
be embedded within SVG elements. Thus SVG can be created and manipulated
with a wide variety of graphics design tools.

Modularization. SVG is an extensive language providing many features. The SVG
1.1 specification consists of 719 PDF pages, defining the SVG elements and attributes in modules. With this approach, vendors can provide implementations covering

only a subset of SVG capabilities or include some SVG definition capabilities together with the definition capabilities for other XML-based languages. SVG subsets are defined by means of SVG *profiles*, where the allowed SVG modules are listed. A profile may introduce a small number of restrictions or extensions on the elements included in the modules to tailor the capabilities for specific needs. W3C has defined two SVG profiles for mobile devices: SVG Tiny and SVG Basic [2].

5.4.1.3   SVG Software

The SVG specification defines three types of SVG software and the criteria for conforming to each of them: SVG generators, SVG interpreters, and SVG viewers. An *SVG generator* is a program that creates SVG document fragments. An *SVG interpreter* is a program that is able to parse and process SVG document fragments. The processing is not limited to any specific kind of processing and may, for example, include converting the fragments into different SVG content or analyzing the text content of the fragments. An *SVG viewer* is an SVG interpreter for which the processing consists of rendering the SVG content onto some output medium.

An SVG viewer is essential for rendering SVG content. The SVG specification divides SVG viewers into two classes:

- *Static SVG viewers* provide support for the static features of the language. These programs can be printers that render SVG content onto paper.
- *Dynamic SVG viewers* support interactivity and dynamic features such as animation (and often called SVG players).

The original intent was that SVG would be implemented in desktop browsers to facilitate viewing SVG content either as separate documents or embedded in HTML/XHTML. Major work has been done in the intervening period, but SVG support still is limited in browsers even though common in mobile devices [14]. Today Mozilla Firefox and Opera have native SVG support, meaning that no plug-in software is needed for those browsers. Both have some limitations, the features of SVG implemented in Opera 9,[4] Opera Presto 2.2,[5] and Mozilla Firefox 3.5[6] are listed on the browsers' websites. However, Microsoft's Internet Explorer, the most widely used Web browser today, does not contain SVG support. Adobe provided an SVG Viewer plug-in for Internet Explorer but, although it is still available for download, Adobe announced that it was discontinuing support for the software as of January 2009.

Figure 5.6 shows how Mozilla Firefox renders the example labeled tspan01 from the SVG 1.1 specification document [3]. The page source is shown in Fig. 5.7. This example shows that Mozilla Firefox is able to render stand-alone SVG Web pages,

---

[4] http://www.opera.com/docs/specs/opera9/svg/

[5] http://www.opera.com/docs/specs/presto22/svg/elements/

[6] https://developer.mozilla.org/En/SVG_in_Firefox

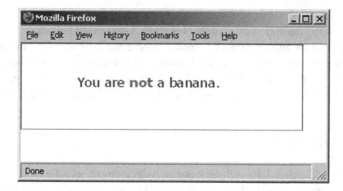

Fig. 5.6   An SVG document example from the SVG specification rendered by Mozilla Firefox

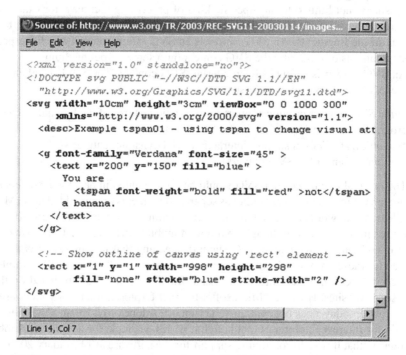

Fig. 5.7   The page source of the document shown in Fig. 5.6

since the SVG document fragment is not embedded in an HTML or XHTML page but defined as an XML document of type svg.

The Apache XML Graphics Project (xmlgraphics.apache.org) is working to provide a set of software modules to support the use and development of SVG solutions. The Java-based SVG toolkit called Batik includes an SVG parser, SVG generator, SVG pretty printer, and SVG rasterizer. The toolkit also includes an SVG browser that facilitates rendering SVG files and viewing SVG content as text and as a tree structure.

SVG content can also be created like any other XML content in either of two ways: automatically transformed from some other content or entered by a human author, such as a graphics designer. For the former, many design tools support export and import of SVG data (see www.w3.org/Graphics/SVG/About). For the latter, SVG content can be created using any editor available for XML authoring. An author can visualize the resulting document with an SVG viewer. For example, Adobe Illustrator is a design tool used for creating complex SVG illustrations [1, 33].

5.4.1.4 Application Areas

SVG has powerful features to describe two-dimensional graphics, and therefore it is a candidate for representing information wherever rendering of two-dimensional graphics is needed, and especially on the Web. Application areas where graphics combined with interactivity is important include technical design, simulations, graphic arts, games, geographic information systems, and graphical user interfaces. In cases where there is a need for storing and handling large amounts of data, SVG is typically used as an export format rather than a native format for the data.

For application areas in which the textual format of SVG is not suitable, W3C has published a binary format, called WebCGM, as an alternative standard for Web graphics. WebCGM is a subset of the Computer Graphics Metafile (CGM), an ISO standard for representing 2D graphical content. WebCGM 2.0 specifies a DOM interface to WebCGM objects and an XML Companion File (XCF) for externalization of non-graphical metadata.

Henderson and Weiderbrueck have published a comparison of the two Web graphics standards [18]. Important differences between the two formats include:

- SVG is particularly well suited to graphic art applications, whereas WebCGM is intended especially for technical applications.
- Scripting is a powerful feature in SVG, but in technical applications where graphics must remain stable for long periods of time, it may cause problems and should be regarded as a security risk.
- The textual format of SVG offers many benefits for some application areas, but not in the technical graphics industry. Hand-editing of the textual format is not an option in case of complex graphics. CGM also provides a textual encoding, but it is prohibited as the delivery format in WebCGM and other technical profiles of CGM.
- CSS styling, which is enabled in SVG, is not available in WebCGM, where styling is thought to increase data integrity and security problems. Thus in WebCGM, the changes required in presentations are left to the applications, not to specifiable by the user.

Mobile phone industries have been active in developing SVG support for mobile devices. Through their participation in the work of W3C, two Mobile SVG Profiles were developed in 2001: SVG Tiny and SVG Basic [2], where the major difference was the inclusion of scripting and styling capabilities in the latter. Compared to desktop computers, mobile devices have limited memory size, processing power, and display real estate, and therefore SVG Full was not implementable on such small devices. As a result, SVG Tiny was developed for highly restricted devices, and SVG Basic was developed for slightly larger devices.

As SVG Tiny 1.1 was adopted by industry, it was seen to be overly restrictive as memory and processing power increased and mobile Web users grew accustomed to attractive visualizations and combining audio and video with graphics. For example, it was recognized that programmatic control of SVG is important for games and sophisticated user interfaces, which led to the design of SVG Tiny 1.2 [4], a superset of SVG Tiny 1.1. The new specification provides support for the use of programming languages and scripting by defining a special lightweight DOM interface called Micro DOM. Since SVG Tiny 1.2 extended SVG Tiny 1.1 to include those features that were previously available in SVG Basic only, there is no longer a need for two mobile versions, and further development of SVG Basic has ceased.

In geographic information systems (GISs) and geospatial services, SVG is particularly useful to visualize maps. An extensive collection of cartographic SVG examples is provided by Andreas Neuman and André M. Winter at http://www.carto.net/papers/svg/samples/. The site introduces and explains the related files, and as such it is informative for learning various SVG features, such as interactivity, use of CSS style sheets, and animation.

5.4.2   Multimedia

In the previous subsection we showed how a document intended to be rendered as a two-dimensional graphic image is described as marked up text using the SVG language. The primary rendering devices for SVG data are computer screens, mobile device screens, or paper. Human access to the graphics information is based on using eyes for visual perception. For people with visual disabilities, alternative rendering may be designed using, for example, a Braille printer or audio support [28]. A *multimedia document* consists of media elements that human users of the document perceive using various senses, for example, graphics with sight, audio with hearing, video with both sight and hearing.

A characteristics feature of multimedia is the presence of time-dependency and the importance of *timing*. Audio and video files consist of time-dependent data, where time duration is important. In using time-dependent data, such as a piece of music, for human-to-human communication the author creates content for a particular duration measured in units of time such as seconds or minutes. The intended message in the communication may be damaged unless the duration constraints are obeyed during the performance of the content by the receiver. In a time-dependent composite object, two component objects can be successive or parallel. For example, notes follow each other in a musical performance but there can be several instruments or voices playing at the same time. In combining two time-dependent objects an important task is *synchronization*, such that the timing of the components of the two objects is appropriately coordinated. For example, when a music soundtrack is added to a movie, the timing of the pieces of music and the flow of images is carefully planned and coordinated.

Several languages have been designed for encoding time-dependent data and multimedia documents as XML marked up text. We begin by highlighting the W3C activities in this area.

SMIL. The Synchronized Multimedia Integration Language (SMIL) [9, 37] is a format for describing interactive multimedia presentations consisting of media objects in various formats. SMIL is not for encoding the media objects themselves, but instead it is used to encode the way the objects are integrated into a single presentation. SMIL provides means to describe the spatial layout and the temporal behavior of the presentation of objects that are each stored in external files. In the first SMIL versions even text was stored in external files, but SMIL 3.0 has defined a new media type, called smilText, to include inline text in a SMIL presentation.

Timing relations are defined in SMIL using three element types collectively known as *time containers*: seq, par, and excl. The child elements of a seq element are played one after another, whereas the child elements of a par element may be played at the same time. The time container excl is new in SMIL 3.0. It allows interactive activation of child elements.

The constructs for defining animation are published in a separate specification, called SMIL Animation [34]. SMIL Animation capabilities are used in SVG to enable the definition of animated graphics. Dick Bulterman, one of the SMIL co-editors, has written an excellent overview of SMIL, which now also includes the description of the enhancements for SMIL 3.0 [43].

For SMIL, as for SVG, modularization and profiling allow the integration of a subset of the features of the language into other languages. Semantically related elements and attributes are defined as a module, and a combination of modules is defined as a profile.

In SMIL 3.0 there are 63 modules grouped into 12 functional areas: *animation, content control, layout, linking, media objects, smilText, metainformation, structure, timing, time manipulations, state,* and *transitions.* The timing group is the largest, with 21 modules.

Each module defines its integration requirements, and the conformance rules define how a DTD can be defined for a SMIL 3.0 profile. When one module requires another one as a prerequisite for integration, a profile must include the second module if it is to include the first. As a start, the SMIL 3.0 specification includes definitions for five profiles: *Language* containing all major SMIL 3.0 features, *Unified Mobile* for mobile devices, *DAISY* for digital talking books that use the Digital Accessible Information System (DAISY) Standards, *smilText* for streaming timed text, and *Tiny* which includes the minimum collection of modules for systems needing only simple SMIL presentations.

As mentioned above, SVG is one of the languages for which SMIL has been used. As a second example, the Open Mobile Alliance (OMA, www.openmobilealliance. org) has chosen SMIL as the format for messaging using the Multimedia Messaging

Service (MMS) by defining a multimedia message as a SMIL presentation [31]. This leads to widespread use of SMIL, since OMA is an industry forum that includes the world's leading mobile operators as well as device, network, software, and service providers.

SMIL's timing features have also been incorporated into HTML. Examples with explanations can be found at the Web developer site http://www.w3schools.com/. Microsoft, Compaq/DEC, and Macromedia submitted a proposal for including SMIL in the Web browsers in 1998 [35], and the principle implementation of the timing features in a browser today is in Microsoft's Internet Explorer [23]. The features described in the proposal created the basis for the development of the XHTML+SMIL profile.

Although this profile has often been mentioned in the literature, the development work has not yet reached a W3C consensus. Three draft versions have been published at W3C [30]: the first in 2000 as a part of an early version of the SMIL 2.0 specification, the second in 2001 as a W3C Working Draft, and the final version in 2002 as a W3C note, where it is described as a note produced by the Synchronized Multimedia Working Group but reflecting only opinions of some members of the group. The lack of interest outside Microsoft is probably related to the interoperability problems discussed by Bulterman and Rutledge [10]: authoring a presentation for one SMIL player and then presenting it in a different player may fail because the players do not share the same media formats. To avoid the problem in the future, the SMIL 3.0 specification has listed five royalty-free media formats that should be supported: for audio the audio/basic and Ogg Vorbis audio, for images image/png and image/jpeg, and for video Ogg Theora video. The W3C SMIL site at http://www.w3.org/AudioVideo/ has listed several SMIL software implementations.

Timed text. Popular multimedia players support their own proprietary timed text formats, but there is a need for an open standard format for timed text on the Web. As mentioned above, a special media type called smilText has been defined for describing inline timed text. This SMIL media type is intended to be a functional subset of another W3C language, and that language is called the Timed Text Markup Language (TTML) [15]. In the specification, timed text is defined as "textual information that is intrinsically or extrinsically associated with timing information." For example, such information could be used for encoding video subtitles that must be synchronized with the video stream.

Voice. Voice refers to the sounds uttered by human beings in the form of speaking, singing, whistling, crying, humming, and so forth. Long before computers there have been activities for building methods and devices to produce human sounds artificially. The term *speech synthesizer* (or *text to speech synthesizer*) refers to the systems capable of rendering digital text as sounds that imitate human speech.

In addition to a speech synthesizer, voice-controlled human-computer interfaces may also include a *speech recognition* system to convert human speech to digital text. Applications using speech in human-computer communication are becoming more common, including speaking navigators in cars and voice-control capability for smart phones. The W3C Speech Interface Framework is a suite of markup

```xml
<?xml version="1.0" encoding="UTF-8"?>
<vxml version="2.0" xmlns="http://www.w3.org/2001/vxml">
<menu accept="approximate">
    <prompt>
        Please choose one of the poems: <enumerate/>
    </prompt>
    <choice  next="http://www.poems.example.com/vxml/hughes.vxml">
        Life Is Fine
    </choice>
    <choice  next="http://www.poems.example.com/ahmatova.vxml">
        I taught myself to live simply
    </choice>
    <choice next="http://www.poems.example.com/vxml/neruda.vxml">
        Walking around
    </choice>
</menu>
</vxml>
```

Fig. 5.8 Example of a dialog in VoiceXML

specifications developed to support building applications that allow people to inter-act with the Web via speech and in particular, by telephone. The framework includes W3C Recommendations for

- *Speech Synthesis Markup Language*, SSML [12] to mark up text that is intended to be synthesized. The markup provides information such as pronunciation, volume, gender and age of the voice, intonation, rhythm, and pausing.
- *Speech Recognition Grammar Specification* [21] to describe grammars for use in speech recognition.
- *Voice Extensible Markup Language*, VoiceXML [29] to create audio dialogs. Using VoiceXML a voice service is specified as a sequence of *dialogs* between a user and an implementation platform. Each dialog may include synthesized speech, recorded audio, recognition of spoken input, recording of spoken input, and recognition of touch-tone keypad input. The text intended to be synthesized is given in SSML format. Every VoiceXML processor must support the Speech Recognition Grammar format for defining the grammar of the spoken input, and other formats are also allowed.

Figure 5.8 shows a simple VoiceXML document. In the example the dialog is defined in a menu. The dialog starts with the voice of the synthesizer: *Please choose one the poems: Life is fine; I taught myself to live simply; Walking around.* If the human user says, for example, "life is fine," the computer proceeds to http://www. poems.example.com/vxml/hughes.vxml. Specifying the value "approximate" for the attribute accept on the menu element allows the user to respond with a subphrase of the choice instead of being required to use the entire phrase.

Multimodal interaction. The users of a multimodal system are able to provide input via such modes as speech, keyboard, mouse, touch, handwriting, and head and body movements. The feedback of the system is provided via output forms such as pre-recorded or synthesized speech, display, or tactile mechanisms such as vibration.

The W3C Multimodal Interaction Activity (www.w3.org/2002/mmi) is developing specifications to support the creation of multimodal Web interfaces. The latest W3C standard in this area is the Extensible MultiModal Annotation markup language (EMMA) [6]. EMMA is intended to be used in a multimodal system where a signal interpretation component is able to convert the user input into EMMA markup for processing of another component. The input may be from a single mode such as speech, natural language text, graphics, or ink input, or from a composite source combining information from multiple modes.

The Ink Markup Language (InkML) [13] is a second language intended for use in multimodal systems. It provides a platform-neutral format to describe text that is written using a pen-based interface. The fundamental element in InkML is trace, which is used to describe a sequence of contiguous ink points. The language can be used to describe static handwritten text and the pen position at various times, as well as information enabling handwriting recognition and authentication. For example, information about pen tilt, pen force, stroke width, and color can be recorded. The InkML specification is still in the Working Draft phase of the W3C standardization process.

Music. Outside W3C there are many additional activities looking for XML-based solutions for multimedia and time-dependent data. One interesting example is IEEE 1599, a standard for encoding music with XML [22] and described in a special issue of the *Journal of Multimedia* [24]. The standard is intended to support building tools for such applications as music education and analysis, music processing and delivery, music browsing on the Web, and for music composition. It enables the integration of various kinds of music information into audio and is organized in six layers:

- *General*: textual description including at least a title, and possibly other information such as authors, dates, genres, related files, and rights.
- *Logical*: description of the events within the music and the layout in pages.
- *Structural*: description of the music objects and their causal relationships from the compositional and musicological points of view.
- *Notational*: description of the graphical representation of the score.
- *Performance*: information about the external MIDI, MPEG4, or Csound files.
- *Audio*: links to the audio material.

With this standard it is possible to create a new encoding using the six layers or to expand the music information in previously encoded media objects by adding new information. The DTD of the language is available from the IEEE standards site at http://standards.ieee.org/downloads/1599/1599-2008/.

Table 5.1 Markup languages for scientific data

Language	Data domain	Developing organization	Specification at
MathML	Mathematics	W3C	www.w3c.org
GML	Geospatial data	Open Geospatial Consortium	www.opengeospatial.org
KML	Geographic data	OGC/Google	www.opengeospatial.org
SBML	Systems biology [20]	SBML Community	sbml.org
PMML	Statistical and data mining models	Data Mining Group	www.dmg.org

5.5   Scientific Data

Scientific data covers a wide range of application areas including mathematics, geographic information, astronomy and astrophysics, genetics, biology, physics, and chemistry, among others. Scientific data is often produced from sensors and as the output of scientific experiments, often yielding enormous quantities of data. Some scientific data requires hierarchical data structures, visualization, and integration of diverse data collections [11]. Often recording historical and evolving versions of data is important to enable the analysis of changes over time.

A few XML-based markup languages have been suggested for scientific data across multiple disciplines. The *Extensible Data Format* (XDF) was developed at the NASA Goddard Space Flight Center (cdf.gsfc.nasa.gov) to support cross disciplinary data interchange [36]. It evolved as a generalization of FITS (Flexible Image Transport System, fits.gsfc.nasa.gov), a standard format used in astronomy. Today XDF has been extended to become a scientific data management package. The related markup language is called the CDF Markup Language (CDFML, http://cdf. gsfc.nasa.gov/html/cdf_xml2.html), most recently published in July 2009. Another effort for a cross-disciplinary markup language for scientific data is the *Extensible Scientific Interchange Language* (*XSIL*), but the development and maintenance of XSIL seems to have ceased (www.cacr.caltech.edu/SDA/xsil).

There are many markup languages designed for the data within individual scientific disciplines. Table 5.1 lists some examples. In the following subsections we examine mathematical data and geospatial data in more detail.

5.5.1   Mathematical Data

The *Mathematical Markup Language* (*MathML*) is the W3C language for mathematical notations [5]. Markup methods for mathematics were developed long before MathML. For example, TeX, the markup language designed by Donald Knuth, was in wide use by the time the World Wide Web became available for distributing and

```
<?xml version="1.0"?>
<html xmlns="http://www.w3.org/1999/xhtml">
<head>
  <title>Our MathML Example</title>
</head>
<body>
  <h4>MathML markup in an XHTML document</h4>
  <p>Here is a simple formula:</p>
  <math xmlns="http://www.w3.org/1998/Math/MathML">
    <mrow>
      <msup>
        <mfenced>
          <mrow>
            <mi>a</mi>
            <mo>+</mo>
            <mn>3</mn>
            <mi>b</mi>
          </mrow>
        </mfenced>
        <mn>2</mn>
      </msup>
    </mrow>
  </math>
</body>
</html>
```

Fig. 5.9 MathML data inside XHTML and rendered by Mozilla Firefox

sharing information in HTML documents. Since HTML did not support the presentation of mathematical expressions, scientists and educators who wished to display mathematical formulae in HTML pages usually included them as GIF or JPEG images. The first version of MathML reached the W3C Recommendation stage in 1999, and today MathML-compliant browsers are able to show the content as mathematical formulae, instead of as images or sequences of characters. Figure 5.9 shows how the expression $(a + 3b)^2$ is expressed in MathML and rendered by Mozilla Firefox as part of an XHTML document.

MathML provides two different forms of markup for mathematics. *Presentation markup* describes the notation structure of the data, intended for programs that render MathML. Alternatively, *content markup* expresses the mathematical semantics in the encoding.

Presentation markup includes about 30 element types that are used to describe the layout of an expression on a page. In the example of Fig. 5.9 all MathML elements are presentational: mi, mn, and mo are elements for identifiers, numeric literals, and operators, respectively, msup for superscripts, mfenced for a pair of fences, and mrow is used for grouping any number of sub-expressions together. Even though presentation markup is provided in visual terms, describing a two-dimensional structure of mathematical symbols, the markup is not a detailed layout language and therefore it supports spoken rendering as well as visual display.

For content markup there are about 120 element types that are used to describe the mathematical meaning of the expressions. The content form for representing the formula $(a + 3b)^2$ is:

```
<math xmlns="http://www.w3.org/1998/Math/MathML">
  <apply>
    <power/>
    <apply>
      <plus/>
      <ci>a</ci>
      <apply>
        <times/>
        <cn>3</cn>
        <ci>b</ci>
      </apply>
    </apply>
    <cn>2</cn>
  </apply>
</math>
```

The apply element captures an operator together with its operands, and every operation is explicitly represented. As such, it can be used as the input language for mathematical applications that are able to manipulate the expressions, such as symbolic algebra engines. As an example, *Maple* is a powerful mathematical computation engine supporting MathML (www.maplesoft.com).

Mathematics is often visualized through graphical images. On Web pages the simultaneous presentation of mathematics and graphics is enabled by integrating MathML, SVG, and XHTML. W3C has defined such an integrated language as an XHTML + MathML + SVG profile, using the XHTML modularization framework [27]. Mozilla Firefox supports the inclusion of MathML and SVG encoding inside XHTML, as does Amaya (www.w3.org/Amaya), an open source software project hosted by W3C and developed jointly by W3C and a research group at INRIA in France. Amaya is not only a browser but also a Web editor, also including an SVG editor. Figure 5.10 shows how Amaya renders an example of the integrated coding from the XHTML + MathML + SVG profile specification [27].

OpenMath (www.openmath.org) is an alternative XML encoding for mathematical expressions for interchange among mathematical software. It is similar to the content markup form of MathML, in that it represents the semantic structure of

Fig. 5.10 MathML and SVG data inside XHTML rendered by the Amaya editor/browser

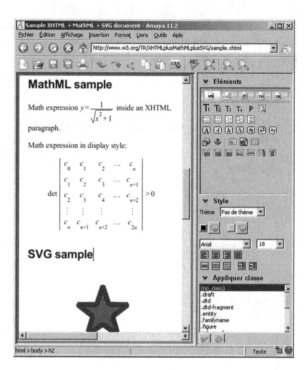

mathematical expressions rather than its presentation form. The formula $(a+3b)^2$ is represented in OpenMath as:

```
<OMOBJ>
  <OMA>
    <OMS cd="arith1" name="power"/>
    <OMA>
      <OMS cd="arith1" name="plus"/>
      <OMV name="a"/>
      <OMA>
        <OMS cd="arith1" name="times"/>
        <OMI name="3"/>
        <OMV name="b"/>
      </OMA>
    </OMA>
    <OMI>2</OMI>
  </OMA>
</OMOBJ>
```

OpenMath relies on *content dictionaries* (CDs) to define collections of mathematical operators, and each operation is encoded in an OMS element that refers to both a content dictionary and an operator name that appears in that vocabulary.

Going beyond mathematical formulae, OMDoc [25] provides structures for encoding larger mathematical entities, such as theorems, examples, and complete mathematical theories. OMDoc can be used, for example, to define the operators that populate the content dictionaries used by OpenMath, so that the content dictionary provides more semantics than is possible by using a mere namespace. OMDoc is intended to be an encoding language for mathematics that is suitable for interchanging information among Web-enabled symbolic computation engines and automatic theorem provers.

5.5.2   Geospatial Data

Geospatial data represents scientific data that is widely used not only for scientific and educational purposes, but also for commercial purposes such as in navigators. As mentioned earlier, SVG can be used for geospatial data in geospatial services and to visualize maps in geographic information systems (GISs) [26]. An alternative XML-based markup language used by several software and service providers for geographic visualizations is KML (formerly Keyhole Markup Language). KML is used to display geographic data, such as in the Google products Google Earth, Google Maps, and Google Maps for mobile [17] (see Fig. 5.11). KML is a standard from the Open Geospatial Consortium (OGC, www.opengeospatial.org), an international organization developing open standards for geospatial and location-based services. These standards are intended to support the building of complex spatial information services accessible through Web applications, as well as through wireless and location-based services and via mainstream information technology.

The schema for KML at schemas.opengis.net/kml/2.2.0/ogckml22.xsd is expressed in XML Schema. For example, type anglepos90Type has been derived from the built-in type double of XML Schema using the minInclusive and maxInclusive facets:

```
<simpleType name="anglepos90Type">
  <restriction base="double">
    <minInclusive value="0.0" />
    <maxInclusive value="90.0" />
  </restriction>
</simpleType>
```

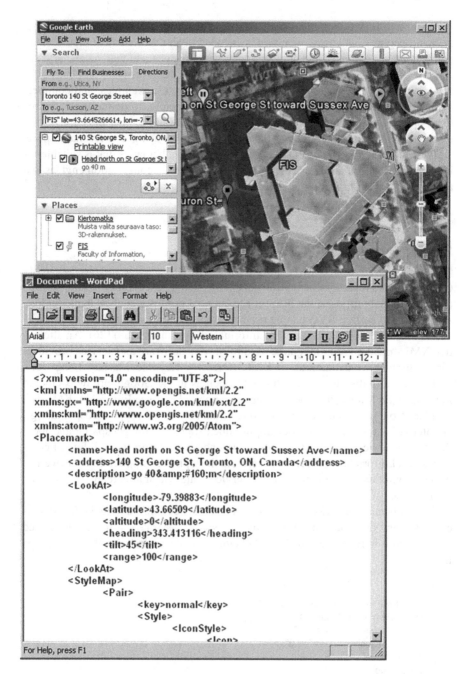

Fig. 5.11 Geographic information copied in the KML format from the Google Earth 3D image to the WordPad text editor

KML extends the OGC family of standards, which also include the following XML-based languages [32]:

- GML (Geography Markup Language): for expressing geographical features and intended to be used as a modeling language for geographic systems and as an exchange format for geographic information on the Internet [19].
- GeoXAML (Geospatial eXtensible Access Control Markup Language Encoding Standard): a geospatial extension of the OASIS Extensible Access Control Markup Language (XACML).
- CityGML (City Geography Markup Language): for representing virtual 3D city and landscape models.
- TML (Transducer Markup Language): for describing sensor data and sensor systems.

5.6 Data for Humanities and Social Sciences

Research in the humanities, including disciplines such as history, literature, religion, philosophy, and languages, often involves analyses of written texts (including novels, plays, essays, and poems) collected into text corpora. Thus, whereas scientific data typically consists of large amounts of measured or calculated numeric data, humanities data characteristically consists of natural language text, possibly enriched with images. Social scientists also rely heavily on texts, but they also study heterogeneous information resources including statistical data, historical texts, maps and other kinds of geospatial data, and videos.

Vast amounts of data for social sciences are available in national statistics agencies as well as national social science data archives such as the Irish Social Science Data Archive (issda.ucd.ie/index.html) or the Finnish Social Science Data Archive (www.fsd.uta.fi/). These data resources, however, are rarely in an XML format, except where markup languages created for other disciplines have been adopted or adapted. For example, Statistics Canada, the United States Census Bureau, and the United Kingdom Ordnance Survey have chosen the Geographic Markup Language to disseminate census data [38].

The heterogeneity and the vast amounts of data resources in the social sciences emphasize the importance of metadata resources for those disciplines. Therefore probably the most important markup vocabulary for social scientists is DDI (Data Documentation Initiative, www.ddialliance.org), the XML-based standard for the documentation of datasets in social and behavioral sciences. Since DDI is not a language for describing primary data resources but rather it is used for metadata, it will not be described in more detail here. In the remainder of this chapter, we summarize XML-based solutions for electronic books and the Text Encoding Initiative, the standard for encoding texts in the humanities and social sciences.

5.6.1   *Electronic Books*

Today books are increasingly published as electronic books (e-books), and there are many e-book vendors. An overview of the e-book marketplace includes information about 20 major companies offering e-books to libraries, as reflected in a survey conducted from May 2007 to May 2008 [42]. Among the companies, nine are publishers and 11 are aggregators offering e-books from a variety of publishers. The most common format of the e-books at that time was PDF, although a few vendors provided the content in HTML or XHTML format as well. Some reading devices, such as Amazon's Kindle (kindle.amazon.com), use their own proprietary formats.

The need for a standard open format for electronic books has been widely recognized. As members of the International Digital Publishing Forum (IDPF, www.idpf. org), an organization for the digital publishing industry that includes major e-book and reading device vendors, over 200 digital publishing organizations have expressed their support for the development of an open XML-based standard for digital books. IDPF has developed a standard called EPUB for digital books and publications. This is intended to enhance interoperability, so that digital content can be distributed over various reading systems with maximum presentational equivalence across hardware and software systems.

The EPUB standard (idpf.org/epub) consists of three specifications: Open Publication Structure (OPS), Open Packaging Format (OPF), and Open Container Format (OCF). OPS defines the format for digital content, OPF defines how various components of a publication are tied together and the way to define and attach metadata to the publication, and finally OCF describes a technology to collect a set of related files into a single file container. For example, OCF defines how files of a container are named and how information about encryption, digital signatures, rights management, and alternative renderings may be provided.

OPS uses vocabularies from three previous document formats, XHTML, SVG, and DTBook, to define a content structure, where DTBook is the DAISY/NISO standard for digital talking books (www.daisy.org). Style information is provided in OPS using CSS 2.0. OPS defines how the three vocabularies should be included in OPS publications, including restrictions on their use and some semantic differences. To support the use of other XML vocabularies, OPS defines the concept of *XML islands*. An *out-of-line XML island* is any complete XML document not using the preferred vocabularies, and an *inline XML island* is an XML fragment using a non-preferred vocabulary and identified using the switch element from the OPS vocabulary.

According to the product descriptions of recent e-book readers (e.g. Reader Pocket Edition™ from Sony at www.sony.com, BeBook from Endless Ideas BV at mybebook.com, and iPhone from Apple at www.apple.com) EPUB has been accepted as one of the supported formats in reading devices. E-book vendors have also started using EPUB as one of their distribution file formats. For example, O'Reilly (oreilly.com/ebooks/) offers books in three formats: pdf, epub, and a Kindle compatible format. The Google Books (books.google.com) repository of

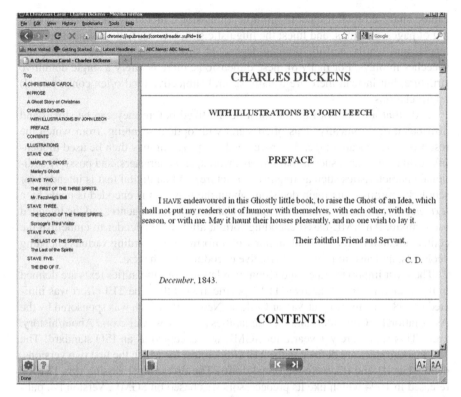

Fig. 5.12 "A Christmas Carol" by Charles Dickens downloaded in the EPUB format from project Gutenberg and displayed by Firefox's EPUB reader

digital books includes some classics such as Grimm's Fairy Tales that are downloadable both in EPUB and pdf formats free of charge. Project Gutenberg (www.gutenberg.org) is another site offering free EPUB books. Figure 5.12 shows a book by Charles Dickens downloaded from the site in the EPUB format as shown using the EPUB reader plug-in for Mozilla Firefox.

5.6.2   Text Encoding Initiative

How to represent natural language text as data has been thoroughly investigated by humanities scholars, especially after it became possible to record the data on digital media. Although today's texts are typically "born digital," humanities researchers investigate texts from all times, written in all languages, and stored using all kinds of media, from stone to silicon. Depending on the area of research, various characteristics of a text might be of interest to scholars, including linguistic, rhetorical, stylistic, or typographical characteristics. Therefore a piece of natural language text can be analyzed with respect to multiple dimensions, including the layout consisting of pages, columns, and lines; the linguistic structure consisting of phrases, sentences, and words; and the domain-dependent structure such as acts, scenes, and speeches in plays. For many of these dimensions, there is rarely a single definitive structure, but instead there are usually several subjective (and often controversial) interpretations.

Texts that are not born digital must be digitized before they can be stored and distributed electronically. This often starts with optical scanning, from which the result is stored as an image. A content analysis program may then be used to identify textual structures such as paragraphs, words, and characters, and possibly additional characteristics such as linguistic structures. When digital text is intended for scholarly purposes the main decisions about the way text is encoded is made by a *text encoder*, a human expert of the particular language, text genre, and the intended use domain. An XML-based encoding format allows the encoder to embellish the content created by the original author with information recording various encoding decisions, and also to provide alternative encodings for the text.

The most important rules and recommendations for humanities texts are defined in the Text Encoding Initiative (TEI) specifications [40]. The TEI effort was initiated in 1987 at a meeting at Vassar College, New York, which was sponsored by the Association for Computers and the Humanities (http://www.tei-c.org/ About/history. xml). This was merely 1 year after SGML was accepted as an ISO standard! The TEI markup rules are defined in the TEI Guidelines, for which the first two versions, denoted as P1 and P2, were unofficial drafts. The first official version was TEI P3, released in 1994 which like its predecessors was based on SGML. Version P4, published in 2001, provided a choice of using SGML or XML, and the most recent version, known as P5, is based solely on XML.

TEI is intended to provide a framework for encoding "any genre of text from any period in any language" (http://www.tei-c.org/Support/Learn/intro.xml). Thus the scope of TEI is extremely wide. To support building markup rules for very different kinds of texts, TEI offers the specification in 22 modules defining more than 500 elements together with attributes. It also includes the procedures by which to choose, customize, and extend the modules for specific needs. The following are examples of modules:

- *Core*: elements common to all TEI documents, including elements for paragraphs, denoting emphasized or foreign text, and quotations. It also includes means to express some editorial information, including alterations performed during encoding.
- *Verse*: verse structures to encode verse lines and line groups
- *Drama*: performance texts for printed dramatic texts, screen plays, or radio scripts
- *Dictionaries*: monolingual and multilingual dictionaries and glossaries
- *Gaiji*: non-standard characters and glyphs
- *Msdescription*: manuscript descriptions for any kind of inscribed artefact
- *Spoken*: transcriptions of speech

As noted above, a characteristic feature in digital texts encoded for humanities research is the structural complexity. It is not rare that the encoder of an old literary work is able to identify several structures that may be interesting and meaningful to the research community. The structures are probably non-hierarchic, overlapping, and discontinuous. For example, the encoder might wish to express the variations in several manuscripts and printed editions of the work. As a second example, the metrical structure in a verse arranged in stanzas and lines may conflict with the linguistic structure of phrases and sentences. The strict requirement that XML elements be nested does not naturally support such non-hierarchic structures. As a result, TEI describes several methods for handling non-hierarchical information, and these are also described in the article by Sperberg-McQueen and Huitfeldt [39]. Interesting encoding use cases and experiences are provided in the collection of essays about electronic textual editing available from the TEI site (www.tei-c.org/About/Archive_new/ETE).

References

1. Adobe White Paper. Creating SVG with Adobe Illustrator CS2. http://www.adobe.com/svg/pdfs/illustrator_svg.pdf, Cited 14 Mar 2011.
2. Anderson, O. et al.: Mobile SVG Profiles: SVG Tiny and SVG Basic. W3C Recommendation (14 January 2003, edited in place 15 June 2009), http://www.w3.org/TR/SVGMobile/, Cited 14 Mar 2011.
3. Anderson, O.: Scalable Vector Graphics (SVG) 1.1 Specification. W3C Recommendation (14 January 2003, edited in place 30 April 2009), http://www.w3.org/TR/2003/REC-SVG11-20030114/, Cited 14 Mar 2011.
4. Anderson, O. et al.: Scalable Vector Graphics (SVG) Tiny 1.2 Specification. W3C Recommendation (22 December 2008), http://www.w3.org/TR/SVGTiny12/, Cited 14 Mar 2011.
5. Ausbrooks, R., Buswell, S., Carlisle, D., Dalmas, S., Devitt, S., Diaz, A., Froumentin, M., Hunter, R., Ion, P., Kohlhase, M., Miner, R., Poppelier, N., Smith, B. Soiffer, N., Sutor, R., Watt, S.: Mathematical Markup Language (MathML) Version 2.0 (Second Edition), W3C Recommendation (21 October 2003) http://www.w3.org/TR/MathML2/, Cited 14 Mar 2011.
6. Baggia, P., Burnett, D.C., Carter, J., Dahl, D.A., McCobb, G., Raggett, D.: EMMA: Extensible MultiModal Annotation markup language, W3C Recommendation (10 February 2009) http://www.w3.org/TR/emma/, Cited 14 Mar 2011.
7. Biron, P.V., Malhotra, A. (eds): XML Schema Part 2: Datatypes Second Edition. W3C Recommendation (28 Oct 2004) http://www.w3.org/TR/xmlschema-2/, Cited 14 Mar 2011.
8. Biron, P.V., Malhotra, A. (eds): W3C XML Schema Definition Language (XSD) 1.1 Part 2: Datatypes. W3C Working Draft (3 Dec 2009). http://www.w3.org/TR/2009/WD-xmlschema11-2-20091203/, Cited 14 Mar 2011.
9. Bulterman, D., Jansen, J., Cesar, P., Mullender, S., Hyche, E., DeMeglio, M., Quint, J., Kawamura, H., Weck, D., Pañeda, X.G., Melendi, D., Cruz-Lara, S., Hanclik, M., Zucker, D.F., Michel, T. (eds): Synchronized Multimedia Integration Language (SMIL 3.0), W3C Recommendation (1 December 2008) http://www.w3.org/TR/SMIL3/, Cited 14 Mar 2011.
10. Bulterman D., Rutledge, L.: SMIL 3.0, Flexible Multimedia for Web, Mobile Devices and Daisy Talking Books, second edition. Series: X.media.publishing. Springer (2009).
11. Buneman, P., Khanna, S., Tajima, K., Tan, W.-C.: Archiving scientific data. ACM Transactions on Database Systems **29**, 1, 2-42 (2004).

12. Burnett, D.C., Walker, M.R., Hunt, A. (eds): Speech Synthesis Markup Language (SSML) Version 1.0, W3C Recommendation (7 September 2004) http://www.w3.org/TR/speech-synthesis/, Cited 14 Mar 2011.

13. Chee, Y.-M., Franke, K., Froumentin, M., Madhvanath, S., Magaña, J—A., Russell, G., Seni, G., Tremlay, C., Watt, S.M., Yaeger, L.: Ink Markup Language (InkML), W3C Candidate Recommendation (11 January 2011) http://www.w3.org/TR/InkML/, Cited 14 Mar 2011.

14. Concolato, C., Le Feuvre, J., Moissinac, J.-C. : Design of an efficient scalable vector graphics player for constrained devices. IEEE Transactions on Consumer Electronics **54**, 2, 895 – 903 (2008).

15. Dolan, M., Freed, G., Hayes, S., Hodge, E., Kirby, D., Michel, T., Singer, D.: Timed Text Markup Language (TTML) 1.0, W3C Recommendation (18 November 2011) http://www.w3.org/TR/ttaf1-dfxp/, Cited 14 Mar 2011.

16. Eichelberg, M., Aden, T., Riesmeier, J., Dogac, A., Laleci, G. B.: A survey and analysis of electronic healthcare record standards, ACM Computing Surveys (CSUR) **37**, 4, 277-315 (2005).

17. Google KML Tutorial. http://code.google.com/apis/kml/documentation/kml_tut.html, Cited 14 Mar 2011.

18. Henderson, L., Weiderbrueck, D.: WebCGM and SVG revisited. XML Europe 2004. http://www.cgmopen.org/technical/webcgm_svg.htm, Cited 14 Mar 2011.

19. Huang, C., Chuang, T., Deng, D., Lee, H.: Building GML-native web-based geographic information systems. Computer & Geosciences **35**, 9, 1802-1816 (2009).

20. Hucka, M. et al. (eds): Systems Biology Markup Language (SBML): Language Specification for Level 3 Version 1 Core (6 October 2010) http://precedings.nature.com/documents/4959/version/1, Cited 14 Mar 2011.

21. Hunt, A., McGlashan, S. (eds): Speech Recognition Grammar Specification Version 1.0, W3C Recommendation (16 March 2004) http://www.w3.org/TR/speech-grammar/, Cited 14 Mar 2011.

22. IEEE Std™ 1599-2008. IEEE recommended practice for defining a commonly acceptable musical application by XML. New York: IEEE Computer Society (2008).

23. Internet Explorer Developer Center. Introduction to HTML+TIME. http://msdn.microsoft.com/en-us/library/ms533099(VS.85).aspx, Cited 3 Oct 2009.

24. Journal of Multimedia **3**, 1, Special Issue: The New Standard IEEE 1599 — Interacting with Music Contents by XML (2009).

25. Kohlhase, M.: OMDoc – An Open Markup Format for Mathematical Documents [version 1.2]. Lecture Notes in Computer Science 4180/2006. Springer Berlin/Heidelberg (2006).

26. Man, Y., Xiuhong, C., Chunling, Y., Jianwei, N.: A practical and light integrated WebGIS based on SVG, WRI International Conference on Communications and Mobile Computing, CMC'09, Volume 3, pp. 142 – 146. IEEE Xplore (2009).

27. Masayasu, I. (ed): An XHTML + MathML + SVG Profile, W3C Working Draft (9 August 2002) http://www.w3.org/TR/XHTMLplusMathMLplusSVG/, Cited 14 Mar 2011.

28. McCathieNevile, C., Koivunen, M.-J. (eds): Accessibility Features of SVG W3C Note (7 August 2000) http://www.w3.org/TR/SVG-access/, Cited 14 Mar 2011.

29. McGlashan, S., Burnett, D.C., Carter, J., Danielsen, P., Ferrans, J., Hunt, A., Lucas, B., Porter, B., Rehor, K., Tryphonas, S.: Voice Extensible Markup Language (VoiceXML) 2.0, W3C Recommendation (16 March 2004) http://www.w3.org/TR/voicexml20/, Cited 14 Mar 2011.

30. Newman, D., Patterson, A., Schmitz, P. (eds): XHTML+SMIL Profile. W3C Note (31 January 2002) http://www.w3.org/TR/XHTMLplusSMIL/, Cited 14 Mar 2011.

31. OMA-MMS-CONF-v1_2-20050301-A. MMS Conformance Document, Approved Version 1.2 – 01 Mar 2005. Open Mobile Alliance. http://www.openmobilealliance.org/technical/ release_program/docs/mms/v1_2-20050301-a/oma-mms-conf-v1_2-20050301-a.pdf, Cited 14 Mar 2011.

32. OpenGIS® Specifications. Open Geospatial Consortium, Inc. http://www.opengeospatial.org/standards/is, Cited 14 Mar 2011.

33. Porter, S.: Using Adobe Illustrator to create complex SVG illustrations. In Geroimenko, V., Chen, C. (eds.), Using Adobe Illustrator to Create Complex SVG Illustrations, pp. 266-284. Springer London (2005).

34. Schmitz, P., Cohen, A. (eds): SMIL Animation. W3C Recommendation (4 September 2001) http://www.w3.org/TR/smil-animation/, Cited 14 Mar 2011.
35. Schmitz, P., Yu, J., Santangeli, P.: Timed Interactive Multimedia Extensions for HTML (HTML+TIME). Extending SMIL into the Web Browser. NOTE-HTMLplusTIME-19980918. http://www.w3.org/TR/NOTE-HTMLplusTIME, Cited 14 Mar 2011.
36. Shaya, E., Thomas, B., Cheung, C.: Specifics on a XML data format for scientific data. In: Harnden, Jr., F.R., Primini, F.A., Payne, H.E. (eds), Astronomical Data Analysis Software and Systems X, ASP Conference Series, Vol. 238 (2001). http://www.adass.org/adass/proceedings/adass00/O6-02/, Cited 14 Mar 2011.
37. SMIL Implementation Reference. Bulterman D., Rutledge, L.: SMIL 3.0, Interactive Multimedia for the Web, Mobile Devices and Daisy Talking Books. Series: X.media.publishing. Springer (2008). http://www.ambulantplayer.org/Docs/SMIL-Ambulant.pdf, Cited 14 Mar 2011.
38. Statistics Canada. Census agricultural regions boundary files for the 2006. Census of Agriculture – Reference Guide. 2006 Census of Agriculture. Catalogue no. 92-174-GIE. Minister of Industry, 2007. http://www.statcan.gc.ca/pub/92-174-g/92-174-g2007000-eng.pdf, Cited 14 Mar 2011.
39. Sperberg-McQueen, C.M., Huitfeldt, C.: GODDAG: A data structure for overlapping hierarchies. Digital Documents: Systems and Principles, Proceedings of the 8th International Conference on Digital Documents and Electronic Publishing. DDEP-PODDP 2000, Lecture Notes in Computer Science 2023, pp. 139-160. Springer Verlag, Berlin Heidelberg (2004).
40. TEI Consortium. TEI P5: Guidelines for Electronic Text Encoding and Interchange. 1.3.0 (February 1, 2009) http://www.tei-c.org/, Cited 14 Mar 2011.
41. Thompson, H.S., Bech, D., Maloney, M., Mendelsohn, N. (eds): XML Schema Part 1: Structures Second Edition. W3C Recommendation (28 October 2004) http://www.w3.org/TR/2004/REC-xmlschema-1-20041028/. Cited 14 Mar 2011.
42. Vasileiou, M., Hartley, R., Rowley, J.: An overview of the e-book marketplace. Online Information Review 33, 1, 173-192 (2009).
43. Zucker, D. F., Bulterman, D.: Open standard and open sourced SMIL for interactivity. interactions 14, 6, 41-46 (2007).

Chapter 6
Metadata

Abstract Metadata has always been important in the management of data collections. This chapter shows how XML can be *interpreted as* metadata and how XML is *used for* metadata, especially in support of resource management, resource discovery, and the Semantic Web. Because the data resources of the Web are huge in size, dynamic in nature, and used both by people and software applications, metadata resources are critical for enabling effective Web communication. Dublin Core was the first initiative to create a standard for metadata to describe Web resources. W3C later created a general metadata model, called RDF which is intended for describing and referencing resources in Web communication and includes an XML-based syntax. The concept of the Semantic Web was then built on the basis established by RDF and XML.

Keywords Dublin Core • Learning objects • Metadata • RDF • Records management • Resource discovery • Resource management • Semantic Web

Metadata is often defined concisely as "data about data." Thus metadata is any data describing, classifying, or characterizing an information object. In the context of data modeling, however, the term *data* is used to describe some real world object, which may itself be an information object. Therefore, when using a broad interpretation, the distinction between the concepts of data and metadata is not clear.

A narrower interpretation for the term *metadata* is achieved by focusing on its intended use. For example, the online guide entitled "Understanding Metadata" defines metadata as "structured information that describes, explains, locates, or otherwise makes it easier to retrieve, use, or manage an information resource" [30]. The information resource can be, for example, a database, a relation in a relational database, an information system, a class of documents, a document, a Web site, or an HTML page.

The term *metadata* is not meaningful in the absence of *data*, nor if it is impossible to separate metadata from data and capture their relationship. In operational information management there may be a physical separation between the two: metadata is *external* to the data. For example, the library catalogue is external to the library collections. On the other hand, metadata can also be *embedded* in the information object it describes. An example familiar to many readers is the META element in an HTML page, which provides some information about the page but is not intended to be visualized by the Web browser unless the user requests the source view of the page. A good introduction to metadata concepts is available through the online site of the Paul Getty Research Library [12].

6.1   XML as Metadata and XML for Metadata

XML can play two distinct roles with respect to metadata: XML markup *as* metadata (with respect to a document's content) and XML-encoded documents *for* storing metadata (with respect to some external data). XML markup in a document serves *as* metadata in relationship to the character data and unparsed entities that together constitute the *primary content* of the document. For example, Fig. 6.1 includes TEI markup from the TEI Guidelines [32] and shows the primary content of the text in bold. The data consists of the first four lines from William Wordsworth's poem *Scorn not the sonnet*:

Scorn not the sonnet; critic, you have frowned,
Mindless of its just honours; with this key
Shakespeare unlocked his heart; the melody
Of this small lute gave ease to Petrarch's wound.

Adding markup to an existing text such as Wordsworth's poems requires expert analysis, and the markup of a piece of text may be done in various ways, depending on the need and the analyst. In the example, the metadata provides information about the metrical lines by means of element tags <l> and </l>, and about sentence boundaries by means of the empty element named anchor [32]. Attributes are used to indicate the type of feature delimited by the empty element and whether the delimiter begins or closes the feature. This example also shows that the markup adds one level to the copyright rules for works under the copyright laws. In the legislation of most countries, old works, such as those of William Wordsworth who died in 1850, are in the public

```
<l>
    <anchor subtype="sentenceStart" type="delimiter"/>
        Scorn not the sonnet;
    <anchor subtype="sentenceEnd" type="delimiter"/>
    <anchor subtype="sentenceStart" type="delimiter"/> critic, you have frowned,
</l>
<l>Mindless of its just honours;<anchor subtype="sentenceEnd" type="delimiter"/>
    <anchor subtype="sentenceStart" type="delimiter"/> with this key
</l>
<l>Shakespeare unlocked his heart;
        <anchor subtype="sentenceEnd" type="delimiter"/>
        <anchor subtype="sentenceStart" type="delimiter"/> the melody
</l>
<l>Of this small lute gave ease to Petrarch's wound.
        <anchor subtype="sentenceEnd" type="delimiter"/>
</l>
```

Fig. 6.1   TEI markup of a piece of William Wordsworth's poem [32]

domain. Thus the primary content of the text in Fig. 6.1 is in the public domain, but the metadata added later by markup can be protected by copyright.

In this example we considered markup embedded in a document instance *as* metadata related to the primary content of the document. A Document Type Definition serves *as* metadata for a class of documents, because it provides information about all documents of the type: how they are structured physically and logically, how the structural components are named, and what kinds of attributes can be attached to elements.

XML can also be used *for* metadata that is related to some external information object. In this situation, the metadata may be represented either as XML attributes or within the content of XML elements. Some standards have been developed for the express purpose of representing and exchanging metadata in XML format. For example, PRISM (Publishing Requirements for Industry Standard Metadata) defines "an XML metadata vocabulary for managing, aggregating, post-processing, multi-purposing and aggregating magazine, news, catalog, book, and mainstream journal content" [31]. On the other hand, XML is also used as a syntactic notation for several metadata standards that allow the use of other notations as well. This is especially applicable to standards that were defined before XML.

In Chap. 3 we briefly introduced the Resource Description Framework (RDF) and Dublin Core. Since both of them have an important role in contemporary information management, more detailed descriptions will be given in this chapter. Other metadata standards having XML syntax in addition to other syntaxes include MARC (Machine Readable Cataloguing) [27], MODS (Metadata Object Description Schema) [29], and METS (Metadata Encoding and Transmission Standards) [28] for the metadata associated with library objects; EAD (Encoded Archival Description) [10] for the needs of archiving; LOM (Learning Object Metadata) [17] for the management of learning objects; and MPEG-7 [22] to describe multimedia content.

Many XML applications have a special element reserved for attaching metadata to a document. For example, the meta element of XHTML is used to identify properties of an XHTML document and to assign values to those properties. This is an empty element in which the metadata is given as attribute values. For example, the elements

```
<meta name="Author" content="Anna Page"/>
<meta scheme="ISO8601" name="date" content="2010-08-06"/>
<meta name="keywords" content="markup languages, XML, metadata"/>
```

are used to provide the author's name and the date of publication and to assign keywords to the page. The scheme attribute informs XHTML software how to determine the value 2010-08-06 properly, that is, as the 6th of August in 2010.

The TEI specification includes the teiHeader element to store metadata that describes a document. The same element type can also be used within an element called teiCorpus to describe a collection of TEI documents. A TEI header has four major parts to record metadata [33]:

- File description for bibliographic information,
- Encoding description for recording the relationship between the electronic text and the source from which it was derived,

- Text profile for the information about the languages used in the text and the context where the text was produced, and
- Revision history.

The remainder of this chapter considers various technologies and applications in which XML is used *for* metadata.

6.2   Resource Discovery

Soon after the advent of the World Wide Web, it was widely realized that as the Internet is a new network of resources, new means are needed for finding appropriate resources to support various tasks. This motivated resource managers to associate metadata with the resources under their control in order that the potential applicability of those resources can be recognized.

The goal of resource discovery is to locate and to access relevant resources from widely distributed heterogeneous networks. Methods and techniques address not only the Web but also other kinds of networks of resources, such as peer-to-peer networks, sensor networks, grids, and library networks.

Following the resource discovery taxonomy of Vanthornout, Deconinck, and Belmans [37], discovery services can be divided into three categories. A *third party service* gathers information on available resources and uses the information to respond to user queries. Examples of such services are Napster, the music file sharing service, and UDDI (Universal Description, Discovery and Integration) registries [35]. A third party service acts as a single, centralized entity, although its implementation can be distributed across several computers. A *genuinely distributed service* has no central, coordinating component. An example of such a fully distributed solution is Gnutella, the file sharing network. *Hybrid services* combine features of centralized and distributed approaches.

XML has been used or proposed to be used for metadata in resource discovery services. For example:

- UDDI defines a framework for defining and querying services [35]. A UDDI service catalogues software services available for other software applications. The UDDI framework is based on the use of XML-based standards both for information representation and for information exchange.
- UPnP enables devices to locate each other and uses the XML-based SOAP protocol for messaging [36]. UpnP is designed especially for "plug-and-play" easy home networking.
- The European Soil Portal maintained by the European Soil Data Center serves as an access point to information about soil data and provides metadata in XML format to describe soil-related Web Map Services [11].
- MusicAustralia is a service provided by the National Library of Australia [34]. It provides an infrastructure to enable institutions to make musical information available through a central discovery service. The participants describe their resources using either MARC21 format [27] or the XML-based Metadata Object Description Schema (MODS) [29].

6.3   Dublin Core

The development of the Dublin Core Metadata Standard (DC) started in 1994 to address the need for facilitating better Web resource discovery. DC was developed by an open organization called the Dublin Core Metadata Initiative (DCMI), and it provides a standardized metadata vocabulary for describing resources. For this purpose, it includes a vocabulary for 15 metadata elements (contributor, coverage, creator, date, description, format, identifier, language, publisher, relation, rights, source, subject, title, and type), and the meaning of the terms has been defined by natural language [9]. For example, creator is defined as "an entity primarily responsible for making the resource" and coverage as "the spatial or temporal topic of the resource, the spatial applicability of the resource, or the jurisdiction under which the resource is relevant" [9]. Definitions are clarified by comments giving examples. For example, the definition of creator is clarified by the comment: "Examples of a Creator include a person, an organization, or a service. Typically, the name of a Creator should be used to indicate the entity."

The DC element set has reached the status of ISO standard, and the vocabulary is identified by the URI http://purl.org/dc/elements/1.1/. DCMI has also recommended how to encode the metadata terms in HTML and XHTML pages by means of the meta and link elements.

Figure 6.2 shows the meta and link elements in the XHTML source code of the DCMI home page at http://dublincore.org/. The first link element identifies the Dublin Core element set as the metadata schema used in the document. The six meta elements provide values for six DC metadata elements by pairing values for the attributes name and content. The DC terms included as attribute values are specified using a namespace label before the period. The preceding link element is similar to an XML namespace declaration, but it does not introduce a true XML namespace. The second link element, after the meta elements in Fig. 6.2, refers to an external metadata description using RDF. That alternative formulation will be described in Sect. 6.5.

Today the Dublin Core has been adopted and adapted widely, but, in spite of its original intent, there is still no evidence that it plays a major role in automated Web resource discovery. This failure results, at least in part, from the dynamics of Internet standardization that affects DC standardization as well as other standards intended to support Web resource discovery. For example, DCMI has seen a need to extend the original set of 15 properties (now referred to as Simple Dublin Core) with new

```
<link rel="schema.DC" href="http://purl.org/dc/elements/1.1/" />
<meta name="DC.title" content="Dublin Core Metadata Initiative (DCMI) Home Page" />
<meta name="DC.description" content="The Dublin Core Metadata Initiative is an open
    forum engaged in the development of interoperable online metadata standards that
    support a broad range of purposes and business models. DCMI's activities include
    consensus-driven working groups, global conferences and workshops, standards
    liaison, and educational efforts to promote widespread acceptance of metadata
    standards and practices." />
<meta name="DC.date" content="2008-08-04" />
<meta name="DC.format" content="text/html" />
<meta name="DC.contributor" content="Dublin Core Metadata Initiative" />
<meta name="DC.language" content="en" />
<link rel="meta" href="index.shtml.rdf" />
```

Fig. 6.2 Dublin Core description in the XHTML source page of the DCMI home page at http://dublincore.org/

properties to be used for characterizing resources. The full set of Dublin Core terms (Qualified Dublin Core) includes 57 property names, names for 20 encoding schemes, and names for 22 classes.

The DC terms are formally defined by means of RDF Schema, a W3C recommendation for describing vocabularies, and the current full set of terms is identified by the URI http://purl.org/dc/terms/. A second RDF schema, identified by the URI http://purl.org/dc/elements/1.1/, is also available for the Simple Dublin Core. Based on these URIs, each of the terms in the two vocabularies has its own URI identifier. For example, in the Simple Dublin Core the identifier for contributor is http://purl.org/dc/elements/1.1/contributor, and the identifier for the term with the same term name is http://purl.org/dc/terms/contributor in the Qualified Dublin Core. Schemas in XML Schema are also available for both variants of DC, and encoding guidelines are available for RDF, XML, and HTML/XHTML.

The changes in the Dublin Core have also been reflected in the DCMI abstract model. (The first recommendation for the abstract model was issued in 2005, and 2 years later a new recommendation version was issued with several changes to the model and the terminology.) It remains to be seen if the formal RDF schema published in the beginning of 2008 will stabilize the Dublin Core and its encoding.

Even though utilization of DC for Web resource discovery seems to have obstacles, the Dublin Core has provided an important basis for the development of domain and community specific metadata standards for resource management and discovery within the domain or community. For example, the metadata standards developed by government agencies in many countries are based on it. Typically these standards introduce some Dublin Core elements as mandatory. For example, the Australian Government metadata standard called AGLS (Australian Government Locator Service) consists of 19 elements: 15 Dublin Core elements and 4 additional elements designed for the Australian context [1]. AGLS is intended to describe both online and offline resources, including services and organizations. It was originally developed for public sector but has spread beyond that especially for cross-sectoral Web portals [1].

The e-Government Metadata Standard (e-GMS) of the United Kingdom [5] is part of the e-Government interoperability framework. In that framework, additional elements, refinements, and encoding schemes to the Dublin Core were introduced to facilitate information and resource management and to support interoperability throughout public sector. The specification also describes mappings between the e-GMS and some other important Dublin Core based metadata standards such as the above mentioned AGLS, the Government Locator Service of the United States (GILS), and the Learning Object Metadata (LOM).

6.4   Resource Management

To facilitate the effective use of structured documents and other online and offline resources in the activities of the enterprise, metadata supports the following activities in addition to resource discovery:

- To organize the resources for storage or archiving;
- To use and track the resources in organizational processes;

- To exchange and share resources between people and across organizations, communities, technical platforms, and software systems;
- To administer the resources, for example, to maintain information about user rights, intellectual property rights, and multiple versions and variants of resources;
- To keep the resources and information in the resources accessible across changes in the technological and organizational environment; and
- To dispose of resources.

The widespread adoption of XML as a format for metadata, and of standards such as the Dublin Core, has been repeatedly motivated by demands for interoperability. Following the lead of the library community, metadata may be regarded as a *surrogate* for the resource it describes [8]. In many cases information sharing and exchange involves the surrogate only, not the real thing. Thus the interoperability of metadata resources is even more important than the interoperability of primary resources.

For example, in a national archive the resources to be managed by means of metadata may include digital files in various formats, paper documents, paper and digital folders, and various kinds of other artifacts. The resources themselves may not all be accessible or subject to exchange. Instead, the digital surrogates describing the various kinds of artifacts in a standardized way, using XML format, can be used by diverse applications and in diverse environments to find information about the archival collection without seeing the artifacts themselves.

Below we describe some influential metadata standards that were developed in various domains to manage resources. In the next section, we then describe RDF, a generalized framework within which any metadata can be recorded.

6.4.1   Learning Object Metadata

Education is a domain where an effective means to manage information resources has the potential to benefit educational institutions, material authors, and learners world-wide. Creation of learning material typically involves reuse of old material. For example, university teachers preparing slides for a course often reuse slides made by themselves for other courses or slides made by other teachers. Slides, figures contained in the slides, and sets of slides are examples of *learning objects* used to build learning material. Similarly paragraphs, sections, chapters, figures, examples, and case studies in this book represent learning objects if they are used for learning, education, or training.

The IEEE Computer Society has created a standard for learning object metadata. The IEEE Standard for Learning Object Metadata (LOM) is intended to facilitate search, evaluation, acquisition, use, reuse, sharing, and exchange of learning objects and their metadata [16]. The standard defines data elements to describe learning objects. These elements are grouped into nine categories: General, Lifecycle, Meta-metadata, Technical, Educational, Rights, Relation, Annotation, and Classification; and each category is itself defined as a data element. A data element in a category is either an aggregate or a simple data element, where an aggregate consists of one or more other data elements. For example, the category

General consists of eight component data elements: General.Identifier, General.Title, General.Language, General.Description, General.Keyword, General.Coverage, General. Structure, and General.AggregationLevel. General.Identifier again is an aggregate consisting of a namespace scheme (General.Identifier.Catalog) and the value of the identifier (General.Identifier.Entry). In a LOM instance all data elements are optional, but the presence of a component of an aggregate automatically implies the presence of the aggregate as well.

The LOM standard defines mappings from the 15 Dublin Core elements to corresponding LOM elements. For example, DC.Identifier corresponds to the LOM element General.Identifier.Entry. However LOM is intended to be extended by data elements tailored for a particular organization or application domain. Some vocabularies for appropriate data element values are recommended in the model, but other values may be used as well. To distinguish between extended and unextended applications of LOM, the concept of conformance is defined at two levels. A *strictly conforming* LOM metadata instance consists solely of LOM data elements, whereas a *conforming* LOM metadata instance may contain extended data elements. Nevertheless, the extended data elements should not replace LOM data elements.

The LOM standard consists of a conceptual model facilitating the use of various representation formats for LOM instances, and the specification of an XML format by means of XML Schema [17]. The conceptual model is referred to as the *LOMv1.0 base schema*. The aggregation relationship between the aggregate and its components in the conceptual model is expressed in XML as parent–child relationships. A LOM XML instance is represented by an element named lom having nine optional child elements corresponding to the nine metadata categories in the conceptual model: general, lifeCycle, metaMetadata, technical, educational, rights, relation, annotation, and classification. The namespace for the XML Schema definition is http://ltsc.ieee.org/xsd/LOM, and a few namespace URIs are reserved for special purposes.

In parallel to the rest of the LOM standard, the XML representation for LOM can also exhibit either of two kinds of conformance: a *strictly conforming* and *conforming* LOM XML instance. In a strictly conforming instance all metadata is represented by elements defined in the standard. On the other hand, three kinds of extensions are permitted to a conforming instance. First, new elements defined in a namespace other than the predefined namespaces may be added to any LOM aggregate data element. Second, attributes may be defined for the LOM data elements. And third, the vocabularies can be extended.

Figure 6.3 shows a piece of a LOM XML instance.

6.4.2   Metadata for Records Management

Records management is an important area of resource management and a prerequisite for building applications that are compliant to governmental and industrial regulations. The International Organization for Standardization defines a *record* as "information created, received, and maintained as evidence and information by an organization or

```
<lom xmlns="http://ltsc.ieee.org/xsd/LOM">
  <general>
    <title>
      <string>XML Family of Languages</string>
    </title>
    <language>en</language>
    <description>
      <string>Classification of W3C specifications related to XML</string>
    </description>
    <keyword>
      <string>XML standards</string>
    </keyword>
  </general>
  <technical>
    <format>text/html</format>
    <location>http://users.jyu.fi/~airi/xmlfamily.html</location>
  </technical>
  ...
</lom>
```

Fig. 6.3 A piece of a LOM XML instance

person, in pursuance of legal obligations or in the transaction of business" [19]. Compared to the more general concept of document management, the evidential nature with respect to a business process is a characteristic feature of records. The ISO standard defines *records management* as "the field of management responsible for the efficient and systematic control of the creation, receipt, maintenance, use and disposition of records, including the processes for capturing and maintaining evidence of and information about business activities and transactions in the form of records."

In government agencies records management has been traditionally controlled via informal recommendations or semiformal standards. In business more controlled and standardized records management practices have recently been mandated, especially after some widely publicized scandals such as those involving Enron/Andersen and Morgan Stanley. In the United States, the Sarbanes-Oxley Act (SOX), also known as the Public Company Accounting Reform and Investor Protection Act, has created new demands for records management not only for US public companies but also for those based in other countries and traded on US stock exchanges [25]. The law from 2002 is administered by the U.S. Securities and Exchange Commission (SEC), and it includes rules about the way companies and their auditors manage information. Effective records management and business reporting practices are essential to ensure SOX compliance. To this end, the XML-based XBRL (eXtensible Business Reporting Language) [38] is intended to improve the accuracy and reliability of business and financial data. Metadata standards are an important means for effective records management.

In the public sector many countries have developed and published standards for records management metadata. Typically they adopt some metadata elements from the Dublin Core and define several additional metadata elements. For example, the Government of Canada Records Management Metadata Standard uses 7 DC elements and introduces 43 elements of its own [13]. In Finland the records management metadata standard has adopted all DC elements and added elements to support the life-cycle management of electronic records [23]. XML is recommended as the representation format, especially to support system integration.

6.4.3   Metadata for Preservation

Metadata is also important in managing the archival and preservation of digital and non-digital resources especially to track and validate authenticity, integrity, and reliability. Many organizations have developed standards for preservation. The variety of solutions developed and adopted is caused by the diversity of archival materials as well as by the varying needs and practices in different countries. The materials, be they digital or non-digital artifacts, may require complicated interrelated descriptive information to enable the finding and understanding the materials. In the development of Encoded Archival Description (EAD, [10]) the complexity of the requirements was the starting point, especially the need for preserving hierarchical relationships and capability to move within hierarchical information structures. The development of EAD started at the University of California, Berkeley in 1993. It took 5 years of work to reach the stability of the metadata specification and publish the first version of the SGML DTD. The latest EAD version from 2002 is defined both for SGML and XML. The standard has been defined using three schema languages: DTD, XML Schema, and Relax NG.

6.5   RDF: Resource Description Framework

In Sect. 3.2.4.2 we introduced the XML applications developed by W3C to support the building of Semantic Web solutions, and among them RDF (Resource Description Framework), a general model for describing Web resources.

The first version of RDF was designed in parallel with the development of XML and published as a W3C Recommendation in February 1999, only 6 months later than XML 1.0. The goal was to provide a model and encoding syntax for metadata describing Web resources, in order to facilitate interoperability between applications that exchange machine-understandable information on the Web. It was intended for a variety of application areas: for example, for resource discovery, to facilitate knowledge sharing by intelligent software agents, and to express privacy preferences, privacy policies or intellectual property rights for Web pages. The first RDF recommendation was superseded 5 years later by a set of six recommendations now constituting the RDF specification:

1. *RDF Primer* [26] gives an overview of the RDF graph data model and its XML syntax, with several examples how to use RDF graphs for describing resources. It also describes how to define RDF vocabularies using the RDF Vocabulary

Description Language (RDF Schema) and gives examples of some RDF applications.

2. *RDF Concepts and Abstract Syntax* [24] describes the RDF graph data model and the RDF graph abstract syntax.
3. *RDF/XML Syntax* [2] describes how RDF graphs are serialized by means of XML.
4. *RDF Semantics* [15] defines the "meaning" of an RDF graph in a precise manner.
5. *RDF Schema* [3] describes a language for defining vocabularies to be used in RDF descriptions.
6. *RDF Test Cases* [14] provides examples corresponding to particular technical concerns and is intended to clarify some of the wording in the specifications.

RDF identifies *resources* using the URI mechanism and describes them in terms of simple *properties* and property *values*. This enables RDF to represent simple *statements* about resources. For example, we can use RDF to make statements about the Cover Pages, a resource hosted by OASIS "to document and encourage the use of open standards that enhance the intelligibility, quality, and longevity of digital information" [7]. Informally we might state that:

"the Cover Pages are hosted by OASIS"
"the Cover Pages are edited by Robin Cover"
"the Cover Pages are located at http://xml.coverpages.org/"

More formally, these statements may be given in the form of triples, such as:

("Cover Pages", "host", "OASIS")
("Cover Pages", "editor", "Robin Cover")
("Cover Pages", "location", "http://xml.coverpages.org/")

All three statements express a relationship between an object and a value, using the form (*resource, property, value*) and often named subject-predicate-object triples.

Referring to all things and the relationships between them using literal strings is problematic in the environment of global communication networks with many natural languages and diverse applications having a need to exchange information. For example, if the three statements are accessed by an application from three different sources and added to a set of other statements, the following problems might appear:

- How could the application reason that "Cover Pages" refers to the same thing in all three statements?
- If there are other statements about the rock band named "Oasis," distinguishing between that band and the organization might require additional analysis (possibly depending on the fact that the band is usually written *Oasis* and the organization is usually written *OASIS*).
- Some statements in the repository might use different terms for the properties indicated by the terms "host", "editor", and "location" in these three statements. For example, if there is the statement ("ebXML standards", "publisher", "OASIS"), a human reader might reason that ebXML standards and Cover Pages have the same publisher, but for automated reasoning to derive this result would require access to additional information.

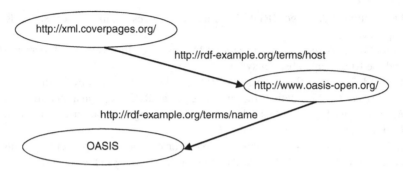

Fig. 6.4 Related RDF statements as a graph

To avoid these kinds of problems, RDF uses URI references as names to identify things as well as relationships between things. Only the third component, values, may be given by literals. For example, to express the statement

"the Cover Pages are hosted by OASIS"

in RDF we must use the URI reference syntax to specify each resource and each property such as, for example:

(http://xml.coverpages.org/, http://rdf-example.org/terms/host, http://www.oasis-open.org/)
(http://www.oasis-open.org/, http://rdf-example.org/terms/name, "OASIS")

In the first statement the current address of the Cover Pages has been used as the identifier of the resource. In the RDF semantics, however, the URI reference is not interpreted as an Internet address of the resource; it is just an identifier. (Any information about the address of the site has to be given by a separate statement.) Instead of providing the value of the property as a literal, the organization is referenced by a URI and its name is provided in a separate triple. With this approach, further statements describing the organization can easily be added.

RDF models a set of statements (triples) as a graph. In the graph representation the subject and object are nodes and the predicate is an arc between the nodes. Figure 6.4 depicts our example triples graphically.

The graph model makes RDF very flexible. Each of the RDF resources can be described in its own way, with their own properties. A graph can be extended by adding new arcs and nodes describing new properties and their values.

The important concept of equivalence is defined for RDF graphs, facilitating software applications to compare two sets of statements and decide if they represent the same things and express the same relationships between the things. Since the graphs consist of triples of URI references and literals, the equivalence of two graphs is determined by comparing pairs of triples, pairs of URI references, and pairs of literals.

In our simple example there still is the problem that applications cannot "know" what we mean by the property for which we use the name http://rdf-example.org/terms/

```
1.          <?xml version="1.0"?>
2.          <rdf:RDF xmlns:rdf="http://www.w3.org/1999/02/22-rdf-syntax-ns#"
3.                  xmlns:ourterms="http://rdf-example.org/terms/">
4.             <rdf:Description rdf:about="http://xml.coverpages.org/">
5.                          <ourterms:host>http://www.oasis-open.org</ourterms:host>
6.             </rdf:Description>
7.             <rdf:Description rdf:about="http://www.oasis-open.org">
8.                          <ourterms:name>OASIS</ourterms:name>
9.             </rdf:Description>
10.         </rdf:RDF>
```

Fig. 6.5 The XML syntax for the graph in Fig. 6.4

host. The URI and terms in it were invented for the purpose of the example. So that applications can interpret URIs in the intended way, the URIs should be taken from well defined vocabularies. Unfortunately widely accepted vocabularies are not available for many application domains. In the example, the property "host" (a site) can possibly be interpreted as "publish" (a site). If so, a well defined interpretation is available in the Dublin Core vocabulary, which we introduced in Sect. 6.3. Using XML syntax, RDF graphs are encoded in a combination of elements, attributes, element content, and attribute values. The XML syntax for the graph in Fig. 6.4 is shown in Fig. 6.5. Line numbers are added to help explain the example. The triples of the graph (the statements) are each represented by an element named rdf:Description. The subject of each triple is given as the value of attribute rdf:about. The property is given as the child element of rdf:Description and the value of the property as the content of the child element. The prefix rdf refers to the namespace for the RDF vocabulary and identified by the URI http://www.w3.org/1999/02/22-rdf-syntax-ns#. The namespace is declared on line 2. Another namespace is declared on line 3 to facilitate the encoding of the property names http://rdf-example.org/terms/host and http://rdf-example.org/terms/name as the qualified element names ourterms:host and ourterms:name, respectively.

Additional RDF statements can be added by using additional rdf:Description elements. To shorten the XML encoding, RDF/XML provides several abbreviations. For example, if several properties are defined for the single resource http://xml.coverpages.org, they need not to be written as separate rdf:Description elements; instead the properties with their values can be given as multiple children of the one parent element included on line 4.

Consider again the Dublin Core metadata associated with the DCMI home page, depicted in Fig. 6.2. The link to an external RDF description associates the same metadata elements to the DCMI home page as the metadata embedded in the page, but now using the RDF/XML format in a separate document. This alternative encoding of the metadata, shown in Fig. 6.6, serves search engines that expect RDF and can interpret XML. Note how several properties (dc:title, dc:description, etc.) are associated with the single resource http://dublincore.org/.

```
<?xml version="1.0"?>
<rdf:RDF xmlns:rdf="http://www.w3.org/1999/02/22-rdf-syntax-ns#"
         xmlns:dc="http://purl.org/dc/elements/1.1/">
<rdf:Description rdf:about="http://dublincore.org/">
    <dc:title>Dublin Core Metadata Initiative (DCMI) Home Page</dc:title>
    <dc:description>The Dublin Core Metadata Initiative is an open forum engaged
        in the development of interoperable online metadata standards that support
        a broad range of purposes and business models. DCMI's activities include
        consensus-driven working groups, global conferences and workshops,
        standards liaison, and educational efforts to promote widespread
        acceptance of metadata standards and practices.
    </dc:description>
    <dc:date>2008-08-04</dc:date>
    <dc:format>text/html</dc:format>
    <dc:language>en</dc:language>
    <dc:contributor>Dublin Core Metadata Initiative</dc:contributor>
</rdf:Description>
</rdf:RDF>
```

Fig. 6.6 External RDF metadata description of the DCMI home page at http://dublincore org/index. shtml.rdf.

6.6 Semantic Web

In Sect. 3.2.4.2 we introduced some basic ideas and technologies for the Semantic Web. The W3C Semantic Web site states:

> The Semantic Web provides a common framework that allows data to be shared and reused across application, enterprise, and community boundaries. It is a collaborative effort led by W3C with participation from a large number of researchers and industrial partners. It is based on the Resource Description Framework (RDF). [39]

In the previous section we explained how RDF is used to describe Web resources. However, the use of RDF alone does not facilitate data to be "shared and reused across application, enterprise, and community boundaries." As we mentioned earlier, the RDF data model is very flexible, and things can be described in many alternative ways. Even though resources and properties are denoted by URIs, different applications, enterprises, and communities may choose distinct descriptions for various resources and distinct names for identical properties. Furthermore, nodes for two resources of the same type in an RDF graph may have completely different properties associated with them. Thus in the absence of any constraints, metadata in RDF format can be as application dependent as any information technology solution.

In order to be understood by diverse applications, metadata requires standardized descriptions to provide shared ontologies. An *ontology* covers the concepts of a domain. For example, the domain might be medicine, legislation, automobile manufacturing, or friendship. Sometimes a simple glossary of terms and their definitions in natural language is called an ontology. Controlled vocabularies, classifications, and thesauri are kinds of ontologies that have traditionally been used in libraries to choose terms to describe publications.

Ontologies for several specific domains have been published on the Web. For example, the biomedical community collects and publishes biomedical ontologies at http://www.obofoundry.org/about.shtml. Any DTD defines a structural ontology for documents of a class by introducing the names of elements in the documents of the class and a containment relationship between the elements.

In the Semantic Web, ontologies must be represented in a computer-usable form and facilitate interpretation of RDF statements over a domain. RDF Schema and OWL (Web Ontology Language), languages of the XML family listed in Sect. 3.2.4.2, are mechanisms for defining ontologies for RDF statements.

RDF Schema provides a way to define *classes*, each of which represents collections of objects of one *type* and is characterized by a set of properties. A *property* applies to one or more classes and has one or more classes as ranges. The predefined property rdf:type is used to specify that a subject (a specific resource) is an *instance* of a *class*, and thus that the associated set of properties for that class apply to the object represented by that resource. In keeping with the rest of RDF, classes are themselves described by means of resources, and therefore they are referenced by URIs.

RDF Schema includes mechanisms for constraining RDF statements, but its support for automated reasoning is weak. For example, RDF Schema lacks definitions for transitive and inverse properties. In contrast, OWL supports stronger automated reasoning. OWL also supports the combination of several ontologies, and a class defined in one ontology can be extended in another ontology. Both RDF Schema and OWL definitions are given by means of RDF graphs, which can be written in any of several syntactic forms, including the XML form RDF/XML.

Research around the Semantic Web has been extensive since the concept was first introduced. However real-life functional cases are still rare. W3C maintains a list of Semantic Web case studies and use cases [40] that are intended to show how organizations use Semantic Web technologies. Currently there are 31 case studies and 13 use cases. The former describe systems being deployed and used within a production environment, and the latter are prototypes that could be useful but not functional in any business environment.

The W3C case studies depict several interesting applications of Semantic Web technologies. Adding semantic data to a computerized environment enhances a system's capability for retrieval and analysis, and in most of the case studies, the primary purpose seems to be to support semantic search by human users across disparate data sources. Table 6.1 summarizes the search-based case studies, and Table 6.2 displays the other cases. In addition to RDF and RDF Schema, three of the other W3C Semantic Web technologies (refer back to Table 3.4) have also been used: OWL in 17 cases, SPARQL in 16 cases, and GRDDL in 2 cases. Additional public vocabularies and ontologies used in the cases are listed in Table 6.3.

Most of the cases aim to integrate data from various applications *within* an enterprise. However, *inter-enterprise* data sharing and reuse could benefit even more from formal ontologies and vocabularies. Therefore those cases where well-planned ontologies and ontology authoring methods are created and published can be expected to become an even richer ground for future Semantic Web solutions.

Table 6.1 W3C case studies serving primarily semantic search and data integration

Case study	Primary purpose
A digital music archive for the Norwegian national broadcaster	Standardization of metadata on music tracks to allow effective access to the production archives in the production process of public broadcasting
An intelligent search engine for online services for public administrations	Semantic search of online services of the city of Zaragoza
Enhancement and integration of corporate social software using the Semantic Web	Querying across different social software at Electricité de France
Enhancing content search using the Semantic Web	Enterprise search engine for the Oracle developer community
Integrated, connected search service for technical standards interface	Integrated search service for the Korean Agency for Technology and Standards
KDE 4.0 semantic desktop search and tagging	Integrated search capability on all information the user has stored on their computer
Online resource for information on aquatic sciences	Multilingual semantic search engine for the aquatic domain, srvvirt2.softeco.it/aquaring_site/
POPS – NASA's expertise location service	Expertise location service, integrates NASA's information about its civil service and contractor workforce. Integrates existing Web content into the POPS browser
Semantic content description to improve discovery	Resource discovery from the Vodafone mobile Web portal, allowing subscribes to use a wide variety of mobile devices, used in "Vodafone live!" portal
Semantic MDR and IR for national archives	Metadata repository for the National Archives of Korea to enable information retrieval from data sources with various metadata implementations, search. archives.go.kr/searcher_semantic_form.htm
Semantic-based search and query system for the traditional Chinese medicine community	Search portal for the Chinese medicine community, search.cintcm.com/TcmSearch/tcmBasicSearch.luc
The Semantic Web for the agricultural domain, semantic navigation of food, nutrition and agriculture journal	Multilingual search engine
Use of Semantic Web technologies in natural language interface to business applications	Natural language question answering interface to business applications

Table 6.2 W3C case studies serving other semantic applications

Case study	Purpose
A linked open data resource list management tool for undergraduate students	Resource list management for students and teachers, launched at the University of Plymouth
A semantic web content repository for clinical research	Querying patient data for generating new knowledge, 54.2 million RDF assertions in 2007
An ontology of Cantabria's cultural heritage	Semantic search, interactive map, tourist applications, etc.
Applied semantic knowledgebase for detection of patients at risk of organ failure through immune rejection	Screening of multiple clinical data sources for detection of individuals at risk of vital organ failure
Composing a safer drug regimen for each patient with semantic web technologies	An ontology of medical conditions for the identification of a safer drug regimen, under development at the time of case publishing in August 2007
CRUZAR, an application of semantic matchmaking for e-tourism in the city of Zaragoza	Building a custom route for each visitor profile, www.zaragoza.es/turruta/Turruta/en/index_Ruta
Geographic referencing framework	Improving data integration at Ordnance Survey, the national mapping agency of Great Britain by means of a topography with sub-ontologies and ontology authoring methods, www.ordnancesurvey.co.uk/ontology
iLaw – intelligent legislation support system	To establish an intelligent legislation support system utilizing text mining and information analysis
Improving the reliability of internet search results using search thresher	Utilizing content labels as metadata associated with Web resources
Prioritization of biological targets for drug discovery	Evaluation and prioritizing drug targets
Real time suggestion of related ideas in the financial industry	Managing innovated ideas of employees at Bankinter
Publishing STW thesaurus for economics as linked open data	Providing a standard format for publishing the STW thesaurus, zbw.eu/stw/versions/latest/about
Semantic tags	A tool for social bookmarking, allowing annotation of Web pages, www.faviki.com/
Semantic Web technology for public health situation awareness	Collection and analysis of data to identify and respond to community health problems, a prototype system implemented in 2007
The swoRDFish Metadata Initiative: better, faster, smarter web content	Web content management of product resources for Sun Microsystems
Twine	Enabling the users to track groups that collectively gather content from a variety of sources
Use of Semantic Web technologies on the BBC Web sites	Creating a Web identifier for every BBC program and for the items interested in the programs, and thus enabling enhanced search and integration of resources and creation of cross program sites

Table 6.3 Public ontologies and vocabularies used in the case studies of [40]

Vocabulary/ontology	Available at	# of cases
BIBO, bibliographic ontology	bibliontology.com	1
Content labels	contentlabel.org/	1
ResearchCyc	researchcyc.cyc.com/	1
DBpedia	dbpedia.org/	2
DOLCE, Descriptive Ontology for Linguistic and Cognitive Engineering	www.loa-cnr.it/DOLCE.html	1
Dublin Core	[9]	4
FOAF	[4]	2
FRBR, Functional Requirements for Bibliographic Records	[18]	1
Geonames	geonames.org/ontology	1
ICRA, internet content rating	www.fosi.org/icra/	1
ISO 21127, reference ontology for the interchange of cultural heritage information	[20]	1
KAON	kaon.semanticweb.org/ontologies	1
MeSH, Medical Subject Headings	www.nlm.nih.gov/mesh/	1
MDR, ISO metadata registry	[21]	1
PRISM, Publishing Requirements for Industry Standard Metadata	[31]	1
SIOC, Semantically-Interlinked Online Communities	sioc-project.org/ontology	1
TCM, Traditional Chinese Medicine	[6]	1
Wikipedia terms	Wikipedia.org/	1

References

1. AGLS Metadata Standard. Part 1: Reference Description. Version 2.0. July 2010. National Archives of Australia. Available at http://www.agls.gov.au/documents/, Cited 19 Apr 2011.
2. Becket, D. (ed): RDF/XML Syntax Specification (Revised). W3C Recommendation (10 February 2004) http://www.w3.org/TR/rdf-syntax-grammar/, Cited 19 Apr 2011.
3. Brickley, D., Guha, R.V. (eds.): RDF Vocabulary Description Language 1.0: RDF Schema. W3C Recommendation (10 February 2004) http://www.w3.org/TR/rdf-schema/, Cited 19 Apr 2011.
4. Brickley, D., Miller, L.: FOAF Vocabulary Specification 0.98. Namespace Document. 9 August 2010 – Marco Polo Edition. http://xmlns.com/foaf/spec/, Cited 19 Apr 2011.
5. Cabinet Office, e-Government Metadata Standard Version 3.1, 29/8/2006. http://interim.cabinetoffice.gov.uk/media/273711/egmsv3-1.pdf, Cited 19 Apr 2011.
6. Chen, H., Mao, Y., Zheng, X., Cui, M., Feng, Y., Deng, S., Yin, A., Zhou, C., Tang, J., Jiang, X., Wu, Z.: Towards semantic e-Science for traditional Chinese medicine. BMC Bioinformatics **8**, 3, published 9 May 2007. http://www.biomedcentral.com/1471-2105/8/S3/S6, Cited 19 Apr 2011.
7. Cover, R. (ed): Cover Pages. Hosted by OASIS. http://xml.coverpages.org/, Cited 19 Apr 2011.
8. Coyle, K.: Understanding metadata and its purpose. The Journal of Academic Librarianship **31**, 2, 160–163 (2005).
9. Dublin Core Metadata Element Set, Version 1.1. 2010-10-11. Dublin Core Metadata Initiative. http://dublincore.org/documents/dces/, Cited 19 Apr 2011.
10. EAD Encoded Archival Description Version 2002 Official Site. The Library of Congress. Updated March 13, 2008. Updated August 6, 2010. http://www.loc.gov/ead/, Cited 19 Apr 2011.

11. European Commission, Institute for Environment and Sustainability, Land management & Natural Hazards Unit. (Updated May 27, 2010) http://eusoils.jrc.it/wms/wms_Metadata.html, Cited 19 Apr 2011.

12. Gill, T., Gilliland, A.J., Whalen, M., Woodley, M.S.: Introduction to metadata. Online Edition, Version 3.0. Edited by M. Baca. Los Angeles, CA: Getty Publications (2008). http://www.getty.edu/research/publications/electronic_publications/intrometadata/index.html, Cited 19 Apr 2011.

13. Government of Canada, Records Management Metadata Standard, Library and Archives of Canada, 2006-02-07, http://www.collectionscanada.gc.ca/government/products-services/007002-5001-e.html, Cited 19 Apr 2011.

14. Grant, J., Beckett, D. (eds): RDF Test Cases. W3C Recommendation (10 February 2004) http://www.w3.org/TR/rdf-testcases/, Cited 19 Apr 2011.

15. Hayes, P. (ed): RDF Semantics. W3C Recommendation (10 February 2004) http://www.w3.org/TR/rdf-mt, Cited 19 Apr 2011.

16. IEEE Standard for Learning Object Metadata. IEEE Std 1484.12.1-2002. New York, NY: IEEE Computer Society.

17. IEEE Standard for Learning Technology – Extensible Markup Language (XML) Schema Definition Language Binding for Learning Object Metadata. IEEE Computer Society. IEEE Std 1484.12.3-2005. New York, NY: IEEE (2005).

18. IFLA, International Federation of Library Associations and Institutions. Functional Requirements for Bibliographic Records. Final Report (September 1997, as amended and corrected through February 2009). http://www.ifla.org/VII/s13/frbr/frbr.htm, Cited 19 Apr 2011.

19. ISO 15489–1:2001. Information and documentation – Records management – Part 1: General. International Organization for Standardization.

20. ISO 21127:2006. Information and documentation — A reference ontology for the interchange of cultural heritage information. International Organization for Standardization.

21. ISO/IEC 11179–1:2004. Information technology – Metadata registries (MDR) – Part 1: Framework. International Organization for Standardization.

22. ISO/IEC JTC1/SC29/WG11, MPEG-7 Overview (version 10), October 2004. http://mpeg.chiariglione.org/standards/mpeg-7/mpeg-7.htm, Cited 19 Apr 2011.

23. JHS 143. Asiakirjojen kuvailun ja hallinnan metatiedot. Versio 3.2.2006. http://docs.jhs-suositukset.fi/jhs-suositukset/JHS143/JHS143.pdf, Cited 19 Apr 2011.

24. Klyne K., Carroll, J.J. (eds): Resource Description Framework (RDF): Concepts and Abstract Syntax. W3C Recommendation (10 February 2004) http://www.w3.org/TR/rdf-concepts/, Cited 19 Apr 2011.

25. Kuhn, J.: Randel, Electronic Records Management and Sarbanes-Oxley Compliance: A Case Study of the COBIT Approach. The Icfai Journal of Audit Practice **4**, 4, 25–39 (2007).

26. Manola, F., Miller E. (eds): RDF Primer. W3C Recommendation (10 February 2004) http://www.w3.org/TR/rdf-primer/, Cited 19 Apr 2011.

27. MARC Standards. Library of Congress – Network Development and MARC Standards Office. Updated April 5, 2011. http://www.loc.gov/marc/, Cited 19 Apr 2011.

28. METS, Metadata Encoding & Transmission Standard, Official Web Site. The Library of Congress (Updated April 12, 2011) http://www.loc.gov/standards/mets/, Cited 19 Apr 2011.

29. MODS Metadata Object Description Schema, Official Web Site, The Library of Congress. (Updated November 19, 2010) http://www.loc.gov/standards/mods/, Cited 19 Apr 2011.

30. NISO, Understanding Metadata. Bethesda, MD: NISO Press (2004). http://www.niso.org/publications/press/UnderstandingMetadata.pdf, Cited 19 Apr 2011.

31. PRISM: Publishing Requirements for Industry Standard Metadata, About PRISM. IDEAlliance Inc. http://www.prismstandard.org/about/. Cited 19 Apr 2011.

32. TEI P5: Guidelines for Electronic Text Encoding and Interchange, Version 1.9.1, "20 Non-hierarchical Structures" (last updated March 5, 2011). TEI Consortium. http://www.tei-c.org/release/doc/tei-p5-doc/en/html/NH.html, Cited 19 Apr 2011.

33. TEI P5: Guidelines for Electronic Text Encoding and Interchange, Version 1.9.1, "The TEI Header" (last updated March 5, 2011). TEI Consortium. http://www.tei-c.org/release/doc/tei-p5-doc/en/html/HD.html, Cited 19 Apr 2011.

34. Thomas, J., Middleton, M., Warren, M.: Preparing resource discovery for digitized music: an analysis of an Australian application. Proceedings of the 7th ACM/IEEE-CS Joint Conference on Digital Libraries (pp. 298–302). New York: ACM Press (2007).
35. Universal Description, Discovery and Integration (UDDI) v2. OASIS, Organization for the Advancement of Structured Information Standards. http://www.oasis-open.org/specs/#uddiv2, Cited 19 Apr 2011.
36. UPnP Forum. http://www.upnp.org/, Cited 19 Apr 2011.
37. Vanthournout, K., Deconinck, G., Belmans, R.: A taxonomy for re-source discovery. Personal and Ubiquitous Computing **9**, 2, 81–89 (2005).
38. XBRL International Home Page, http://www.xbrl.org/, Cited 19 Apr 2011.
39. W3C Semantic Web. W3C Semantic Web Activity. http://www.w3.org/2001/sw/, Cited 19 Apr 2011.
40. W3C Semantic Web. Semantic Web Case Studies and Use Cases. http://www.w3.org/ 2001/ sw/sweo/public/UseCases/, Cited 19 Apr 2011.

Chapter 7
Data Interchange

Abstract Automated communication on the Web requires not only standardized ways to represent data assets, but also standardized ways to exchange information between software applications that use their own internal structures to represent information. In this chapter we concentrate on the adoption of XML to support data exchange in business. We describe the shift from the traditional EDI (Electronic Data Interchange) document standards to XML-based standards and frameworks, and furthermore, to the standards for Web services. At the end of the chapter we introduce XML-based solutions for supporting security in data interchange.

Keywords ebXML • EDI • Frameworks • Interchange standards • RosettaNet • Security • Web services

In the previous three chapters, we considered the use of XML for three kinds of data assets in organizations: documents, other primary data, and metadata. These assets are important facilitators of communication and these assets, their structures, and their management provide one perspective on communication. Another is that of data interchange. Before XML, SGML-based markup languages were seen as a notation for electronic documents to separate layout from content in order to provide flexible publishing, to add semantic and linguistic information to digitized historical texts, and to retrieve structural components from large document collections. XML was designed to be an important advancement to solve problems related to data interchange between software applications having their own ways to represent data in their systems and information repositories. In this chapter we consider the use of XML from the perspective of data interchange.

Communication between organizations usually takes place in business processes, such as those used to manage a supply chain. Each process is divided into communicative actions called transactions taking place between two parties and involving data exchange between the parties. Transactions and transaction management can be considered on various levels in information management and communication: one level is that of a database system, and another is the level of business interaction. In database systems a transaction is a sequence of database activities that is isolated from all other concurrent database activities. In spite of comprising several smaller activities, a transaction must be atomic, in the sense that either all component activities are performed or none of them is performed, and *durable*, meaning that after completion a transaction's effect should not be accidentally lost. Finally, the execution of a transaction on a consistent database should transform the database into a consistent state. The atomicity, consistency, isolation, and durability requirements are challenging for XML databases [15], and these problems will be addressed in the next chapter.

Business interaction involves the exchange of business documents between software applications controlled by two business partners. Electronic Data Interchange (EDI) standards were developed for this purpose. In the next section we describe the shift from traditional EDI document standards to XML-based standards. Electronic business requires from the participating partners not only rules for business documents, but also well-defined rules for business processes and for message exchange between software applications in different organizational and technological environments. The goal of the development of business frameworks has been to create a package of rules to support the planning, initiation, and operation of electronic business. Section 7.2 introduces some of those frameworks and the role that XML plays.

Recently models, methods, and techniques have been developed to automate business processes and data interchange by means of Web services. Section 3.2.4.3 introduced the XML-based languages developed by W3C for this purpose, and in Sect. 7.3 we further elaborate the role for XML.

Finally, data interchange in communication networks must be secure from unauthorized access and unauthorized tampering. Section 7.4 introduces some XML-based solutions to support security in data interchange, especially in the context of Web services.

7.1   EDI

Business-to-business solutions in electronic commerce require agreements about the language used for business documents exchanged between applications controlled by the participating partners. The language has to be formal so that it can be interpretable by computer software. Starting as early as the 1960s, Electronic Data Interchange (EDI) standards have been developed for the purpose. The standards created by the United Nations Economic Commission for Europe (UN/ECE) are called EDIFACT standards [32]. They define the syntax rules for messages to be exchanged between applications, code lists, descriptions of atomic and composite data elements, and finally descriptions of whole messages that represent business records, such as invoices and purchase orders.

In 1979, the American National Standards Institute (ANSI) independently chartered a committee now known as Accredited Standards Committee (ASC) X12 to create cross-industry rules for data interchange in the domestic trade within the

United States. The first ASC X12 standards were published in 1983. The message structures in the standards developed by these two bodies are basically the same, but there are differences in the terminology. In spite of their differences, the standards from these two standardization bodies have been widely used since the 1980s to develop more specific rules for particular business sectors and for particular business partners.

Over the years there have been attempts to converge the UN/ECE standards and the North American ANSI ASC X12 into a single international EDI standard [28]. The convergence has not succeed, but the dialogue and collaboration between the standardization organizations is active and the need for commonality is enforced by the pervasiveness of global business activities promoted by the Web.

To compare the difference between an XML format and the traditional EDI formats, consider the following piece of an EDIFACT message related to selling something from one organization to another:

NAD+SE+++KEURUUN LANKA OY++KEURUU++42700+FI'

The fragment includes a composite data element used to exchange the name and address of the seller in a message. The type of the composite is indicated by the symbol NAD (Name and Address). The structure of NAD elements is defined in the UN/ECE data element directory. As opposed to XML notation, component data elements of a composite element are not marked up explicitly by any data element identifier. They must instead be written in the order defined in the directory, using the plus symbol (+) as a separator. Successive plus signs refer to missing optional elements, and the semantics of a piece of data is derived from its position. For example, the NAD element begins with a mandatory party qualifier, taken from a code list. The code SE in the example refers to the seller party. The string KEURUUN LANKA OY is interpreted as the name of the seller because it appears in the location reserved for the party name. In a similar way, KEURUU is interpreted as the name of the city, 42700 as its postal code, and FI as the country code. The apostrophe (') ends the composite element.

When compared to the EDIFACT and ASC X12 formats, XML-based formats may be considered to be merely an alternative syntax for describing business documents. XML-based EDI languages, however, have important characteristics of their own, gained from being based on XML:

1. XML markup is human readable, or at least much more easily human readable than the traditional EDI messages. In particular, all parts of the logical structure are explicitly marked up with named tags, which is an effective way to improve human readability.
2. XML is designed for Web communication and can easily be used with other Web standards. Integration with other systems is therefore easier than in the traditional EDI solutions built for Value Added Networks (VAN) and special telecommunications software. XML is supported by generic, and often public domain, XML software and other open Web technologies.

3. The minimum rules constraining XML documents are few. Thus XML offers much more flexibility for sectoral or local level standardization than is available when using traditional EDI formats.
4. The wide deployment of XML simplifies writing translators from any particular language to another and simplifies interaction between people developing message standards for specific domains or business partners.
5. The XML-related specifications developed at W3C are available to be used in the EDI standardization and in specifying message transformations, queries, and the layout for messages.
6. There are different levels at which the XML-based standardization can be deployed. In the lightest form of adoption, a vocabulary can be agreed for element and attribute names. If there is a need to constrain the values of elements and attributes, then XML Schema is available for that purpose.

These characteristics have motivated the design of XML support for EDI. The Communications and Controls Sub-committee X12C of X12 has published several XML schemas and developed a reference model for XML design [1]. The model provides guidelines for the design of XML messages. The recommendations are targeted not only at the X12 community but at all message designers, and they are intended to align with the parallel United Nations Centre for Trade Facilitation and Electronic Business (UN/CEFACT) standardization efforts. The standardization activities within both ASC X12 and UN/ECE organizations are strongly targeted to support the specification and use of varying vocabularies and information structures in diverse contexts and situations. In alignment with this approach, several repositories offering business message standards in XML form have evolved. Examples of these are eBIS-XML (the electronic Business Interchange Standard) by BASDA [3] and UBL (Universal Business Language) by OASIS [2].

BASDA eBIS-XML. Since 1999, the Business Application Software Developers Association (BASDA) has provided XML standards for orders and invoices. BASDA represents its members as the voice of the business applications software industry to governments and policy making groups worldwide, but it is especially active in the UK where it is located. The standards have been designed to allow large corporate accounting systems to communicate with small business systems. XML schemas are available for downloading free of charge from www.basda.org. A special variant of the standard, called eBIS-XML-UKGov has been designed for the electronic procurement needs of the UK Government using a subset of the core eBIS-XML.

OASIS UBL. The UBL specification includes a library of XML schemas for reusable data components, such as Address and Payment, and for general document types. Version 2.0, published in 2006, includes 31 document types, among them catalogue, catalogue request, catalogue deletion, catalogue item specification update, order, and order response. The language is specified according to the rules defined in the UN/CEFACT Core Components Technical Specification. Therefore the context of each document type is described by showing the related business processes, party roles, and business rules. The context definition is intended to provide the semantics for document types. The schemas for document types are intended to be extended to meet the requirements of specific industries. The OASIS site also provides an update package for UBL 2.0, to be applied to all new UBL 2.0 installations. The update package includes, for example, the latest code lists.

7.2 Frameworks for Business Interactions

Standards for business documents are merely a subset of the standards needed in business interactions on the Web; people, organizations, processes, and other aspects of business must also be represented using sharable techniques. In electronic commerce (e-commerce) the major processes involve selling and buying products over the Internet, but business interactions on the Web cover a wide range of other activities as well.

Interactions may take place in inter-organizational business processes, involving several parties and many software systems. The interaction relationships can be characterized as business-to-business (B2B), business-to-consumer (B2C), business-to-government (B2G), government-to-business (G2B), and government-to-government (G2G) relationships. To support these relationships, business communities have developed frameworks intended to enhance interoperability in business processes.

There has been a clear tendency away from mere document standardization toward wider frameworks that cover not only documents but also business processes and messaging on the Internet. Even though a business process often involves several parties, the frameworks usually consider the interaction between two communicating partners at a time, as shown in Fig. 7.1. The frameworks typically include standards for the following aspects [20]:

Business processes: what kinds of actions are included in business processes, what are the roles of business partners in the processes, what are conditions whereby they interact, and what kinds of documents are exchanged between the partners.

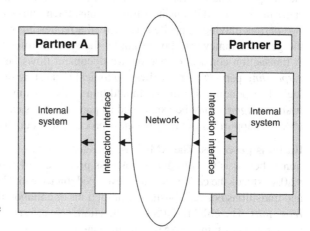

Fig. 7.1 Business interaction between two partners over the Internet

Business documents: what kinds of components are contained in the business documents and how the business documents are structured in the data exchange.

Messaging: how business documents are exchanged securely between software systems.

XML is utilized in the standards for all three aspects.

The frameworks can be roughly divided into cross-sectoral and industry-specific frameworks, with a gradual shift from industry-specific frameworks to cross-sectoral. For example, RosettaNet was originally focused on electronic component and consumer electronics industries; then the standards expanded to semiconductor manufacturing, telecommunications, and logistics industry; and today, according to the RosettaNet homepage at www.rosettanet.org, RosettaNet is intended to help "companies of all sizes that represent multiple industries meet the demands of today's global supply chain by addressing the challenges of increasingly complex, global trading networks." Here we first introduce two cross-sectoral frameworks: ebXML and RosettaNet, and then we describe some industry-specific standardization activities.

7.2.1   ebXML

The ebXML [11], developed collaboratively by UN/CEFACT and OASIS, is a generic, cross-industry framework, not defining particular business processes or business documents but rather providing the means for particular industries and domains to define the processes and documents they need. In the case study presented in Sect. 3.7, we briefly introduced the five parts of ebXML that have been approved as ISO standards. An overview of the whole ebXML framework can be found in the OASIS white paper "The Framework for eBusiness" [30].

In the ebXML framework *business collaboration* consists of a set of business activities executing *business transactions* between collaborating partners. Each partner plays one or more roles in the collaboration, and the roles exchange messages in the context of business transactions. Each transaction is conducted between two parties playing opposite roles, called a requesting role and responding role in the generic framework. For example, the specific roles may be buyer and seller. A transaction consists of one or two document flows between the *requesting* and *responding* parties: there is always a logical requesting document, and optionally a logical responding document. In addition to the document exchange, one or more *business signals* may be exchanged as part of a transaction. Below we summarize ebXML support for defining business processes, documents, and messaging:

Business processes. The XML-based language BPSS (Business Process Specification Schema) is used to define business processes [9]. The latest OASIS standard v2.0.4 extends the earlier standard developed jointly with UN/CEFACT. The ordering and transitions between business transactions or collaborations are defined in a *choreography*. The ebXML BPSS specification, also referred to as ebBP, is available as a schema written in the XML Schema language.

Business documents. The ebXML framework does not define particular document structures. Instead, each ebBP business process definition refers to a set of business document definitions that may be given by an XML schema language or by some other definition language. For example, a partner can document that it will use the OASIS UBL, the Universal Business Language defining 31 document types through XML schemas, as summarized in Sect. 7.1. The framework is intended to ensure that two trading partners using different syntaxes for business documents (for example, one using XML syntax based on the OASIS UBL and another using UN/EDIFACT syntax) interpret the document components in the same way. The method for specifying those components in a standardized, syntax-independent way is provided in the ebXML Core Components Technical Specification (ebCCTS, Part 5 in the ISO approved ebXML). In fact, this approach has been adopted for defining the UBL document types.

Messaging. The framework also provides the Message Service Specification (ebMS), an XML-based language to define various formats for *envelopes* that can hold business messages (Part 2 in the ISO approved ebXML).

In addition to these facilities, the ebXML framework also provides support for registering eBusiness artifacts (Registry Information Model and Registry Services Specification, Parts 3 and 4 in the ISO approved ebXML) and for configuring the technical contract between business partners (Collaboration Protocol Profile and Agreements, Part 1 in the ISO approved ebXML).

7.2.2 RosettaNet

Whereas ebXML is a generic framework that provides tools to define XML-based standards for particular business sectors, RosettaNet defines structures and vocabularies for particular kinds of business interactions. The RosettaNet community was founded in 1998 by 40 major high technology companies, including Microsoft, Intel, and SAP, to create standards that would enhance interoperability in managing the supply chains for information technology companies. Since, just like the automotive, construction and other industries, high tech companies are in business relationships with many other companies, RosettaNet now provides a common language across different industries [25]. Here we summarize the RosettaNet support for defining business processes, documents, and messaging:

Business processes. RosettaNet provides several *Partner Interface Process* (*PIP*) specifications expressed in XML and defining standards for automating business processes [27]. Each PIP defines the roles of business partners (e.g. buyer, seller), the business activities involved between the roles, and the types of business documents exchanged in the activities. Constraints on time, security, authentication, and performance of the interactions are also specified in PIPs. In all, 149 PIPs are defined in the version published in April 2010. These PIPs are divided into eight classes called *clusters*:

Cluster 0: Five PIPs for administering and testing RosettaNet connections
Cluster 1: Two PIPs to request an account setup and to maintain an account
Cluster 2: Thirty-seven PIPs for the distribution of product information
Cluster 3: Fifty-four PIPs for quotation and order management
Cluster 4: Thirteen PIPs for inventory management
Cluster 5: Nineteen PIPs for marketing information management
Cluster 6: Ten PIPs for service management and technical support
Cluster 7: Nine PIPs for distributing manufacturing information

Each PIP is also described graphically using a UML activity diagram. In the most recent PIP descriptions, XML Schema definitions are also provided. In the same way as in ebXML, the messages exchanged between partners in business processes can be divided into two categories: business documents and business signal messages. For each PIP one or more business document types are specified.

Business documents. The business document types related to PIPs are defined using either a DTD, the XML Schema language, or both. The RosettaNet Business Dictionary defines common terms used in the schemas.

Messaging. The RosettaNet Implementation Framework (RNIF) [26] defines how to package a business document into a RosettaNet business message so that it contains the headers and features needed for secure processing of the message. The definitions are provided as a set of DTDs. RNIF is defined for various transport protocols, but the capability to exchange messages using HTTP is mandatory in all RNIF software. RNIF also defines means for authentication, authorization, non-repudiation, packing, and unpacking of messages.

7.2.3   Industry-Specific Frameworks

In addition to the cross-industry e-business frameworks, there are frameworks describing how particular business sectors can use XML [19]. Most of the industry-specific frameworks evolved from traditional EDI standardization work by defining XML syntax for documents, adopting messaging standards suitable for Internet communication, and providing support to negotiate standardized business processes between business partners. As part of their design, the industry-specific frameworks often adopt one or more components from the general cross-industry frameworks. The Web sites related to industry-specific standardization give an impression of fragmented efforts, and it is difficult to find well-documented specifications, even though standardization work is going on in many areas. We summarize the current situation in three areas:

Textile and clothing industries. The EDIFACT-based EDITEX standardization of the European textile industry has ceased, and various replacements have begun to evolve in its place. Most illustrative is *Moda-ML* (Middleware tools and documents to enhance the textile/clothing supply chain through XML), a project developed in Italy from 2001 to 2003. The basis of Moda-ML is ebXML: the business process descriptions are provided using BPSS and the messaging uses ebMS. The Moda-ML home page at www.moda-ml.org states that Moda-ML is "an initiative that aims to publicly offer tools and format specifications for the data exchange based on XML and Internet and to stimulate convergence and consensus of associations and firms." The site and the specifications are available in both Italian and English.

Financial services. Within this sector there are at least four sets of standards: *FIX* (Financial Information eXchange defined at www.fixprotocol.org), *SWIFT* (Society for Worldwide Interbank Financial Telecommunications at www.swift.com), *OFX* (Open Financial Exchange Protocol at www.ofx.net), and *IFX* (Interactive Financial eXchange at www.ifxforum.org). FIX and SWIFT originally used non-XML syntax, but both have extended their standards to include specifications for XML syntax (FIXML [14] and SWIFT MX [29], respectively). OFX was originally defined using SGML DTDs, and the new versions use XML Schema instead. It provides document and messaging standards, but not standards for business processes [22]. The first version of IFX was released in 2000 and defined using a set of DTDs. Later XML Schema was adopted to define document types.

A comparison of IFX, OFX, SWIFT, and a proprietary format identified various semantic incongruities among the standards and showed that mediation between them is not a trivial task [17]. As a result, the existence of several standards has unfortunately caused high costs to banks and other financial institutions.

Chemical industry. CIDX (Chemical Industry Data Exchange) is an example of an industry-specific standardization organization that has faced many challenges common to other sectors as well [4]. CIDX was originally a standardization organization for the North American chemical industry, developing EDI standards based on ASC X12. In 2003 CIDX committed to converting the CIDX standards to XML Schema. At that time, version 4.0 of the Chem eStandards consisted of 60 message types. During the following years, CIDX extended its standards to support global business, developed business process guidelines, and created alliances with standardization organizations from other industries, from Europe, and from Asia. Thus the standards and standardization work reflected the globalization of the industry. Like some other industries, CIDX specified the RosettaNet Implementation Framework, but omitting RosettaNet PIPs, as its message service standard.

The CIDX standards were not adopted as widely as expected, and CIDX conducted a study for identifying obstacles to its adoption. The CIDX annual report of 2007 summarizes the results of the study. Among the most serious problems were these two:

- The lack of cross-industry standards was seen as a serious problem in the industry, where 75% of business is conducted with partners in other sectors.
- The cost and time needed for the adoption of electronic business was regarded as being too high, especially for small and medium size enterprises. In particular, the RosettaNet Implementation Framework was acceptable by big companies but regarded as too complicated for small and medium sized companies.

CIDX attempted to find less complicated standards without success. As an alternative approach, it instead started to consider the possibility of providing standards-compliant software tools to its members, which had been successful in some other industries, such as agriculture. At the end of 2008 CIDX transferred its standards and standardization work to OAGi (Open Application Group, Inc., www. oagi.org), a standards development organization focusing on building cross-industry standards. At the same time, chemical industry-specific operations and activities were transferred to the American Chemistry Council's Chemical Information Technology Center (www.americanchemistry.com/s_chemITC/). Subsequently, in early 2009, CIDX ceased operations.

7.3   Web Services

The frameworks discussed in the previous section support interoperability among information systems and automation of business processes between existing partners by means of XML-based standards. There is also some support for formalizing new relationships, such as the Collaboration Protocol Profile and Agreements of ebXML, but the creation of new relationships assumes human contacts. The idea in Web services is to use well-defined descriptions of the services to find and create business relationships, as well as to conduct business activities, automatically.

In Sect. 3.2.4.3 we introduced the languages of the XML family developed at W3C to support the building and use of Web services. In this section we describe XML-based solutions and proposals for Web services at the four layers of the Web service interoperation framework proposed by Yu et al. [33]. Security, which is critical for Web services, will be discussed in the next section.

Messaging layer. W3C's SOAP provides the standard for exchanging messages between Web services as XML documents, and the predominant protocol combined with SOAP is HTTP. To support messaging with different network protocols and to improve the reliability of messaging, some complementary specifications have been developed, including W3C's WS-Addressing [16] and the OASIS standard WS-ReliableMessaging [7].

Representation layer. WSDL, defined by W3C, provides the syntax to specify mechanisms to access a Web service and interact with it using SOAP. W3C has also published some recommendations to extend the representation capabilities of WSDL. One of them is Web Services Policy, which can be used to describe policy information relevant to service selection and usage, e.g. privacy policy [34]. Semantic information about a service can be added to a WSDL description by means of a standardized annotation mechanism [13]. An alternative approach for describing semantics of Web services is to use ontologies instead of WSDL. In particular, OWL-S [24] and Web Service Modeling Ontology [6] have been attempts to define ontologies that could be used to extend Web services to Semantic Web services. The special issue of the *Communications of the ACM* published in December 2005 describes the vision of semantic e-business and includes an interesting collection of articles on the topic.

Discovery layer. The discovery layer facilitates the publishing and discovery of Web services. The OASIS standard UDDI specifies how to represent data and meta-data about Web services in registries and how to classify, catalog, and manage the services so that they can be discovered and consumed. The UDDI data structures are defined using XML Schema.

Process layer. The process layer facilitates the construction of complex Web service processes, including conversations between a service and its requester and the development of composite services from component services. OASIS has developed several specifications to facilitate the construction of business processes based on Web services, including Web Services Business Process Execution Language, Web Services Context, and Web Services Coordination. All OASIS specifications are available at the OASIS site www.oasis-open.org.

7.4 Security in Data Interchange

Security is important in all Web communication and a critical concern in the design of electronic commerce solutions. In Sect. 3.2.4.3 we listed the XML applications developed at W3C to enhance security: XML-Signature for associating digital objects with digital signatures in XML format, XML Encryption for encrypting data and representing the result in XML format, and XKMS (XML Key Management Specification) to distribute and register public keys. OASIS also actively creates and promotes security standards, focusing on security needs in electronic business and particularly in the use of Web services.

The foundations for the OASIS work on Web services security are provided in a standard named Web Services Security. The most important component of the standard is defined in the WS-Security Core Specification consisting of a set of SOAP extensions [18]. The goal of the core specification is to enable secure SOAP message exchange by providing a set of mechanisms that can be used to construct various security protocols. Several related profiles have been specified as part of the Web Services Security package. Additional OASIS work on security is continuing, for example, in the following areas [21]:

Digital signature services. XML request/response protocols have been defined for signing and verifying XML documents and other data [8]. The protocols are associated with profiles to meet the needs of various applications. For example, OASIS has specified profiles for the following purposes:

- Creating and verifying time-stamps,
- Signing a software program,
- Using the Universal Postal Union's Electronic PostMarking service in compliance with the OASIS digital signature specifications, and

- Creating and validating qualified signatures in compliance with the guidelines given by the German signature law.

Enterprise key management infrastructure. The infrastructure includes a set of methods, languages, policies, and procedures for managing cryptographic keys in enterprises. Work is progressing to create the Symmetric Key Services Markup Language (SKSML), by which applications may request and receive symmetric key management services from centralized servers over networks.

A framework for creating and exchanging security information between online partners. Several software systems collaborating as business partners deal with various subjects in common. The systems may operate in different technical environments, but they are all concerned with the same security attributes of the subjects. If the subject is a person, the most important security attribute is the identity of the person. If the person has been authenticated by one party whom the other parties trust, they can rely on that authentication if there were a way to communicate information about the subject between the parties.

The Security Assertion Markup Language (SAML) enables one party to assert security statements about a subject and submit assertions in request/response protocols to other parties [23]. SAML is designed especially for the following situations:

Single Sign-On. In communicating with multiple systems, it can benefit both the user and the system providers if re-authentication can be avoided after authentication has been completed by a trusted party.

Federated identity. Instead of using their different proprietary ways to identify a mutual user, business partners may agree to refer to that user with a federated identity.

Needs for security assertion constructs in other standards. SAML specification defines how SAML assertions and request-response protocol messages can be exchanged between systems using common underlying protocols such as SOAP and HTTP.

SAML assertions are information packages that can be flexibly exchanged between trusted parties. Therefore each assertion uses XML to capture information about the issuer (who has issued the assertion), subject, and conditions under which the assertion is valid (such as validity period and audience restriction). Assertions can be exchanged in request/response protocols using various protocol mechanisms. For example, consider a situation where three parties, the University of Jyväskylä, the University of Waterloo, and the University of Toronto all have some activities involving "Maija Ek." If the University of Jyväskylä has authenticated this person, then the University of Waterloo might trust it enough to be willing to depend on the authentication done in Jyväskylä, instead re-authenticating on its own. Furthermore, the University of Toronto might trust Waterloo enough to request authentication of that person from Waterloo.

Figure 7.2 shows a SAML assertion expressing that the University of Jyväskylä has authenticated "Maija Ek" using a password-protected authentication mechanism. Line 1 contains the declaration of the SAML namespace. Lines 2 through 5 provide information about the SAML version used, when the assertion was created, and who issued it. Timestamps in SAML use the dateTime data type of XML Schema.

```
1. <saml:Assertion  xmlns:saml="urn:oasis:names:tc:SAML:2.0:assertion"
2.       Version="2.0" IssueInstant="2009-03-17T12:00:00Z">
3.   <saml:Issuer Format="urn:oasis:names:SAML:2.0:nameid-format:entity">
4.       http://jyu.fi
5.   </saml:Issuer>
6.   <saml:Subject>
7.       <saml:NameID
8.        Format="urn:oasis:names:tc:SAML:1.1:nameid-format:emailAddress">
9.        maija.ek@jyu.fi
10.       </saml:NameID>
11.   </saml:Subject>
12.   <saml:Conditions
13.       NotBefore="2009-03-17T12:00:00Z"
14.       NotOnOrAfter="2009-03-17T12:30:00Z">
15.   </saml:Conditions>
16.   <saml:AuthnStatement
17.       AuthnInstant="2009-03-17T12:00:00Z" SessionIndex="1234512345">
18.        <saml:AuthnContext>
19.          <saml:AuthnContextClassRef>
20.           urn:oasis:names:tc:SAML:2.0:ac:classes:PasswordProtectedTransport
21.          </saml:AuthnContextClassRef>
22.        </saml:AuthnContext>
23.   </saml:AuthnStatement>
24. </saml:Assertion>
```

Fig. 7.2 An example of a SAML assertion

Lines 6 through 11 identify the subject to which the statement applies. The subject has a name identifier in the form of an email address, one of the various name identifier formats defined by SAML. Lines 12 through 15 show the validity period of the assertion, and lines 16 through 23 contain an authentication statement about the subject. The statement shows that the subject was originally authenticated using a password-protected authentication mechanism at the date and time shown. The assertion can be exchanged between the University of Jyväskylä and the University of Waterloo using SOAP, for example. Furthermore, the University of Waterloo might send the assertion to the University of Toronto using HTTP.

The statement in the assertion of Fig. 7.2 is an example of an *authentication statement*. Another kind of statement is an *authorization decision statement*, declaring that the subject is entitled to do something (for example, a person is permitted to buy some item). A third type of statement is an *attribute statement*, which is used to provide some specific attributes about the subject (for example, that a person has a certain type of credit card). An assertion may contain multiple statements of various types about a subject [23].

Access control. Access control involves three kinds of entities: subjects, resources, and actions; a subject may or may not have permission to perform an action on a resource. Access control mechanisms are needed not only for data exchange, but for all resource management more generally. When organizations have resources in XML format, access control can also be applied to document fragments as well as complete resources [5].

Organizations are often required to establish and follow policies that dictate the acceptability of requests by specific subjects to execute specific actions on specific resources. This is particularly important when an organization must ensure compliance to governmental and sectoral regulations, such as legislation regarding financial and privacy obligations. The heterogeneous proprietary solutions in use in many large organizations, where each department (e.g. Legal, Finance, Human Resources, Information Systems) manages its own security enforcement, hinder obtaining systematic ways to enforce access control.

A goal in the development of the Extensible Access Control Markup Language (XACML) [12] has been to provide a method for combining individual rules and policies into a single policy set that applies to each individual access request. Expressing the policies in a standard format, specifically as XML documents, provides a basis for uniform management of access control throughout the enterprise. The common mechanism also allows the organization to make authorization decision based on combining rules that originate from multiple departments.

Recording the policies as text documents brings many benefits. For example, policy statements may be written by several policy writers, combined from several components, and distributed in multiple ways. The XACML specification provides many illustrative examples showing how to express policies, rules, decision requests, and responses to decision requests using XACML. For example, as part of the access control policy of a health care centre, XACML might be used to express a rule stating that *a person is allowed to read any record of a patient under 16 years of age if the person is the designated parent or guardian of the patient.*

7.5   The Status of Interchange Standards

As this chapter has shown, research and development for XML-based solutions to support data exchange has been extensive. The work in international, national, and sectoral standardization organizations has produced hundreds of standards, many with multiple versions. The standards of many organizations are available free of charge, some without registration. Finding information about the operational use of the standards is much more difficult. There are case studies available on some sites, but often the case study sites seem outdated. For example, the case studies on the ebXML site are dated 2003 [11].

Information about the use of standards in the public sector can be found in the standards catalogues published in some countries to support interoperability in e-Government. For example, the standards lists published in the interoperability frameworks of Great Britain and New Zealand include many of the standards mentioned in this chapter. Some examples of the standards and their status levels in the frameworks are given in Table 7.1.

Table 7.1 Standards for data interchange and security in Great Britain and New Zealand

Standard	Great Britain [31]	New Zealand [10]
SOAP	v1.2 adopted	v1.1 adopted, v1.2 recommended
WSDL v1.1	Adopted	Adopted
XML Signature	Adopted	Future consideration
XML Encryption	Adopted	Future consideration
XKMS 2.0	Adopted	
ebXML Registry Services Specification v2.1	Recommended	Adopted
ebXML registry information model v2.1	Recommended	Adopted
UDDI v3	Recommended	Adopted
OASIS Web Services Security	Parts of it either adopted or recommended	Recommended
OASIS SAML	v 2.0 recommended	v 1.1 recommended
OASIS SAMS 2.0		NZ SAMS profile developed

References

1. ASC X12 Reference Model For XML Design. 2002. ASC X12C Communications and Controls Subcommittee, Technical Report Type II, ASC X12C/2002-61. Data Interchange Standards Association, Inc. http://www.x12.org/x12org/xmldesign/index.cfm, Cited 19 Apr 2011.
2. Bosak, J., McGrath, T., Holman, G.K. (eds): Universal Business Language v2.0. OASIS Standard (12 December 2006) http://docs.oasis-open.org/ubl/os-UBL-2.0/, Cited 19 Apr 2011.
3. Business Application Software Developers Association, eBIS-XML http://websites.uk-plc. net/BASDA/eBIS-XML-35485.htm, Cited 19 Apr 2011.
4. CIDX Home Page http://www.cidx.org/, Cited 19 Apr 2011.
5. Damiani, E., De Capitani di Vimercati, S., Paraboschi, S., Samarati, P.: A fine-grained access control system for XML documents. ACM Transactions on Information System Security (TISSEC) **5**, 2, 169–202 (2002).
6. de Bruijn, J., Fensel, D., Keller, U., Lara, R.: Using the web service modeling ontology to enable semantic e-business. Communications of the ACM **48**, 12, 43–47 (2005).
7. Davis, D., Karmarkar, A., Pilz, G., Winkler, S., Yalçinalp, Ü. (eds): Web Services Reliable Messaging (WD-ReliableMessaging) Version 1.2, OASIS Standard (2 February 2009) http:// docs.oasis-open.org/ws-rx/wsrm/200702/wsrm-1.2-spec-os.html, Cited 19 Apr 2011.
8. Drees, S. (ed): Digital Signatures Service Core Protocols, Elements, and Bindings Version 1.0. OASIS Standard, (11 April 2007) http://docs.oasis-open.org/dss/v1.0/oasis-dss-core-spec-v1.0-os.html. Cited 19 Apr 2011.
9. Dubray, J.-J., Amand, S.St., Martin, M.J. (eds): ebXML Business Process Specification Schema Technical Specification v2.0.4. OASIS Standard (21 December 2006) http://www. oasis-open.org/specs/#ebxmlbpv2.0.4, Cited 19 Apr 2011.
10. E-government in New Zealand, http://www.e.govt.nz/, Cited 19 Apr 2011.
11. ebXML Home Page. http://www.ebxml.org/. Cited 19 Apr 2011.
12. eXtensible Access Control Markup Language (XACML) Version 2.0. OASIS Standard (1 Feb 2005) http://www.oasis-open.org/specs/#xacmlv2.0, Cited 19 Apr 2011.

13. Farrell, J., Lausen, H. (eds): Semantic Annotations for WSDL and XML Schema, W3C Recommendation (28 August 2007) http://www.w3.org/TR/sawsdl/, Cited 19 Apr 2011.
14. FIXML Resources for FIX 5.0 Specification http://www.fixprotocol.org/specifications/fix5.0fixml, Cited 19 Apr 2011.
15. Grabs, T., Böhm, K., Schek, H.-J. : XMLTM: efficient transaction management for XML documents. Proceedings of the Eleventh International Conference on Information and Knowledge Management, CIKM'02, pp. 142–152. New York: ACM Press (2002).
16. Gudgin, M., Hadley, M., Rogers, T. (eds): Web Services Addressing 1.0 – Core, W3C Recommendation (9 May 2006) http://www.w3.org/TR/ws-addr-core/, Cited 19 Apr 2011.
17. Jayasena, S., Madnick, S., Bressan, S.: Financial information mediation: A case study of standards integration for Electronic Bill Presentment and Payment using the COIN mediation technique. Working Paper CISL# 2004–12. Cambridge, MA: Composite Information Systems Laboratory (CISL), Sloan School of Management, Massachusetts Institute of Technology (2004) http://web.mit.edu/smadnick/www/wp/2004-12.pdf, Cited 19 Apr 2011.
18. Nadalin, A., Kaler, C., Monzillo, R., Hallam-Baker, P. (eds): Web Services Security: SOAP Message Security 1.1 (WS Security 2004). OASIS Standard Specification (1 February 2006) http://www.oasis-open.org/committees/download.php/16790/wss-v1.1-spec-os-SOAPMessageSecurity.pdf, Cited 19 Apr 2011.
19. Nurmilaakso, J.-M..: EDI, XML, and e-business frameworks: A survey. Computers in Industry **59**, 4, 370–379 (2008).
20. Nurmilaakso, J.-M., Kotinurmi, P., Laesvuori, H.: XML-based e-business frameworks and standardization. Computer Standards & Interfaces **28**, 5, 585–599 (2006).
21. OASIS Committees by Category: Security http://www.oasis-open.org/committees/tc_cat.php?cat=security, Cited 19 Apr 2011.
22. Open Financial Exchange, Specification 2.1.1 (May 1, 2006). http://www.ofx.net/DownloadPage/Files/OFX2.1.1.zip, Cited 19 Apr 2011.
23. Ragouzis, N., Hughes, J., Philpott, R., Maler, E., Madsen, P., Scavo, T. (eds): OASIS Security Assertion Markup Language (SAML) V2.0 Technical Overview, Committee Draft (25 March 2008) http://www.oasis-open.org/committees/download.php/27819/sstc-saml-tech-overview-2.0-cd-02.pdf, Cited 19 Apr 2011.
24. Martin, D. (ed): OWL-S: Semantic Markup for Web Services. W3C Member Submission (22 November 2004) http://www.w3.org/Submission/OWL-S/, Cited 19 Apr 2011.
25. RosettaNet Home Page http://www.rosettanet.org/, Cited 19 Apr 2011.
26. RosettaNet Implementation Framework: Core Specification, Version V02.00.01 (Revised: 6 March 2002). Available at RosettaNet site http://www.rosettanet.org/, Cited 19 Apr 2011.
27. RosettaNet, Overview. Clusters, segments, and PIPs. Version 02.10.00. RosettaNet Program Office (20 April 2010) Available at RosettaNet site http://www.rosettanet.org/, Cited 19 Apr 2011.
28. Salminen, A.: EDIFACT for business computers: Has it succeeded? StandardView **3**, 1, 33–42 (1995).
29. SWIFT Standards MX, General Information, SWIFT (08 April 2011) https://www2.swift.com/uhbonline/books/public/en_uk/mxgi_20110408/title.htm, Cited 19 Apr 2011.
30. The Framework for eBusiness. An OASIS White Paper (Last revision 24 April 2006) http://www.oasis-open.org/committees/download.php/17817/ebxmljc-WhitePaper-wd-r02-en.pdf, Cited 19 Apr 2011.
31. UK GovTalk, Schemas and Standards (last updated 29 May 2010) http://interim.cabinetoffice.gov.uk/govtalk/schemasstandards.aspx, Cited 19 Apr 2011.
32. UN/EDIFACT Main Page, United Nations Directories for Data Interchange for Administration, Commerce and Transport (last updated 13 December 2010) http://www.unece.org/trade/untdid/welcome.htm, Cited 19 Apr 2011.
33. Yu, Q., Liu, X., Bouguettaya, A., Medjahed, B.: Deploying and managing Web services: issues, solutions, and directions. The VLDB Journal **17**, 3, 537–572 (2008).
34. Vedamuthu, A.S., et al.: Web Services Policy 1.5 – Framework. W3C Recommendation (04 September 2007) http://www.w3.org/TR/ws-policy/, Cited 19 Apr 2011.

Chapter 8
Adopting XML for Large-Scale Information

Abstract This book has presented many different ways to encode information in XML format and the purposes for doing so. In this concluding chapter we consider problems related to managing XML information assets and the methods available to address those problems. Approaches for persistently storing XML data can be divided into file storage and database storage, and the research community has been especially active in designing new solutions for XML databases. However, adoption of XML often means massive migration procedures from some legacy data into the XML format; examples of migration cases are given. While describing the problems related to adopting XML, we give examples of the kinds of data for which XML is not suitable. As a case study we consider the large scale adoption of XML in the public sector.

Keywords Content management systems • Government applications • Migration • Persistent storage • XML databases

During recent years there has been a strong migration to XML. Sometimes it means the transfer of legacy data into XML format, but more often XML replaces some older format for authoring new documents or other new artifacts. For instance, instead of composing documents using a traditional word processor (and thus producing text in its proprietary format), new documents may be authored with an XML editor. XML also emerges when the creation of data is facilitated by XML technologies. Examples of these new kinds of information artifacts are RSS feeds, RDF descriptions on the Semantic Web, WSDL descriptions of Web services, schemas written in XML Schema, and style sheets written in XSLT. All these situations require decisions about the way XML artifacts should be organized and managed, and they cause rapid and extensive growth of persistent XML data repositories.

In the first section of this chapter we introduce methods for storing XML data persistently and their related problems. The previous chapters in the book have shown the variety of areas where XML-based solutions have been developed, but XML is not suitable for some kinds of data. Therefore, in Sect. 8.2 we give examples

A. Salminen and F. Tompa, *Communicating with XML,*   185
DOI 10.1007/978-1-4614-0992-2_8, © Springer Science+Business Media, LLC 2011

of cases where the use of XML is not recommended, and for some of them it is not even possible. Finally, Sect. 8.3 summarizes two cases of large-scale adoption of XML in the public sector.

8.1   Persistent Storage of XML Data

Considering the variety of XML data in different environments and use cases, it is obvious that the needs for storing and managing persistent XML data are quite diverse. Sometimes XML data consists of text only, sometimes it consists of facts similar to traditional database data, and sometimes it consists of complex multimedia data and associated metadata. The requirements for document-centric cases (repositories of XML documents) differ from the requirements for data-centric cases (collections of traditional enterprise data encoded in XML format). Furthermore, the requirements for metadata storage differ from the requirements for primary data storage.

For some purposes, XML documents can simply be stored in a file system, accessible on a server in hierarchical directories or folders, in the same way as documents have traditionally been organized. The benefit of this solution is easy implementation.

For large data repositories, however, there are drawbacks to this solution: inefficiency in data access and minimal support to deal with security, versions, integrity, consistency, and crash recovery. The database systems community has worked for decades to design and develop systems for large-scale information management, especially to enable efficient data access and to ensure consistency and reliability. Traditional database systems with XML-enabling extensions may be natural solutions for data-centric repositories. However, XML data has features very different from traditional relational data, and therefore the storage and management solutions often require careful consideration.

8.1.1   Special Characteristics and Requirements

In this section we discuss the characteristics common to much XML data, although none of them appears in all XML data. The features derive partly from the characteristics of XML and partly from the typical application domains of XML, and they create the basis for the requirements for XML data management systems. Much of this material is based on our earlier analysis of general requirements for XML document database systems [35]. In addition, Westermann and Klas's analysis of XML database solution for the management of MPEG-7 media descriptions [47] provides many requirements that extend beyond MPEG-7.

Modeling challenges. A traditional database uses a well-defined data model to describe some enterprise in the real world. For example, a student database is an idealized description of a group of people that constitutes the enterprise, and all its important characteristics can be represented as a collection of tables in the relational

```
<?xml version="1.0"?>
<extract>
    <author>Charles Berlitz</author>
    <title>Native Tongues</title>
    <passage>
        &lquot;Beserk,&rquot; meaning &lquot;violently crazy,&rquot; comes from the
        term applied to the furious warriors among the Norsement&mdash the
        Bezerkers, who kept slaying until their enemies were literally cut apart.&ellip;
        the word really means <span lang="norse">behr sekr</span> (&lquot;bear
        skin&rquot;), &ellip; a rough &ellip; coat &ellip; the warriors habitually wore.
    </passage>
</extract>
```

Fig. 8.1 XML document without explicit modeling of the real-world data

model. An important principle is to use logical data modeling to provide the idealized description of the enterprise, and to keep this separate from the actual, physical representation of the data in the computer and separate from the external forms presented to human beings.

The complexity of XML-related data repositories and the need to integrate the management of structured documents with the management of other types of data create a special challenge for the underlying data model. In most research papers and some W3C specifications (as summarized in Sect. 2.5.2), the XML data model is simplified to be a labeled tree, including elements with their character data and attributes with their values. Occasionally, to emphasize shared data or to encode ID-IDREF pairs explicitly, the model is instead a directed graph, and each document or the whole collection of documents is treated as a hypertext [12]. Although usually the elements in the models are ordered, sometimes they are not. Such simplifications are often sufficient for developing capabilities dealing with the hierarchical structure of elements.

However, XML includes the physical structure consisting of entities as well as the logical structure that captures the relationships among elements. Furthermore, the data in XML is interpreted by humans using external presentations involving the text, figures, and possibly other kinds of objects produced from the logical *and* the physical structure. It is possible to separate the description of the external presentation by using style sheets, but it is not possible to separate the logical and physical structure because each XML document inexorably includes them both.

In contrast to storing data in relational databases, when storing a collection of documents, we are in a situation where the documents themselves are often used as a means to describe some real-world data. For example, consider the document fragment in Fig. 8.1, where the document structure, but not the real-world data, is reflected in XML elements. Alternatively, XML structures could be added to capture the linguistic data (what does "bezerk" mean? what is its etymology?) and perhaps also the historical data (who slayed whom? what did they wear?). However, the management of multiple document structures is a major challenge for text data and document modeling [34]. As a result, designers of document databases must consider the question of what to model even more carefully than designers of relational databases.

To make things even more complicated, it is well known that understanding the meaning of documents requires not only understanding their contents, but also understanding, at least to some extent, the context in which the documents have been created. This is especially apparent in records management and archives [27].

In summary, in contrast to traditional databases, document repositories require the management of both the physical document structure built from the documents' storage units and symbols, as well as the description of the "enterprise" reflected by the information in the documents' contents. Since the documents are intended for human perception, to be understood as information pertaining to some topic, it is also necessary to enable the management of the external forms presented to human beings. In addition, closely related W3C specifications that extend the capabilities specified in XML 1.0, such as XML Namespaces, XML Schema, and XLink, should be accommodated when developing XML database solutions, and this accommodation must adapt to the continuing development and re-development of the specifications. Finally the role of metadata to provide contextual information is important, and managing metadata together with the documents they describe is critical for document repositories.

Natural language content. Document-centric XML data contains primarily natural language text. It consists of successive symbols of an alphabet, constituting sentences of some language. Based on some criteria, the structure relates individual text fragments to other text pieces or to some other types of data. Operations on the document must be able to access and manipulate individual natural language elements ("words"), the sequential placement of those elements, the repeated occurrence of any elements, the structural units containing those elements, and the relationships among those units. Useful capabilities include operations to define constraints on text, to specify subsets to be retrieved, to arrange the results of retrieval, provide browsing facilities over those results, and to update instances of text [34]. In the contemporary world of global communication, the documents of a repository may be created using many languages, with diverse alphabets of symbols. The appropriateness of a full-text indexing method to a specific document repository depends on the language and content domain of its documents. For example, the indexing terms that are effective for a repository of English novels will perform poorly when used against a repository of Finnish technical documentation.

Granularity. Fine-grained fragmentation is a common feature in XML data. Any data management solution should include the capability to access data on all granularity levels and support access control and maintenance at the element level. An XML database including data for a variety of purposes and diverse users typically requires fine-grained, role-based access control [4]. The combination of role hierarchies, the hierarchic structure of XML documents, and nested nature of document containers (such as folders) requires complex inheritance and conflict resolution rules to determine access rights [10]. The challenge for XML database systems is to support such fine-grained access control efficiently in very large database environments with tens or thousands of users, each shifting among many possible roles.

Order. The order of document parts is important in document-centric XML data. For example, the steps in following some directions (whether finding a museum in a strange city, preparing a recipe, or knitting a pattern) cannot be reordered arbitrarily. The order of the components in a document must be maintained in the storage solution.

Versatile collections of data. Structured document management often requires a versatile collection of document types, even for the same material. For example, case studies confirm that production and publication of structured documents often requires multiple document type definitions that represent various *versions* developed over time as well as several *variants* covering different phases of document production [15, 33]. Furthermore, these studies confirm that the data content should be preserved in its variant forms corresponding to diverse document type definitions. The Data Definition Language (DDL) of an XML database system should provide capabilities to manage diverse document type definitions for versions and variants and do so as new document type definitions are created and existing ones are updated.

Role of schemas. There is much more heterogeneity in the role of schemas in XML data management than in the management of relational data. One advantage in adopting XML as opposed to SGML was that document structure could be represented without any associated schema. Consequently, the document instances stored in a database may have been created without any schema, as instances of a shared schema, or as instances of several diverse schemas.

The need for several document type definitions for the same material and for various versions of some of those document type definitions requires software support, which has greatly matured since the early experimental times of SGML and XML applications for document creation. In light of the growing use of XML for various types of data and the simultaneous increase in the diversity of presentation media, the need for managing rich collections of document type definitions in a single environment will increase. Since XML involves many forms of data manipulation, many forms of media, and many persons having diverse qualifications and application needs, all in the presence of continually changing international and industry-level standards, document type definitions will be "alive," and the database system should support the management of their evolution. In summary, elaborating on the needs to support versions and variants, the Data Definition Language for an XML database system should support the definition of multiple document type definitions, their organization into manageable collections, their presentation as data (typically in XML format), and their role as metadata constraining other data in the database instance.

Multiple levels of validity. A database should support multiple levels of validity for XML data. For example, we may wish to define either subcollections or views consisting of:

1. Non-XML data values from a set of types (e.g., numbers, dates, strings, images, tables),
2. Well-formed XML documents,

3. Valid XML documents, each associated with its own document type definition provided by a user or application,
4. Valid XML documents, each associated with a document type definition from a closed set known to the database system (either predetermined by the database administrator or pre-registered by some application), or
5. Fragments of well-formed or valid XML documents.

Queries. In an XML data management system users should be able to express their information needs in terms of any data in the repository, including element and attribute types and content, entities, URIs, tags, comments, processing instructions, schemas and other metadata [23]. Furthermore, the query capabilities should include fine-grained retrieval of fragments.

Update. As for traditional database systems, the update operations for an XML data repository include insertion, deletion, and replacement. The data affected can be a whole document, part of a document, a file, a URI, a style sheet, or any other unit. Furthermore the affected component may be either basic data or metadata, such as a DTD, a set of RDF descriptions for resources within the database or outside it, or a set of links. The Data Manipulation Language (DML) should provide mechanisms for applications to distinguish updates that cause the creation of new documents from those that create new *versions* or new *variants* of existing document parts. For example, Iwaihara et al. have described a version model and a method for access control on versioned documents [22]. In many environments multiple users in various roles maintain the content of structured document repositories through a complicated process in which documents are developed gradually and collaboratively. Such processes rely on XML editors and support for *workflow management and collaboration*, which should be integrated with XML database systems.

An XML database may contain various forms of reference: entity references, intradocument IDREFs, and inter-document links, where the links can be embedded HTML-like links or richer XLink-type links. The requirement of *referential integrity* is an important goal for an XML database, restricting updates such that all entity references, IDREFs, and links to documents within the database have existing targets. Traditional mechanisms to disallow or to cascade updates that would otherwise violate referential integrity should be supported.

A major concern in updating traditional databases has been transaction management. Relational database systems include capabilities for applications to specify the scope of each transaction, and this must also be available as part of the data manipulation languages for XML database systems [19]. For example, the DML may include a mechanism in which an application request is presented to the database system in the form of an XML document, which is a natural unit for specifying the collection of operators that must be executed as an atomic transaction (whether the data units to be updated are documents, document fragments, or nodes).

Web as the environment. XML was designed for use on the Internet. References in XML documents refer to Internet resources, and thus XML database systems should support Internet resource management, which includes accommodation for other kinds of data.

Table 8.1 Summarization of Bourret's XML database product listings [6]

Product category	Application type	Number of products	Open-source
Middleware	Data-centric	45	18
IDEs and editors	Data-centric	6	–
Data integration software	Data-centric	23	–
XML-enabled databases	Primarily data-centric	24	3
Native XML databases	Data- and document-centric	41	12
Web application servers	Data-centric	8	4
Wrappers	Data-centric	4	1
Content (document) management systems	Document-centric	34	1
XML query engines	Data- and document-centric	Not listed	
XML data binding	Data-centric	56	37

8.1.2 XML Management Solutions

No widely accepted single model or technology for managing XML document repositories has evolved. The generic names for candidate management systems have varied, and the boundaries between types of systems are fuzzy. For example, under the title of "XML database products," Ronald Bourret distinguishes the following categories: middleware, integrated development environments and editors, data integration software, XML-enabled databases, native XML databases, Web application servers, wrappers, content (document) management systems, XML query engines, and XML data binding [6]. For each of the categories, Bourret lists several products and indicates whether the products of the category are intended for data-centric applications, document-centric applications, or both. Table 8.1 shows for each category the intended application type, the number of products, and the number of open-source products. As Bourret warns, this product listing is not complete, accurate, or up-to-date. The products, vendors, and their Web sites change continuingly, and the information available on the Web is often geared primarily for marketing. In spite of their weaknesses, Bourret's product tables provide an interesting snapshot of a dynamically changing business and development area, and they can be used, as Bourret suggests, as a starting point for research.

In the remainder of this section, we consider three broad categories of systems: content management systems, XML-enabled database systems, and native XML database systems.

8.1.2.1 Content Management Systems

The term *content management system* originally referred to a Web-based publishing system. Now the term has been widely adopted by software product vendors, practitioners, and researchers in the context of *enterprise content management systems* to refer to technologies used to manage diverse assets such as documents, Web sites, intranets, and extranets in organizational or inter-organizational contexts [17, 41].

Content management systems with XML support typically provide functionality for

- Authoring structured documents;
- Organizing information in an XML store, workspaces, and folders;
- Integrating and reusing XML components and data from diverse sources in various formats;
- Applying rich metadata, including full-text and structure indexes;
- Searching based on hierarchic structures and links;
- Managing versions;
- Managing workflows;
- Maintaining audit trails;
- Managing access control;
- Publishing and distributing documents and data.

Vendors of content management systems often provide this functionality as a suite of software components from which a system can be customized to meet the needs of a particular customer. Examples of suites enabling the storage and management of XML documents and their parts are Astoria (www.astoriasoftware.com) and Documentum (www.emc.com). Other companies specialize as service providers rather than product vendors: Tieto (www.tieto.com) with their TRIP suite and Excosoft (www.excosoft.se) are two examples.

The XML storage in a content management system can be based on a file system, a database system, or some proprietary storage format. A characteristic feature of many content management systems is efficient text search. Often the role of XML schemas is limited.

To illustrate the role of content management systems, we summarize a case study performed by Mats Broberg [8], who describes how a new XML-based documentation management system was implemented for the Swedish division of FLIR, a large, multinational manufacturing company. Until 2000, product documentation consisting of text and images had been created using FrameMaker. At that time, FrameMaker was able to import and export XML files, but it did not provide facilities for writing XML content directly nor support the use of full Unicode.

Broberg reports that early in 2001 the business environment and procedures changed, requiring more modular specifications for variations of product platforms. Simultaneously globalization of businesses created new demands for translations into many languages with less lead time. A process for changing the documentation system was started, with the following critical requirements: smooth transfer from the old documentation system to the new; flexible management of translations among up to 17 languages; and traceability of versions arising from variations in product lines as well as translations.

After evaluating bids from 15 suppliers of documentation systems, a contract was signed in November 2002 with Excosoft, a Swedish consulting and software development company specializing in content management solutions. The implementation was gradual, and in the beginning manuals were maintained using both FrameMaker and the new system. In December 2002 all technical documentation was converted to XML. At the end of January 2003 the implementation enabled the production of manuals in PDF format from the new system and automated processing of XML files that were delivered from the translation agency. The XML and image files were organized in folders, and a SQL database was used for version management. When a master manual was ready to be translated, separate folders were created for the translation project.

The software of the new system for FLIR consisted of (a) an XML editor and authoring system from Excosoft, (b) a version management system from Excosoft, (c) a formatting tool from Excosoft incorporating the XSL-FO formatting engine XEP from RenderX, (d) a translation management tool from Excosoft, (e) the XML parser Xerxes from Apache Software Foundation, and (f) the XSLT processor Xalan from Apache Software Foundation. Information retrieval was primarily based on links and navigation, in a similar manner as on the Web.

At the time of Broberg's report in 2004, approximately 10,000 XML and image files were included, and one person in the company was responsible for the management of all user documentation. This is an example of a rather small XML data set, but it represents a typical situation in international manufacturing companies.

8.1.2.2   XML-Enabled Database Systems

The database research community has been actively investigating XML since the end of the 1990s (see, for example, [1] and [44]). Much of the effort has been directed at using XML as a database wrapper and mediation medium, using XML to describe Web resources, storing and indexing XML in traditional database systems, understanding the interaction of DTDs with constraint and typing mechanisms, and designing query languages for XML. In an influential paper, Maier examined XML query language proposals from the database perspective [26], but broader management issues peculiar to XML databases have not yet received much attention.

A relational or object-oriented database system can be extended to support XML data management [13]. All current commercial database systems provide some XML support, such as through Oracle's XML SQL Utility and IBM's DB2 XML Extender or DB2 pureXML.

When conventional database systems are used for XML, the data model of the original system is typically extended to encompass XML data, but the extensions define simplified tree models rather than rich XML documents. A problem in using the systems is the need for parallel understanding of two different kinds of data models. In the DB2 XML Extender, for example, the whole document can be stored either externally as a file or as a whole in a column of a table. Elements and attributes can also be stored separately in side tables, which can be accessed independently or used for selecting whole documents. DTDs, which are stored in a special table, can be associated with XML documents and used to validate them.

8.1.2.3   Native XML Database Systems

Native XML database systems are designed especially for the management of XML data. Some content management systems, including Astoria, are also designed to manage SGML or XML data. Ideally, such systems include capabilities to define, create, store, validate, manipulate, publish, and retrieve XML (or SGML) documents and their parts.

Native XML database systems have been compared to other kinds of XML data management systems, for example by Vakali et al. [43], and several benchmarking methods have been developed to test the performance of database management systems that are capable of storing, searching and retrieving XML data. In contrast to XML-enabled database systems, native XML systems provide more comprehensive document management capabilities, including front-ends for users to manipulate documents. Related offerings, such as Tamino [45], are software packages intended for building applications for the management of SGML/XML data. A few systems, especially those designed to support semi-structured data, such as Lore [18] and a more recent study of storage strategies for semi-structured data [5], provide native support for tree-structured data but are limited in their support of rich XML documents because they do not rely extensively on DTDs or other document type definitions and they do not support physical entities.

As we discussed in Sects. 2.5.2 and 8.1.1, there is no universal, well-defined conceptual data model for XML data. This causes problems for native systems: for example, the underlying model for XML data is not explicitly defined in Tamino, making it difficult to write robust applications. Many of the systems consist of packages of tools that do not share a common data model, and this may limit the kind of XML documents they are able to store and manipulate. Unfortunately, because the systems do not spell out the details of the data model, such inconsistencies and constraints are often difficult to detect.

8.1.3 Migration into XML Format

An XML data store is often created from some earlier data store in some other format. In this section we consider some common situations where such migration is needed.

Migration for digital preservation. Because of the explosive growth of digital information repositories, their preservation has become a major concern. The information publicly available on the Web, in various organizations, and in private digital repositories is stored using many diverse file formats and various databases, and it is often embedded in proprietary formats in software systems. Many digital artifacts are needed for longer than the time during which they are accessible in their original environments. The archival and records management communities have been active in creating methods to migrate digital objects from unstable or proprietary formats into more stable and open formats.

There are several ways XML can be used in the migration process. Often it is the target file format; for example, a relational medical database [29] and the social security law guides [30] were migrated into XML. Sometimes it is the format for recording users' guides, such as for documents containing instructions for using and interpreting the objects with which they are encapsulated. Finally, any metadata created as part of the migration process can be expressed in XML.

Migration from SGML for forward compatibility. Extensive SGML-based document repositories have been created, especially for technical documentation and for scholarly texts adopting the TEI standard [39]. However, migration from SGML to XML is needed before XML tools can be applied or for flexible integration with other XML data. TEI established a working group to support the migration from SGML to XML and collected reports from nine migration case studies [40], including the British national corpus, the collection of Japanese texts at the University of Virginia Library, and the collection of women writers' texts at Brown University.

SGML document repositories are marked up with the same general principles as XML, but since XML is a restricted form of SGML, legacy SGML documents dating from the pre-XML era are not necessarily XML documents. A W3C note by James Clark explains the differences between SGML and XML [11], and although TEI version P3 was defined for SGML, versions since P4 have been for XML. Most of the SGML features not present in XML can be removed from the data source by automated means, and thus the documents can be transformed to fulfill XML's constraints. A well-known open-source converter program is osx for Linux (linux.die.net/man/1/osx). Unfortunately not all XML restrictions can be handled automatically by transformation rules [11]. For example, names may cause problems in the transformation because SGML allows characters that are not permitted in XML names.

Migration from HTML. Among the resources using SGML, the majority are HTML documents, which usually migrate to XHTML. An important motivation for the migration from HTML to XHTML is for archival preservation, for which the Smithsonian Institution Archives published recommendations [38].

In some cases there is a need to identify the semantics of HTML page contents and therefore to transform HTML resources into an XML format through which the structure reflects the semantics. For example, DITA (Darwin Information Typing Architecture) is one such format, originally developed at IBM and now an OASIS standard. Its specification, reachable from www.oasis-open.org/specs/, includes the architectural specification, the language specification, and a set of schemas. DITA is designed to organize topic-oriented information, and Joaquim Baptista has reported on the use of DITA for technical documentation in an enterprise requiring multi-channel publishing [3]. Upgrading from HTML to DITA has occasionally been useful, and IBM has published instructions for such migration [2].

8.2 When Not to Use XML

During its first 15 years XML has become a powerful Web technology and has been repeatedly referred to as the *linga franca* of the Web. However, this does not mean that XML is preferable for all data on the Web. Even when XML might have many benefits, the adoption environment may not necessarily enable design and implementation of a successful solution.

8.2.1   Not to Replace Database Technology Universally

XML technology does not replace database technology. The evolution of databases is closely aligned with the development of modeling methods. Database design starts from describing the entities and relationships of an enterprise in the real world. The modeling involves the design of schemas on the conceptual, logical, and physical levels. Optimization, transaction processing, concurrency control, recovery, consistency, and security are essential components of database systems and proven technologies have been developed for them. XML on the other hand evolved from SGML, a representation format and the meta-markup language intended for documents used in human communication. Tim Bray, who co-edited the first XML Working Draft [7] with C. Michael Sperberg-McQueen, says: "The idea was to take SGML and throw away the 95% that never got used and retain the 5% that did" [20]. By restricting the language designed for electronic publishing, the goal was to improve its usability for that task and, at the same time, extend its use to some other areas:

> XML is primarily intended to meet the requirements of large-scale Web content providers for industry-specific markup, vendor-neutral data exchange, media-independent publishing, one-on-one marketing, workflow management in collaborative authoring environments, and the processing of Web documents by intelligent clients. It is also expected to find use in certain metadata applications. XML is fully internationalized for both European and Asian languages, with all conforming processors required to support the Unicode character set in both its UTF-8 and UTF-16 encodings. The language is designed for the quickest possible client-side processing consistent with its primary purpose as an electronic publishing and data interchange format [46].

Today XML is often critical as an import/export format for databases, and the solutions developed for databases are necessary in implementing XML data management. Thus database technologies provide solutions to some XML data management problems, but they have many other application domains as well. XML cannot replace the adoption of database concepts and solutions for those applications.

8.2.2   Not to Replace Other Proven Technologies Arbitrarily

Even though XML has replaced other data representation formats in many environments, there remain many situations where there is no need to use XML. For example, compared to many other data formats, XML is verbose. Therefore, binary data or comma-delimited text may be a more efficient format than XML for data exchange between two systems. W3C has published a recommendation for a binary format called XOP (XML-binary Optimized Packaging) to provide efficient serialization of XML Infosets [21]. Furthermore, the Efficient XML Interchange (EXI) Working Group of W3C has conducted performance tests with several high-performance XML interchange encoding formats and their associated processors [48] and the development of an EXI format has started [36]. Although there is wide agreement on the need for a more efficient XML format, creating a new format for XML introduces new incompatibility problems [16, 24].

8.2.3   Risks in the Development and Deployment of New XML Applications

XML is an enabling technology, but, even in cases where the benefits are evident, its deployment often requires hard work, versatile knowledge, and close collaboration. Therefore before initiating a new development activity, the expected benefits should be critically compared to the expenses needed and possible risks. The development process for new solutions may be too challenging and complex given the resources available.

Going through the applications listed at the OASIS Cover Pages at xml.cover-pages.org, it is not difficult to encounter standardization activities that have ceased, although some may have evolved into or may have been folded into some other standardization activities. Examples of the activities that seem to have ceased include:

1. Open Content Syndication Directory Format (OCS), "to enable channel listings to be constructed for use by portal sites, client based headline software and other similar applications";
2. Portable Site Information (PSI), to enable the creation of portable Web sites;
3. Controlled Trade Markup Language (CTML), to provide a unified XML vocabulary for business documents;
4. Weather Observation Markup Format (OMF), to encode weather information reports.

Even within standardization organizations, some activities cease. For example, at W3C there have been language developments that seem to have ended prematurely, at least without any new published results. Examples of these are:

1. XML Fragment Interchange, to facilitate sending fragments of XML documents, not always whole documents. The W3C Candidate Recommendation was published in February 2001.
2. A P3P Preference Exchange Language (APPEL), for describing collections of preferences regarding P3P policies. The last Working Draft version was published in April 2002.

There are many reasons why the activities for designing new XML applications cease. Quite often the activities are initiated in a temporary project, by a group of enthusiastic people with some temporary funding. When the funding ends, the development work also ends.

Another problem is that the whole universe of XML-related languages is evolving and changing continuingly. Each language development activity is dependent on some other XML-related languages and their development activities. As mentioned in Sect. 3.1, sectoral standardization is typically based on universal standards, and local standards usually depend on sectoral standards. Furthermore, standards at each level often depend on other standards at the same level – for example, representations for shipping records might involve standards for other transportation modes and standards for financial processes. Maintaining the necessary knowledge

and understanding of the evolving context may be extremely difficult and
time-consuming.

When deploying XML at the local level, challenges are caused not only by the
choice of language to adopt or develop, but also by the unavailability of robust
software. Research has shown that early adopters of any innovation sometimes face
tremendous obstacles because the tools and technology are immature, and this has
been experienced by some early adopters of XML [9]. Even when implementation
and initial deployment can be considered successful, the solution may require major
maintenance efforts.

Finally, the benefits accruing from XML adoption may not be apparent to the
individuals who must endure critical changes in their work. The cost of ensuring
that the new tools are usable and investing in employee motivation must be included
in assessing the costs for planning new schemas and work processes.

8.3   Case Study: Government Applications

The recommendations and standards provided by various public domain agencies
clearly show that there is an increasing interest in extending the use of XML-based
standards, e.g. SAGA in Germany [31] and the guidelines of the Library and
Archives Canada [25]. Table 7.1 listed the XML-based standards adopted or recommended for data interchange and security in two countries: Great Britain [42] and
New Zealand [28]. Together with showing the extent of interest in XML-based standards, the standard listings of government agencies also show the areas where XML
standards are not recommended.

For over 10 years public domain agencies have shown interest in the adoption of
open structured document standards, based on first SGML and later XML. However,
creating and implementing policies and practices for such adoption has faced many
obstacles. Unfortunately, there are few reported large-scale SGML/XML adoption
cases besides those that involve HTML only. In the remainder of the chapter, we
describe two pioneering cases.

8.3.1   The Case of the Finnish Parliament and Government
         Ministries

Among the public sector adopters of the open document standards, the Finnish
Parliament was a pioneer before the time of XML. In the early 1990s, the Finnish
Government and Parliament started looking for a standard document format to
replace the various proprietary formats then in use. The need for an application-
independent standard for digital documents activated collaboration between the
Parliament, some Government ministries, and researchers at the University of
Jyväskylä. A project called RASKE (coming from the Finnish phrase "Rakenteisten

AsiakirjaStandardien KEhittäminen," meaning the development of standards for structured documents) commenced in 1994 ([32, 33], www.it.jyu.fi/raske). The researchers created a framework in which document standardization was not restricted to the development of document formats only, but considered as the holistic development of document management environments related to business or administrative processes. It was realized that effective implementation of an approach to manage structured documents will evidently change not only the documents themselves, but also the processes that involve documents, the roles of people in the processes, and the tools for working with documents. A set of methods for analyzing and describing document management within a given domain were adapted from existing information systems development methods.

During 1994–1998 researchers analyzed document production in Parliamentary processes, problems related to document management, and requirements for future solutions. The document analysis encompassed four domains: the enquiry process, national legislative work, Finnish participation in EU legislative work, and the creation of the state budget. At the early stage of the project, SGML was chosen as the basis for the future document standards, and the researchers designed preliminary DTDs for 21 document types, including, for example, Government Bill, Government Decision, Government Communication, Private Bill, Special Committee Report, Budget Proposal, and Communication of Parliament.

The research project was followed by practical development projects in which selected companies designed and implemented SGML solutions for specific subsets of documents while the Parliament and Government ministries redesigned their work processes. The first implementation was the archive of laws and statutes in SGML form (www.finlex.fi), published by the Ministry of Justice in 1997. An SGML-based budgetary system was implemented in 1998 in each ministry, and in 1999 the Parliamentary State Budget was handled in SGML format. During 1998–2002 SGML was adopted for all Parliamentary document types produced in Parliament. The format of the State Budget Proposal was shifted from SGML to XML in 2004.

The Government Bill was the most important document type in the interorganizational legislative process, and the original goal at the beginning of the standardization work was for each originating ministry to create the content of a Bill in SGML format. However, this goal was not achieved. Each Government Bill is currently authored by using Microsoft Word templates with a custom-designed style editor, documents produced with the templates are stored in a document database of a decision support system, and later they are converted into SGML format in the Parliament.

The Parliamentary documents produced in the Parliament are authored in SGML format using Adobe FrameMaker+SGML. Connections to other applications provide retrieval of data from databases; for example, names of Parliament Members and common phrases can be imported from corresponding databases. The export function provides document storage to Trip, a document archive system from Tieto Corporation, which has been used in the Parliament for document storage since the time before the shift to SGML. Automated transformation from SGML to ASCII and PDF formats can also be performed during export. Today Trip has expanded into a software package supporting the storage and access of SGML and XML documents.

For Parliament it was decided at the start of the standardization review that legacy documents were not to be transformed into the new standard formats. From 2011 on, the Parliament is planning to migrate from SGML to XML, extending the migration gradually also to pre-SGML documents.

Despite the shared understanding of the needs for document standardization, standardization progressed independently in the Parliament and in the Government ministries. Each organization made its own decisions concerning the technological systems to adopt, and therefore the technology solutions for supporting document management became heterogeneous. Disparate solutions in the Parliament and Government led to some difficulties in inter-organizational document management processes. In the budgetary domain, the document structure is controlled from the beginning by a schema, and therefore structurally faulty documents are rare. However, elsewhere, manual work is needed to correct errors in automated conversions, and the tracking of the technical author of a faulty document may be troublesome.

The shift to structured document production caused major changes to government processes. Some civil servants and Members of Parliament still use traditional text editing, and their secretaries manually convert the resulting texts into the templates. At first, understanding the idea of structured documents was hard for some authors, but to most, schema-directed authoring has since become a natural part of their job. Schema design and maintenance has been a continuing process. In addition to the schemas, various style sheets and transformation definitions have also been designed, implemented, and maintained. Furthermore, since many definitions of terms are deeply interrelated, versioning and maintenance of the terminology require special expertise.

In spite of the problems, the implementation of SGML/XML for Finnish Parliamentary documents has had several positive effects: the consistency and layout of documents have improved, content reuse is more effective, and the translation from Finnish to Swedish is semi-automated. The dependence on a publishing house is not as strong as it used to be, and publishing costs are significantly lower. For citizens, the implementation of the structured document approach has meant better accessibility to Parliamentary information. Compared to the situation prior to standardization, capabilities for defining queries have significantly improved. In the budgetary domain, there is no longer a need for manual conversions. In summary, the new solution allows last minute changes, speeds up editing and publishing, improves versioning, and decreases the dependence on the publishing house.

Even though the Finnish Government was less successful than Parliament in meeting the original standardization plans, the idea of developing and adopting open document standards in collaboration with Parliament has not been discarded. In fact, a new standardization project has been initiated. The goal is to design and adopt new XML-based document standards in the Government in 2011 and to shift Parliament document procedures from SGML to XML. If successful, the result will be increased interoperability for the joint processes of Parliament and the Government.

8.3.2 The Case of Massachusetts

IT policy development for the state government of Massachusetts in the United States is an important case with wide implications outside Massachusetts as well. The "Enterprise Open Standards Policy" and the first version of the "Enterprise Technical Reference Model" (ETRM) were published in 2004. The policy stated that

> All prospective IT investments will comply with open standards referenced in the current version of the Enterprise Technology Reference Model.... Existing IT systems will be reviewed for open standards compatibility and will be enhanced to achieve open standards compatibility where appropriate. Open standards solutions will be selected when existing systems are to be retired or need major enhancements.

The current ETRM version is numbered 5.0 and was published in September 2008 [14]. It describes the service oriented architecture of Massachusetts and identifies the standards, specifications and technologies that support the computing environment in the state government. The architecture is divided into 6 domains: access, information, applications, integration, management, and security. XML has an important role in all domains. For example, in the security domain, identity assertion is based on SAML version 1.1, Web service authentication is based on XML Signature, and encryption is based on XML Encryption. For the large-scale adoption of XML, the most important domain is information. It defines standards and guidelines for 4 areas, called disciplines in ETRM: data formats, data management, data interoperability, and (yet to be finalized) records management. Even though the format for long term conservation of files remains to be addressed in the records management discipline, the file format discipline and the data interoperability discipline show the core role of XML:

> The adoption of XML is the cornerstone of the Commonwealth's Service Oriented Architecture (SOA) vision of a unified enterprise information environment. Agencies should consider the use of XML for all projects, and should implement XML, unless there are compelling business reasons not to do so.

Probably the most well-known and discussed component of ETRM has been the list of acceptable document formats. In Sect. 3.4 we briefly described the progress of the two XML-based document formats into ISO approved office standards: OpenDocument Format (ODF) developed at OASIS and Office Open XML File Formats (OOXML) originating from Microsoft. Shah, Kesan and Kennis provide an interesting and detailed report of the historical battle related to the two standards in Massachusetts [37]. ETRM version 2.0, published in 2004, listed the acceptable document formats to include plain text format, rich text format (RTF), HTML, PDF, and XML, but excluded all Microsoft formats, even though Microsoft had at the time its own XML format for office documents. This exclusion caused Microsoft to negotiate with the Massachusetts government to make several changes in the patent license of Microsoft's XML formats. Later Microsoft made this license publicly available. The draft version 3.0 of ETRM posted for public review included both ODF and Microsoft Office XML formats as acceptable document formats, but Microsoft's document formats were excluded from the official final version, as well as from the next version numbered 3.5. In November 2005 Microsoft responded by announcing the submission of its new XML format, now called Office Open Extensible Markup Language (OOXML), to two international standards bodies, ECMA International and the International Organization for Standardization (ISO). Furthermore, Microsoft posted on the Internet a "covenant not to sue" regarding the OOXML formats.

Before the next version (4.0), the Massachusetts Information Technology Division responsible for the development and maintenance of ETRM received opposition from a new direction, representatives of disabled workers in Massachusetts. They voiced their concerns about the planned changes because disabled workers were dependent on extra technologies built for the Microsoft products. This concern was covered by the local press and was followed by Microsoft's announcement of sponsoring the development of plug-in translators between OOXML and ODF. There was a period of developing and testing the plug-ins and a "production-ready" plug-in by Sun was licensed in Massachusetts in May 2007.

Even though many reservations about the openness of OOXML were raised by critics of Microsoft, Massachusetts decided to include OOXML in the list of accepted document formats, together with ODF, in version 4.0 of ETRM. The latest version (5.0) defines ODF, OOXML, plain text, HTML, and PDF as open formats. PDF may be used for documents whose content will not undergo further modifications and need to be preserved in their current presentation, and plain text is confined to documents where formatting is not important and which are not part of any official record. XML is the primary format: "All agencies are expected to migrate away from proprietary, binary office document formats to open, XML-based office document formats". HTML is the preferred format for documents accessible using a Web browser. RTF is regarded as an acceptable format in special cases.

Public administration agencies world-wide will observe with great interest the consequences of the Massachusetts open standards policy, especially the ruling concerning office documents. We are not aware of any statistics on the numbers of documents created in the XML formats since the publication of ETRM. Since all offices in Massachusetts now use XML based formats, the numbers should be at new levels in the coming years.

8.4   Conclusions

The Finnish Parliament and the Massachusetts government have been pioneers in the adoption of SGML/XML technologies and suffered problems of early adopters. Immaturity of the technology is only one of the problems encountered by pioneers in the public domain. Information technology policies and standards in the public domain may have important consequences in the work of people in business sectors involved. Experiences in the Finnish case emphasized the need for inter-organizational co-operation from the early phases of standardization [33]. The involvement of many organizations in legislative work increased the complexity of the planning and implementation of new solutions. Changes in document production caused changes in the work of several groups of people. Motivating the needs for changes and demonstrating future benefits was seen to be extremely important, and one tool for motivating authors in the Parliament to adopt new working practices was the customized editor that simplified authoring. The detailed analysis of documents and work processes at the beginning of standardization and the involvement of diverse and representative stakeholders were seen as valuable means to elicit information about the requirements and needs from all parties involved. One of the lessons that emerged from Massachusetts after the unexpected and strong objections of the disabled workers was the importance of considering the full spectrum of direct and indirect stakeholders. Based on their analysis, the authors of the Massachusetts case study conclude: "The history of the open standards policy around document formats is long and tortured." In the large-scale migration to XML, pioneers experience obstacles that later XML technology adopters may avoid – as long as the lessons learned are successfully communicated.

References

1. Abiteboul, S., Buneman, P., Suciu, D.: Data on the Web. San Francisco, CA: Morgan-Kaufmann (2000).
2. Anderson, R., Day, D., Hennum, E.: Migrating HTML to DITA, Part 1: Simple steps to move from HTML to DITA (31 Jan 2005) http://www.ibm.com/developerworks/xml/library/x-dita8a/, Cited 19 Apr 2011.
3. Baptista, J.: Pragmatic DITA on a budget. Proceedings of the 26th Annual ACM International Conference on Design Communication, SIGDOC'08 pp. 193–198. New York: ACM Press (2008).
4. Bertino, E., Castano, S., Ferrari, E., Mesiti, M.: Controlled access and dissemination of XML documents. Proceedings of the 2nd International Workshop on Web Information and Data Management pp. 22 – 27. New York: ACM Press (1999).
5. Bhadkamkar, M., Farfán, F., Hristidis, V., Rangaswami, R.: Storing semi-structured data on disk drives. ACM Transactions on Storage, 5, 2, 6:1–6:35 (2009).
6. Bourret, R.: XML Database Products (20 June 2010) http://www.rpbourret.com/xml/XMLDatabaseProds.htm, Cited 19 Apr 2011.
7. Bray, T., Sperberg-McQueen, C.M. (eds): Extensible Markup Language (XML), W3C Working Draft (14 Nov 1996) http://www.w3.org/TR/WD-xml-961114.html, Cited 19 Apr 2011.
8. Broberg, M.: A successful documentation management system using XML. Technical Communication 51, 4, 537–546 (2004).
9. Chen, M.: Factors affecting the adoption and diffusion of XML and Web services standards for E-business systems. International Journal on Human-Computer Studies 58, 3, 259–279 (2003).
10. Chinaei, A. H., Chinaei, H. R., Tompa, F. W.: A unified conflict resolution algorithm, Proceedings of the 4th VLDB Workshop on Secure Data Management 2007 (SDM'07), Springer LNCS 4721, September 23, 2007, 1–17.
11. Clark, J.: Comparison of SGML and XML. W3C Note (15 Dec 1997) http://www.w3.org/TR/NOTE-sgml-xml-971215, Cited 19 Apr 2011.
12. Conklin, J.: Hypertext: an introduction and survey. IEEE Computer 20, 9, 17–41 (1987).
13. Draper, D.: Mapping between XML and relational data. In: Katz, H. (ed.) XQuery from the Experts: A Guide to the W3C XML Query Language, pp. 309–352. Addison-Wesley, Boston (2004).

14. Enterprise Technical Reference Model - Service Oriented Architecture (ETRM v. 5.0). Information Technology Division, Commonwealth of Massachusetts (16 Sep 2008) http://www.mass.gov, Cited 19 Apr 2011.
15. Fahrenholz, S: SGML for electronic publishing at a technical society – Expectations meets reality. Markup Languages: Theory and Practice 1, 2, 1–30 (1999).
16. Geer, D.: Will binary XML speed network traffic? IEEE Computer 38, 4, 16–18 (2005).
17. Glazier, D., Jenkins, T., Schaper, H.: Enterprise Content Management Technology. What You Need to Know, Waterloo, Ontario: Open Text Corp. (2005).
18. Goldman, R., McHugh, J., Widow, J.: From semistructured data to XML: Migrating the Lore model and query language. Proceedings of the International Workshop on the Web and Databases, WebDB'99 pp. 25–30. New York: ACM Press (1999).
19. Grabs,T., Böhm, K., Schek, H.-J.: XMLTM: Efficient transaction management for XML documents. Proceedings of the Eleventh International Conference on Information and Knowledge Management, CIKM'02, pp. 142–152. New York: ACM Press (2002).
20. Gray, J.: A conversation with Tim Bray. ACM Queue 3, 1, 16–25 (2005).
21. Gudgin, M., Mendelsohn, N., Nottingham, M., Ruellan, H. (eds): XML-binary Optimized Packaging, W3C Recommendation (25 January 2005) http://www.w3.org/TR/xop10/, Cited 19 Apr 2011.
22. Iwaihara, M., Hayashi, R., Chatvichienchai, S., Anutariya, C., Wuwongse, V.: Relevancy-based access control and its evaluation on versioned XML documents. ACM Transactions on Information and System Security 10, 1, 1–31 (2007).
23. Kamps, J., Marx, M. de Rijke, M., Sigurbjörnsson, B.: Articulating information needs in XML query languages. ACM Transactions on Information Systems 24, 4, 407–436, 2006.
24. Kangasharju, J. (ed): Efficient XML Interchange (EXI) Impacts, W3C Working Draft (03 Sep 2008) http://www.w3.org/TR/exi-impacts/, Cited 19 Apr 2011.
25. Library and Archives Canada (LAC), Local Digital Format Registry (LDFR), File format guidelines for preservation and long-term access, Version 1.0 (October 2010) http://www.collectionscanada.gc.ca/obj/012018/f2/012018-2200-e.pdf, Cited 19 Apr 2011.
26. Maier, D.: Database desiderata for an XML query language. QL'98 – The Query Language Workshop, W3C, (Boston, Dec. 1998) http://www.w3.org/TandS/QL/QL98/pp/maier.html, Cited 19 Apr 2011.
27. McKemmish, S., Acland, G., Ward, N., Reed, B.: Describing records in context in the continuum: the Australian Recordkeeping Metadata Schema. Archivaria 48 (Fall 1999), 3–43 (1999).
28. New Zealand E-government Interoperability Framework (NZ e-GIF), Version 3.3., Introduction (February2008)StateServiceCommission,http://www.e.govt.nz/standards/e-gif/e-gif-v-3-3/e-gif-v-3-3-complete.pdf, Cited 19 Apr 2011.
29. Pons, A., Millet, J., Gijarro, E., Mainteiga, M.: Medical database migration using new XML Internet standard. Computers in Cardiology 26, 93–96 (1999).
30. Reuben, E.: Migrating records from proprietary software. Computers in Libraries 23, 6, 30–33 (2003).
31. SAGA Version 4.0, Standards und Architectures für E-Government-Anwendungen. Bundesministerium des Innern (March 2008) http://gsb.download.bva.bund.de/KBSt/SAGA/SAGA_v4.0.pdf, Cited 19 Apr 2011.
32. Salminen, A., Lehtovaara, M., Kauppinen, K.: Standardization of digital legislative documents – a case study. Proceedings of the Twenty-Ninth Hawaii International Conference on System Sciences 5, pp. 72–81. Los Alamitos, CA: IEEE Computer Society Press (1996).
33. Salminen, A., Lyytikäinen, V., Tiitinen, P., Mustajärvi, O.: Implementing digital government in the Finnish Parliament. In W. Huang, K. Siau, & K.K. Wei (eds), Electronic Government Strategies and Implementation (pp. 242–259). Hersley, PA: IDEA Group Publishing (2004).
34. Salminen, A., Tompa, F.W.: Grammars++ for modeling information in text. Information Systems 24, 1, 1–24 (1999).

35. Salminen, A., Tompa, F.W.: Requirements for XML document database systems. Proceedings of the First Document Engineering Conference, DocEng'01, pp. 85–94. New York: ACM Press (1999).

36. Schneider, J., Kamiya, T. (eds): Efficient XML Interchange (EXI) Format 1.0, W3C Candidate Recommendation (8 December 2009) http://www.w3.org/TR/exi/, Cited 19 Apr 2011.

37. Shah, R., Kesan, J., Kennis, A.: Implementing open standards: A case study of the Massachusetts open formats policy. Proceedings of the 2008 International Conference on Digital Government Research pp. 262–271. Los Angeles, CA: Digital Government Society of North America (2008).

38. Smithsonian Institution Archives. Archival presentation of Web resources. HTML to XHTML migration test technical considerations, Evaluation, and recommendations (1 July 2002) http://siarchives.si.edu/pdf/dollarrpt2.pdf, Cited 19 Apr 2011.

39. TEI Consortium (eds.): TEI P5: Guidelines for Electronic Text Encoding and Interchange. 1.9.1 (Last updated March 5, 2011) http://www.tei-c.org/P5/. Cited 19 Apr 2011.

40. TEI MI W 06 Migration Case Study Reports. http://www.tei-c.org/Activities/Workgroups/MI/miw06.xml, Cited 19 Apr 2011.

41. Tyrväinen, P., Päivärinta, T., Salminen, A., Iivari, J.: Characterizing the evolving research on enterprise content management. European Journal of Information Systems **15**, 6, 627–634 (2006).

42. UK GovTalk, e-GIF Technical Standards Catalogue (Last updated 02 October 2009) http://interim.cabinetoffice.gov.uk/govtalk/schemasstandards/e-gif/tsc_rtf_and_pdf_versions.aspx, Cited 19 Apr 2011.

43. Vakali, A., Catania, B., Maddalena, A.: XML data stores: emerging practice. IEEE Internet Computing **9**, 2, 62–69 (2005).

44. Vianu, V.: A Web odyssey: from Codd to XML. Proceedings of the 20th ACM Symposium on Principles of Database Systems pp. 1–15. New York: ACM Press (2001).

45. webMethods Tamino XML server. Software AG. http://www.softwareag.com/fr/images/SAG_TaminoXML_FS_Jul09-web_tcm46-5580.pdf, Cited 19 Apr 2011.

46. W3C Issues XML1.0 as a Proposed Recommendation (30 December 1997) http://www.w3.org/Press/XML-PR, Cited 19 Apr 2011.

47. Westermann, U., Klas, W.: An analysis of XML database solutions for the management of MPEG-7 media descriptions. ACM Computing Surveys **35**, 4, 331–373 (2003).

48. White, G., Kangasharju, J., Brutzman, D., Williams, S. (eds): Efficient XML Interchange Measurements Note, W3C Working Draft (25 July 2007), http://www.w3.org/TR/exi-measurements/, Cited 19 Apr 2011.

Appendix A: Introduction to XHTML

HTML (HyperText Markup Language) is the authoring language created for the World Wide Web, to support the distribution of information over the Internet by means of Web pages. Authoring of an HTML document requires only a primitive text editor. To prepare a document for presentation to anyone in the world, it must be stored on a *Web server* which associates the document with an address and responds to page requests from software applications called *Web clients* or *user agents*. The user agent commonly used by humans for browsing the Web and for accessing resources is called a *Web browser*.

An HTML document is a structured document consisting of three components: the HTML version information, the header, and the body. The header contains the title of the page and possibly some metadata. Web browsers usually show the title as the window title. The body includes the content intended to be displayed in the browser window as the Web page. The structure of the Web page is indicated by means of textual elements including headings at several levels, paragraphs, various types of lists, and tables. Multimedia features enable pages' authors to include images, video clips, other HTML pages, and other objects in their pages. For example, a page may include interactivity provided by software applications called applets.

The language includes hyperlinks (or links) so that pages can be connected to each other and to other kinds of digital information resources. A link has a direction and two ends called anchors, a source anchor and a destination anchor. The example below creates two links: one from the document to the description of the p element in the HTML 4 specification, another from the end of the document to the top of the same document. Element a is used both for the source and destination anchors.

A. Salminen and F. Tompa, *Communicating with XML*,
DOI 10.1007/978-1-4614-0992-2, © Springer Science+Business Media, LLC 2011

```
<html><head> <title>Simple html example</title></head>
<body>
<h3><a name="beginning">Example with two links</a></h3>
<p>
A  paragraph on a Web page is delimited by the element
<a href="http://www.w3.org/TR/html401/struct/text.html#h-9.3.1">p</a>.</p>
<p><a href="#beginning">top</a></p>
</body>
</html>
```

XHTML (Extensible HyperText Markup Language) provides the same capabilities as HTML 4, but instead of being an SGML application, XHTML is an XML application. This means that XHTML pages follow the rules of XML and may thus be processed using XML software.

The XHTML 1.0 specification defines three language variants, each corresponding to one of the three variants of HTML 4: Strict, Transitional, and Frameset. Strict is the variant that does not include styling capabilities but is instead based on the idea that the styling information is provided in style sheets. Strict is the variant that is recommended for most uses. Transitional includes style attributes to support legacy pages from browser environments, where style attributes were commonly used. The Frameset variant includes the description of frames.

The example above could be a piece of markup in either an HTML or an XHTML document. However, HTML allows the same information to be provided in ways that are not accepted in XHTML. For example, the end-tags of the p elements could be omitted and both upper case and lower case letters could be used in element and attribute names. In XHTML, like in all XML documents, all element and attribute names must be in lower case, and end-tags are required in all non-empty elements.

An important feature in XHTML is that the specification is modularized so that various XHTML languages can be defined from the standard building blocks for different types of devices. Thus XHTML is not a single language with three variants, but instead a family of current and future languages and modules that reformulate, subset, and extend HTML 4. The document XHTML Modularization defines sets of elements in modules so that arbitrary module combinations can be used, and probably extended, to define XHTML conforming languages for various platforms. This is intended to enable easy exchange of data across platforms.

The core modules must be present in any language considered to be a language in the XHTML family. These modules contain the basic structural and text elements, as well as the anchor element a enabling the creation of links. For example, all elements in the previous example are included in the core modules. In addition, special modules are available for images, frames, forms, and scripting, among other features.

As an example, XHTML 1.1 defines XHTML 1.0 Strict using modules. Alternatively, XHTML Basic is designed especially for small appliances, such as mobile phones, car navigation systems, and digital book readers, to replace the various HTML variants that have been designed for those devices.

Appendix B: History of XML

The history leading to the development of XML is summarized in Table B.1, and some milestones in the development of XML are depicted in Table B.2. The story behind these two tables is provided by the narrative in this appendix, which is divided into four parts: *Origins of the Internet, Origins of SGML, From the Internet to the World Wide Web*, and *From SGML to XML*. A list of historical readings, which have also served as our main information sources, can be found at the end of the appendix.

B.1 Origins of the Internet

Computer networking started in the United States in the 1960s, at the time of the Cold War. The Soviet Union's success in launching Sputnik into space in the previous decade activated technological research and development in U.S. In 1958 the U.S. Department of Defense established a new organization called ARPA (the Advanced Research Projects Agency, which was subsequently called DARPA, the Defense Advanced Research Projects Agency) to support research on computer networking. The ARPANET network was created in 1969, interconnecting four computers at four universities by the end of that year. At first ARPANET was used for file transfer and remote computing. To activate collaborative development of technical specifications, a practice called RFC (Request for Comments) was initiated. This practice was based on open publication of specifications and an open request for comments.

Besides ARPANET, several other computer networks were developed in the 1970s. Their architectures and connection protocols differed from those of the ARPANET. The idea of "Internetworking Architecture," a network of interconnected networks with various architectures, evolved. To implement this idea, a new transmission protocol was needed. TCP/IP (Transmission Control Protocol / Internet Protocol) was developed for this purpose, and it formed the underpinnings of today's Internet. This activated wide interest in further development of network technologies in many countries. Because the researchers needed effective means of communication to support collaboration, electronic mail was created.

B.2   Origins of SGML

Automated text processing of documents was well-established by the 1960s [20], and the problems with embedded formatting instructions were soon identified. In a meeting of the Canadian Government Printing Office in 1967, William Tunnicliffe pointed out the importance of separating information content in documents from their format. The idea of "generic document coding" was an important feature in the language Charles Goldfarb, Ed Mosher, and Ray Lorie designed at IBM. In his article in the ACM SIGPLAN/SIGOA conference in 1981, Charles Goldfarb adopted the term Generalized Markup Language (GML) for the language developed at IBM and the term *descriptive markup* for the document coding style in GML. In the same article Goldfarb emphasized the importance of rigorous markup if the processing of sets of documents of certain types were to be automated.

The work towards standardized rules for descriptive markup started in a committee of the International Organization for Standardization (ISO). The first chair of the committee was William Tunnicliffe, and the concrete development work was done primarily by Charles Goldfarb. The work resulted in the Standard Generalized Markup Language (SGML), accepted as ISO standard 8879 in 1986.

B.3   From the Internet to the World Wide Web

Even though the U.S. Department of Defense was the principal force behind the Internet, the technical specification documents were public and development work was open for university researchers worldwide. Therefore networking soon expanded to other countries. The World Wide Web (WWW) was introduced in 1991, and that same year the Internet Society was organized to coordinate the development of the Internet. WWW was a hypermedia application designed by Tim Berners-Lee and Robert Cailliau for CERN (the European Organization for Nuclear Research) to support collaboration among the physicists working around the world.

The information published in the World Wide Web was accessible throughout the Internet via documents linked to each other by hyperlinks. The system was based on a client–server architecture and incorporated three major technological innovations: HTML (HyperText Markup Language) as the presentation language for documents and hyperlinks, HTTP (Hypertext Transfer Protocol) as the rules for exchanging documents between computers, and URI (Uniform Resource Identifier) as the notation for identifying objects uniquely throughout the Internet.

In 1992, more than one million computers were connected to the Internet. WWW proved to be extremely convenient, and its adoption expanded rapidly. New kinds of businesses evolved, based on the connectivity of people and the connectivity of software applications all over the world.

B.4   From SGML to XML

The World Wide Web advanced globalization rapidly, connecting a rich variety of people and software applications. Communication among applications, however, was often hindered by differences in the representation of data. This was a great barrier for effective use of the Internet, particularly for business purposes. It became urgent to find some common rules for representing information and information structures within the Internet and for exchanging information between applications over the Internet.

SGML essentially offered such rules, but the flexibility of SGML and its inherent ambiguity were too complicated for the needs of the Internet. One of the problems of SGML was the difficulty of building robust software supporting SGML in general, so that it interpreted not only a particular SGML application such as HTML. The development of a restricted form of SGML for the purposes of the Internet communication started in the mid 1990s. A major goal was to simplify the language so that the design and implementation of software for it would not be too tedious.

In July 1996 Jon Bosak from Sun Microsystems called for a W3C working group to derive from SGML a simpler format. The design principles were drafted by August and the first draft for the XML specification was published before the end of the year. Tim Bray and Michael Sperberg-McQueen served as co-editors of the specification and introduced XML at the SGML '96 Conference in Boston.

The specification development did not advance without problems, however. The working group was large, with members from several (often competing) companies and other organizations, including representatives from Adobe, ArborText, DataChannel, Fuji Xerox, Grif, HP, INSO, ISOGEN, Microsoft, Muzmo, NCSA, Netscape, SoftQuad, Sun, Textuality, the University of Illinois, Vignette, and W3C. At that time W3C did not provide much support for the work. Finally a perceived conflict of interest evolved when Tim Bray, originally representing a small Canadian firm Textuality, joined Netscape. In response, Microsoft requested Bray's resignation as co-editor. In August, however, Netscape and Microsoft found a compromise through the nomination of Jean Paoli as a third co-editor, who could represent Microsoft's interests. Thus the first W3C Recommendation for XML 1.0 was published in February 1998, co-edited by Tim Bray, Jean Paoli, and Michael Sperberg-McQueen.

Important XML-related development work started in parallel with the creation of the specification. Rapid progress in software development was enabled by the creation of W3C's Document Object Model (DOM), which provided a standard for application programming interfaces for XML. Two other important early standards were XPath and Namespaces for XML, both of which were incorporated into many of the later standards.

Table B.1　Milestones before XML

1960s: Origins of networking and descriptive markup

1962	MIT's J.C.R. Licklider presents a vision of globally interconnected computers
1965	A non-local connection of two computers (Massachusetts ↔ California)
1967	William Tunnicliffe introduces the idea of "generic coding" of documents in a meeting of the Canadian Government Printing Office
1969	First nodes of ARPANET get connected; RFC (Request for Comments) series of notes established for developing and publishing technical specifications
1969	Generic document coding implemented at IBM by Charles Goldfarb, Ed Mosher, and Ray Lorie

1970s: Beginning of the Internet

1972	Idea about "Internetworking architecture" presented at DARPA
1973	TCP/IP (Transmission Control Protocol/Internet Protocol) implemented; internationalization started: Great Britain and Norway join ARPANET

1980s: From ideas to practice

1981	Generalized Markup Language (GML) introduced
1983	ARPANET adopts TCP/IP
1985	U.S. National Science Foundation's NSFNET established to serve all higher education
1986	SGML accepted as ISO standard 8879
1989	Several countries joined NSFNET: AU, CA, DE, DK, FI, FR, IL, IS, IT, JP, MX, NL, NO, NZ, PR, SE, UK

1990s: Globalization

1990	ARPANET closed
1991	WWW and HTML introduced; Internet Society organized, Unicode 1.0.0 published
1992	The number of computers connected to the Internet exceeds one million
1993	The universal character set published as ISO 10646–1:1993
1994	W3C organized
1998	URI syntax published as RFC 2396

Table B.2 Early milestones during the development of XML

1996	Jon Bosak (Sun Microsystems) organizes a W3C working group in July to derive from SGML a simple format to be used as the metalanguage of the Web.
	The name Extensible Markup Language invented by James Clark.
	The design principles for XML drafted in August, the same design principles have remained in the subsequent specifications.
	The first draft for the XML specification published in November, co-edited by Tim Bray (Textuality) and Michael Sperberg-McQueen (University of Illinois at Chicago).
	Tim Bray and Michael Sperberg-McQueen introduce XML at the SGML '96 Conference in Boston.
1997	The first XML Conference held in San Diego in March.
	Two versions of the W3C Working Draft for XML published, with Tim Bray and Michael Sperberg-McQueen as co-editors.
	Some conflicts between Netscape and Microsoft, especially after Tim Bray joined Netscape. Tim Bray temporarily dismissed from the co-editorship of the XML language, but in August Netscape and Microsoft find a compromise and Bray returns.
	Jean Paoli added to the co-editors to represent Microsoft for developing the W3C Working Draft for XML published in August.
	W3C Proposed Recommendation for XML in December.
1998	The first W3C Note for the namespace mechanism published in January, co-edited by Tim Bray (Textuality and Netscape), Dave Hollander (Hewlett-Packard), and Andrew Lyman (Microsoft).
	The first W3C Recommendation for XML 1.0 released in February.
	W3C Recommendation for Document Object Model (DOM) Level 1, with editors and principal contributors from ArborText, IBM, iMall, Inso EPS, Microsoft, Netscape, Novell, SoftQuad, Sun, Texcel Research, and W3C
1999	W3C Recommendation for Namespaces in XML.
	W3C Recommendation for XML Path Language (XPath).

Historical Readings

1. Berners-Lee, T., Fielding, R., Irvine, U.C., Masinter, R.: Uniform Resource Identifiers (URI): Generic syntax. Network Working Group, Request for Comments: 2396 (August 1998) http://www.ietf.org/rfc/rfc2396.txt, Cited 19 Apr 2011.
2. Berners-Lee, T.: The World Wide Web: A very short personal history (May 1998) http://www.w3.org/People/Berners-Lee/ShortHistory.html, Cited 19 Apr 2011.
3. Bosak, J.: XML, Java, and the future of the Web (March 1997) http://www.ibiblio.org/pub/sun-info/standards/xml/why/xmlapps.htm, Cited 19 Apr 2011.
4. Bosak, J., Bray, T.: XML and the second-generation Web. Scientific American (May 1999) http://www.fhi.rcsed.ac.uk/rbeaumont/virtualclassroom/hig1/scientific_american_xml_web_may_1999.pdf, Cited 19 Apr 2011.
5. Bray, T.: Annotated XML specification (1998) http://www.xml.com/axml/testaxml.htm, Cited 19 Apr 2011.
6. Bray, T.: Opinion piece (July 1997) http://www.textuality.com/xml/Opinion.html, Cited 19 Apr 2011.
7. Bray, T., Sperberg-McQueen, C.M. (eds): Extensible Markup Language (XML), W3C Working Draft (14 Nov 1996) http://www.w3.org/TR/WD-xml-961114.html, Cited 19 Apr 2011.
8. Connolly, D.: XML development history (January 2003) http://www.w3.org/XML/hist2002, Cited 19 Apr 2011.
9. Design principles for XML, Draft DD-1996-0001 (August 1996) http://www.textuality.com/sgml-erb/dd-1996-0001.html, Cited 19 Apr 2011.
10. Furuta, R.: Important papers in the history of document preparation systems: basic sources. Electronic Publishing – Origination, Dissemination, and Design **5**, 1, 19–44 (1992).
11. Goldfarb, C.F.: The roots of SGML – A personal recollection (1996) http://www.sgmlsource.com/history/roots.htm, Cited 19 Apr 2011.
12. Goldfarb, C.F.: SGML: The reason why and the first published hint. Journal of the American Society for Information Science **48**, 7, 656–661 (1997). The article is a commentary of the article by Goldfarb, C.F., Mosher, E.J., Peterson, T.I.: An online system for integrated text processing. Proceedings of the 33rd Annual Meeting of the American Society for Information Science **7**, pp. 147–150. (1970).
13. Goldfarb, C.F.: A generalized approach to document markup. Proceedings of the ACM SIGPLAN SIGOA Symposium on Text Manipulation, ACM SIGOA Newsletter **2**, 1–2, 68–73 (1981).
14. Gonnet, G. H., Tompa, F. W.: Mind your grammar: a new approach to modeling text. Proceedings of the 13th International Conference on Very Large Data Bases, pp. 339–346. San Francisco, CA: Morgan Kaufmann Publishers (1987).
15. Gray, J.: A conversation with Tim Bray. ACM Queue **3**(1), 16–25 (2005).
16. Kennedy, D.: XML Conference 1997 (March 1997) http://xml.coverpages.org/kennedyXML97a.html, Cited 19 Apr 2011.
17. Leiner, B. M., Cerf, V. G., Clark, D. D., Kahn, R. E., Kleinrock, L., Lynch, D. C., Postel, J., Roberts, L. G., Wolff, S.: A brief history of the Internet. ACM SIGCOMM Computer Communication Review **39**, 5, 22–31 (2009).
18. Sperberg-McQueen, C.M.: Back to the frontiers and edges. Closing remarks at SGML '92: the quiet revolution (October 1992) http://cmsmcq.com/1992/edw31.html, Cited 19 Apr 2011.
19. Sperberg-McQueen, C.M.: Reports from the W3C SGML ERB to the SGML WG and from the W3C XML ERB to the XML SIG (December 1997) http://www.w3.org/XML/9712-reports.html, Cited 19 Apr 2011.
20. van Dam, A., Rice, D.E.: Computers and Publishing: Writing, Editing, and Printing. In F.L. Alt, M. Rubinoff (eds), Advances in Computers **10**, 145–174 (1970).

Appendix C: Extended Backus-Naur Form (EBNF)

Syntactic metalanguages are used to define which linear sequences of symbols are valid sentences in a language, what is the syntactic structure of those sentences, and how those syntactic structures are named. The most common syntactic metalanguage adopted in the computing world is Extended Backus-Naur Form (EBNF). There are many slightly different variants of EBNF, but all of them are based on Backus-Naur Form (BNF), developed in the 1960s by John Backus and Peter Naur for describing the syntax of the Fortran and Algol 60 programming languages. An extension of BNF was introduced by Niklaus Wirth in 1977, containing explicit iteration constructs that were missing from BNF and thus causing the need for extensive use of recursion for expressing repetition [2]. The International Organization for Standardization published an EBNF standard [1] based on Wirth's extension, but there still is some diversity among the notations called EBNF.

EBNF is used in XML for two purposes: to describe the accepted constructs in XML specifications and to define the valid structure of child elements in the content models in DTDs. The notation used in content models, as described in Section 2.4.2, constrains the element structure through use of the metasymbols '+', '*', '|', '?', ',', '(', and ')'. The first two symbols, * and +, represent iteration; | represents the alternation of two content particles; ? represents optionality; a comma represents concatenation of two successive content particles; and parentheses indicate grouping.

The notation used in the XML specifications to describe the formal grammar of XML is illustrated in Chapter 2 of this book and introduced in Section 6 of W3C's XML specification. The grammar consists of a set of rules, each defining one named part of the language. Each rule is of the form

```
symbol ::= expression
```

The symbol on the left side is the name of the part, and the expression on the right side describes the structure of the part, using the following notations:

- Literal character strings from the Unicode character set are quoted either as "string" or 'string', for example, "ELEMENT" or ' < !['.

- Names of other parts are written underlined to indicate that in the electronic version of the specification the name is also a hyperlink leading to the productions defining the part, for example, the symbol <u>Attribute</u> on the right side of a rule leads to the rule defining the syntax of the part called Attribute.
- Subexpressions of the form #xN, where N is a hexadecimal integer, refer to Unicode characters with the code value equal to N.
- *Metasymbols* [, [^,], (,), -, ?, |, *, and + are used to indicate the following constraints:

  - Square brackets [and] to specify a range or a set of characters or [^ and] to exclude a range or a set of characters,
  - Round brackets (and) for grouping,
  - Symbols ?, * , and + as postfix unary operators to indicate optionality (?) and iteration (* for zero or more occurrences, + for one or more occurrences),
  - The symbol | as a binary infix operator to denote alternatives,
  - The symbol – to indicate a range of characters when used inside square brackets [and], and as a binary operator to refer to intersection when used outside square brackets.

  Other notations used in the productions are

/* ... */	for comments,
[wfc: ...]	for well-formedness constraints; names a constraint on well-formed documents associated with a production, and
[vc: ...]	for validity constraint; names a constraint on valid documents associated with a production.

No explicit metasymbol is used to indicate concatenation in the XML grammar of the specifications.

1. ISO/IEC 14977:1996. Information technology – Syntactic metalanguage - Extended BNF.
2. Wirth, N.: What can we do about the unnecessary diversity of the notations for syntactic definition? Communications of the ACM **20**, 11, 822–823 (1977).

Index

A

Access control, 14, 181, 182, 188, 190, 192
American National Standards Institute (ANSI), 170, 171
Anonymous type, 53, 56
ANSI. *See* American National Standards Institute (ANSI)
API. *See* Application programming interface (API)
Application programming interface (API), 62, 63, 84
Archives, 73, 120, 141, 164, 188, 195, 198
ARPANET, 2, 210–212
ASCII, 4, 32, 199
Atom, 17–19, 122
Attribute
  list, 63
  list declaration, 39, 43–46, 48, 52, 58
  name, 30, 32, 33, 38, 39, 43, 46, 53–55, 74, 75, 106, 172, 208
  specification, 30, 31, 43
  type, 37, 44, 45, 48, 49, 53, 61, 76, 190
  value, 30, 37, 39, 44–46, 49, 50, 52, 53, 55, 58, 63, 114, 116, 151, 153, 161
Authoring, 36, 84, 85, 93, 95, 102, 125, 129, 132, 163, 165, 185, 192, 193, 196, 200, 203

B

Backus, John, 216
Base type, 57, 59, 118–120
Berners-Lee, Tim, 2, 3, 213
Bosak, Jon, 211, 213
Bray, Tim, 196, 214

Browser, 6, 7, 12, 16, 26, 78, 81, 84, 86, 87, 100, 101, 104, 127, 129, 132, 136–138, 150, 164, 202, 207, 208
Business application, 88–90, 164, 172
Business process, 82, 87–90, 95, 157, 169, 170, 172–179

C

Cailliau, Robert, 213
Candidate Recommendation, 71, 72, 197
Canonical XML, 73, 76, 77, 96
Cascading Style Sheets (CSS), 13, 31, 73, 74, 76, 77, 84, 96, 102–104, 124, 126, 129, 130, 142
CC/PP. *See* Composite capabilities/preference profiles (CC/PP)
CDATA, 29, 39, 43, 44, 50
Character
  data, 4, 26, 27, 29, 40–42, 45, 55, 59, 115, 123, 125, 150, 187
  encoding, 27, 37–38
  entity reference, 7
  reference, 37, 47, 49
Chemical Industry Data Exchange (CIDX), 177, 178
Child element, 28–30, 32, 40–42, 53, 55, 65, 66, 98, 125, 131, 156, 161, 216
CIDX. *See* Chemical Industry Data Exchange (CIDX)
Clark, James, 61, 211
Comment, 24, 31, 37, 65, 79, 99, 153, 190, 210, 212, 217
Complex type, 53, 56, 57, 59, 61, 114, 115, 119
Compliance, 10, 96, 157, 180, 182

Composite capabilities/preference profiles
        (CC/PP), 73, 82, 83
Content management, 13, 192
    system, 191–193
Cover Pages, 159–161, 197
Cover, Robin, 77, 159
CSS. *See* Cascading Style Sheets (CSS)

D

Data
    interchange, 14–16, 88, 135, 169–183
    model, 13, 65, 77, 89, 114, 149, 158, 159,
        162, 186, 187, 193, 194
    open data, 87, 165
    type, 13, 39, 43, 44, 52, 61, 89,
        114–123, 180
Database
    schema, 10, 14, 95
    system, 3, 13, 26, 95, 107, 121,
        169, 186, 188–194, 196
Data-centric, 113–145, 186, 191
DC. *See* Dublin Core (DC)
Declaration
    attribute, 59
    attribute list, 43–46
    document type, 24, 38–40
    element, 55–58
    element type, 39–43, 52, 53, 55, 58
    entity, 34, 46–48, 50–52
    global, 57, 58
    local, 57
    markup, 31, 38–40, 53
    namespace, 32, 33, 153
    notation, 39, 46–48, 52, 53
Deep Web, 11, 86
Descriptive markup, 8–10, 96, 210, 212
Dictionary encoding, 110
Digitize, 144, 169
DocBook, 79
Document
    centric, 186, 188, 189, 191
    element, 29, 64, 95, 124
    management, 12, 13, 84, 93–110,
        157, 189, 191, 194, 199, 200
    repository, 96, 105, 188
    transformation, 97
    type, 25, 38, 45, 74, 79, 172, 173,
        175–177, 189
    type declaration, 24, 38–40
Document Object Model (DOM), 13, 65,
        73, 76, 84, 85, 126, 129,
        130, 211, 214

Document type definition (DTD), 10, 12, 13,
        21, 24–26, 33–63, 74, 76, 84, 89,
        95, 101, 114, 116, 131, 134, 151,
        158, 163, 176, 177, 189, 190, 193,
        194, 199, 215
DOM. *See* Document Object Model (DOM)
DTD. *See* Document type definition (DTD)
Dublin Core (DC), 153, 154, 156–158

E

EAD. *See* Encoded Archival Description
        (EAD)
EBNF. *See* Extended Backus-Naur Form
        (EBNF)
E-book. *See* Electronic book (e-book)
ebXML. *See* Electronic Business using XML
        (ebXML)
ECMA, 76, 85, 86, 126, 202
E-commerce. *See* Electronic commerce
        (e-commerce)
EDI. *See* Electronic Data Interchange (EDI)
Editor, 84, 129, 131, 137, 138, 140, 159, 185,
        190, 191, 193, 199, 203, 207, 211
E-government. *See* Electronic government
        (e-government)
Electronic book (e-book), 142–143
Electronic Business using XML (ebXML)
    ebCCTS, 89, 175
    ebCPP, 88
    ebMS, 89, 175, 177
    ebRIM, 89
    ebRS, 89
Electronic commerce (e-commerce), 1, 71, 72,
        81, 88, 170, 173, 179
Electronic Data Interchange (EDI), 15, 88,
        170–173, 176
Electronic government (e-government), 1, 16,
        72, 87, 154, 182
Element
    child element, 28–30, 32, 40–42, 53, 55,
        65, 66, 98, 125, 131, 156, 161, 216
    content, 30, 35, 36, 42, 45, 50, 52, 58, 61,
        125, 161
    content model, 42
    declaration, 55–58
    empty element, 7, 124, 150, 151
        tag, 24, 27, 43
    hierarchy, 9
    name, 7, 8, 10, 17, 27, 30, 32, 39, 40, 54–56,
        58, 65, 102, 108, 150, 156, 161
    root element, 29, 40, 45
    sibling element, 28, 64, 109

tag, 7, 24, 27, 43, 150
type, 24, 27, 32, 37–45, 52, 53, 55, 58, 65,
    109, 125, 131, 151
type declaration, 39–43, 52, 53, 55, 58
EMMA. *See* Extensible Multimodal
    Annotation markup language
    (EMMA)
Encoded Archival Description
    (EAD), 158
End-tag, 5, 7, 9, 24, 27, 29, 30, 35, 40, 208
Entity
    declaration, 34, 46–48, 50–52
    external entity, 38, 47, 50
    general entity, 34–36, 46, 47, 49, 50
    internal entity, 35, 46, 49
    literal entity value, 46, 49, 50
    parameter entity, 34–37, 46, 47, 49, 50
    parsed entity, 34, 35, 37, 47, 48, 50
    reference, 7, 13, 24, 25, 35, 36, 46, 49,
        50, 190
    unparsed entity, 34, 36, 44, 48, 49, 63
    value, 46, 49, 50
Enumerated type, 44–46, 60
EPUB, 142, 143
Exchange, 3, 15, 16, 21, 70, 81, 82, 87–89,
    141, 152, 155, 157–159, 169–171,
    173–177, 179–182, 196, 197, 208
Extended Backus-Naur Form (EBNF), 23, 40,
    61, 216–217
Extensible Access Control Markup Language
    (XACML), 141, 182
Extensible HyperText Markup Language
    (XHTML)
    basic, 79
    modularization, 79, 208
    print, 79
Extensible Multimodal Annotation markup
    language (EMMA), 73, 83, 84,
    114, 134
External entity, 38, 47, 50
External subset, 38, 48
Extranet, 15, 191

F
Facet, 57, 94, 117–120, 122, 139
Feed
    aggregator, 16
    reader, 16, 17
Financial Information eXchange
    (FIX), 177
FIX. *See* Financial Information eXchange
    (FIX)

Formal grammar, 22, 23, 216
Formal language, 3, 22–24
Framework, 3, 80, 87, 88, 151, 152, 154,
    155, 158–162, 174, 175, 177,
    180, 199

G
General entity, 34–36, 46, 47, 49, 50
Geography Markup Language (GML), 135,
    141, 210, 212
Gleaning Resource Description from Dialects
    of Languages (GRDDL), 73, 80,
    81, 163
Glyph, 125, 144
GML. *See* Geography Markup Language (GML)
Goldfarb, Charles, 210, 212
Government application. *See* Electronic
    government (e-government)
Grammar
    formal, 22–24, 216
    tree-regular, 61
Granularity, 188
Graph, 3, 158–163, 187
Graphics, 2, 48, 78, 80, 114, 123–135, 137
GRDDL. *See* Gleaning Resource Description
    from Dialects of Languages (GRDDL)

H
HL7, 14
Hollander, Dave
HTML. *See* HyperText Markup Language
    (HTML)
HTTP. *See* HyperText Transport Protocol (HTTP)
Hyperlink, 75
Hypertext, 2, 3, 187, 207, 208, 213
HyperText Markup Language (HTML), 2 ff, 21,
    22, 26, 31, 32, 75, 76, 78, 79, 85, 86,
    100–104, 106, 126–128, 132, 136,
    142, 149, 150, 153, 154, 190, 195,
    198, 201, 202, 207, 208, 210–212
HyperText Transport Protocol (HTTP), 3, 176,
    178, 180, 181, 213

I
IANA. *See* Internet Assigned Numbers
    Authority (IANA)
ID, 44, 45, 61, 76, 120
IDREF, 44, 45, 61, 66, 116, 120, 190
IEC. *See* International Electrotechnical
    Commission (IEC)

IEEE, 121, 134, 155
IETF. *See* Internet Engineering Task Force
    (IETF)
IFX. *See* Interactive Financial eXchange (IFX)
Index
    element, 105, 106, 108, 109
    indexing, 105–108, 188, 193
    term, 105, 106, 108, 109
Information
    asset, 11, 14
    retrieval, 105, 193
    reuse, 12
Infoset, 52, 64, 65, 196
Interactive Financial eXchange (IFX), 177
Interchange, 182–183, 196, 197
Internal entity, 34–36, 46, 49
Internal subset, 38
International Electrotechnical Commission
    (IEC), 61, 85, 86, 217
Internationalization, 76
Internationalization Tag Set (ITS), 73, 75, 76
Internationalized Resource Identifier (IRI),
    32, 33
International Organization for Standardization
    (ISO), 21, 61, 70, 71, 85, 86, 88,
    89, 122–124, 129, 142, 144, 153,
    157, 166, 174, 175, 201, 202,
    210–213, 217
Internet Assigned Numbers Authority
    (IANA), 71
Internet Engineering Task Force (IETF), 17,
    46, 71
Internet, the, 2, 3, 15, 70, 78, 81, 173, 210,
    212, 213
Interoperability, 72, 87–88
Intranet, 15, 191
IRI. *See* Internationalized Resource Identifier
    (IRI)
ISO. *See* International Organization for
    Standardization (ISO)
ITS. *See* Internationalization Tag Set (ITS)

K
KML (formerly Keyhole Markup Language),
    135, 139–141

L
Layout, 94–95
Learning Object Metadata (LOM), 151,
    154–157
Lexical space, 114, 115, 117, 118
Link. *See* Hyperlink

Literal entity value, 46, 49, 50
Localization, 75, 76
Logical structure, 26, 27, 31, 33, 38, 39, 52,
    76, 171, 187
LOM. *See* Learning Object Metadata
    (LOM)
Lorie, Ray, 210, 212
Lyman, Andrew, 211

M
Marked up text, 123
Markup
    content markup, 136
    descriptive markup, 8–10, 96, 210, 212
    markup declaration, 31, 38, 39, 53
    markup language, 2, 6, 8, 10, 21, 22, 38,
        78, 79, 83, 86, 169
    presentational markup, 8
    procedural markup, 8
Mathematical Markup Language (MathML),
    14, 32, 73, 74, 78, 83, 84, 114,
    135–138
MathML. *See* Mathematical Markup Language
    (MathML)
Metadata
    external metadata, 153
    metadata embedded metadata, 161
    XML as metadata, 12
    XML for metadata, 11, 74
Metalanguage, 2, 38, 216
Metasymbol, 41, 217
Migration
    for digital preservation, 194–195
    from HTML, 195
    from SGML, 195
Mixed content, 40–42
Mosher, Ed, 210, 212
Multimedia, 14, 113–145, 207
MusicXML, 14

N
Namespace
    namespace declaration, 32, 33, 153
    namespace label, 32, 33, 153
    target namespace, 54–56, 59
    XML Names, 32, 33, 54, 73–75
Native XML database system, 193–194
Natural language, 22, 188
Naur, Peter, 216
Nesting, 28, 52, 61, 64
    proper, 29
News feed. *See* Feed

Nillable, 61
Non-hierarchical information, 145
Notation declaration, 39, 48, 52, 53
Numeric data, 121–122

O
OASIS. *See* Organization for the Advancement of Structured Information Standards (OASIS)
ODF. *See* OpenDocument Format for Office Appications (ODF)
OED. *See* Oxford English Dictionary (OED)
Office Open XML File Format (OOXML), 86, 201, 202
OFX. *See* Open Financial Exchange Protocol (OFX)
OMA. *See* Open Mobile Alliance (OMA)
OMDoc, 139
Ontology, 163, 178
OOXML. *See* Office Open XML File Format (OOXML)
Open data, 85–86
OpenDocument Format for Office Appications (ODF), 85, 201, 202
Open Financial Exchange Protocol (OFX), 177
OpenMath, 137–139
Open Mobile Alliance (OMA), 131, 132
Open source, 84, 86, 137, 191, 195
Open standard, 84, 201
Open XML. *See* Office Open XML File Format (OOXML)
Organization for the Advancement of Structured Information Standards (OASIS), 61, 85, 86, 88–90, 141, 159, 160, 172–175, 178, 179, 183, 195, 197, 201
OWL. *See* Web Ontology Language (OWL)
Oxford English Dictionary (OED), 109

P
Paoli, Jean, 211, 214
Parameter entity, 34–37, 46, 47, 49, 50
Parent element, 28, 97, 161
Parsed entity, 34, 35, 37, 47, 48, 50
Parser, 25, 26, 63, 66, 84, 128, 193
Parsing, 41, 66, 76, 96
Partner Interface Process (PIP), 90, 175–177
#PCDATA, 40, 41, 44, 53, 61
Persistent storage, 186–195
Physical structure, 27, 33–37, 39, 48, 52, 187

PIP. *See* Partner Interface Process (PIP)
Platform for Privacy Preferences (P3P), 73, 82, 83, 197
POWDER. *See* Protocol for Web Description Resources (POWDER)
P3P. *See* Platform for Privacy Preferences (P3P)
Precision, 12, 107, 108, 115, 121–123
Presentational markup, 8
Preservation, 158, 194–195
Pretty printing, 7, 28
Procedural markup, 8
Processing
    processing instruction, 31, 63, 65, 75, 99, 190
    processing model, 22, 62–66, 74
    stream processing, 22, 63–64, 66
    tree processing, 22, 64–66
Production rule, 23, 24, 40
Protocol for Web Description Resources (POWDER), 73, 80
Public domain, 16, 73, 84, 87, 120, 151, 171, 198, 202
Public sector, 10, 71, 72, 85, 88, 154, 157, 182, 186, 198

Q
Qualified name, 33, 116
Querying, 13, 76, 81, 93, 94, 96, 104, 108–109, 152, 164, 165
Query language, 13, 71, 77, 80, 81, 110, 193

R
RDF. *See* Resource Description Framework (RDF)
Really Simple Syndication (RSS), 17, 185
Recall, 49, 107
Recommendation, 22, 36, 71–77, 79, 80, 82, 83, 124, 136, 154, 158, 196, 197, 211, 214
    Candidate, 71, 72, 197
    Proposed, 71, 211
    Working Draft, 36, 71, 72, 196, 211
Records management, 73, 120, 156–158, 188, 194, 201
Relational database, 13, 61, 96, 149, 187, 190
RELAX NG, 18, 61–62, 76, 86
Rendering, 31, 41, 75–77, 94, 97, 100–106, 110, 113, 124, 126, 127, 129, 130, 132, 136, 142
Replacement text, 49–51

Resource Description Framework (RDF),
        74, 84, 151, 153, 155, 158–163,
        165, 190
    RDF schema, 73, 80, 81, 154, 158, 159, 163
    RDF Site Summary, 17, 185
        (*see also* Really Simple Syndication
        (RSS))
Resource discovery, 152–154, 158, 164
Resource management, 154–158, 181, 190
Retrieval
    effectiveness, 107–108
    engine, 105
    ranking, 107–108
Root, 29, 33, 34, 38, 40, 45, 48, 65, 119, 124
RosettaNet, 90, 174–177
RSS. *See* Really Simple Syndication (RSS)
RTF, 201, 202
Ruby annotation, 73, 83
Rule, production, 23, 24, 40

S
SAML. *See* Security Assertion Markup
        Language (SAML)
SAX. *See* Simple API for XML (SAX)
SBML. *See* Systems Biology Markup
        Language (SBML)
Scalable Vector Graphics (SVG), 73, 78,
        83, 84, 104, 114, 123–131,
        137–139, 142
    Basic, 127, 130
    generator, 127, 128
    interpreter, 127
    Tiny, 127, 130
    viewer, 127
Schema
    component, 53, 55
    language, 13, 18, 45, 52, 74, 76, 81, 86, 89,
        95, 114, 158, 174, 175
Scientific data, 135–141
Search engine, 101, 106, 108, 161, 164
Searching, 125, 192, 194
Sectoral, 70–73, 154, 172, 174, 182, 197
Security, 22, 77, 96, 129, 170, 175, 178–183,
        186, 194, 196, 198, 201
Security Assertion Markup Language
        (SAML), 180, 181, 183, 201
Semantic Web, 15, 73, 74, 78–82, 158,
        162–166, 178, 185
Semi-structured data, 194
Server, 13, 82, 180, 186, 191, 213
Service Modeling Language (SML), 73, 82, 83
SGML. *See* Standard Generalized Markup
        Language (SGML)

Sibling element, 28, 64, 109
Simple API for XML (SAX), 63, 84, 85
Simple Object Access Protocol (SOAP), 16,
        73, 82, 83, 89, 152, 178–181, 183
Simple type, 53, 55, 59, 114, 115, 117,
        119, 120
SKSML. *See* Symmetric Key Services Markup
        Language (SKSML)
SMIL. *See* Synchronized Multimedia
        Integration Language (SMIL)
SML. *See* Service Modeling Language (SML)
SOAP. *See* Simple Object Access Protocol
        (SOAP)
Society for Worldwide Interbank Financial
        Telecommunications (SWIFT), 177
SPARQL, 73, 80, 81, 163
Speech
    recognition, 132, 133
    synthesizer, 102, 132
Speech Synthesis Markup Language (SSML),
        73, 83, 114, 133
Sperberg-McQueen, Michael, 211, 213, 214
SSML. *See* Speech Synthesis Markup
        Language (SSML)
Standard Generalized Markup Language
        (SGML), 2, 8–12, 21, 22, 38, 54,
        78, 84, 88, 113, 144, 158, 169,
        177, 189, 194–196, 198–200,
        202, 208, 212
Standardization
    local, 70, 72
    sectoral, 71–73, 182, 197
    universal, 70, 71
Standards, 15, 17, 18, 69 ff, 94–96, 120–122,
        129, 131, 134, 139, 141, 151 ff,
        164, 169 ff, 189, 197–203, 211
Start-tag, 7, 24, 27–33, 35, 39, 40, 43–45, 49,
        54, 63, 116
Storing, 13, 93, 109–111, 129, 150, 185–187,
        193, 194
Stream processing, 22, 63–64, 66
String type, 44, 45, 56, 57, 115,
        116, 118, 120
Structured document, 9, 12, 76, 78, 93–96,
        102, 106, 109, 154, 187, 189, 190,
        192, 199, 200
Style sheet, 31, 50, 73–77, 84, 85, 95–97,
        101–104, 124, 126, 130, 185, 187,
        190, 200, 208
Surrogate, 155
SVG. *See* Scalable vector graphics (SVG)
SWIFT. *See* Society for Worldwide Interbank
        Financial Telecommunications
        (SWIFT)

Symmetric Key Services Markup Language
        (SKSML), 180
Synchronized Multimedia Integration
        Language (SMIL), 14, 73, 83, 114,
        123, 126, 131, 132
    SMIL animation, 73, 83, 126, 131
System identifier, 39, 47, 48
Systems Biology Markup Language (SBML),
        10, 14, 135

T
Tag
    empty-element tag, 24, 27, 43
    end-tag, 5, 7, 9, 24, 27, 29, 30, 35, 40, 208
    start-tag, 7, 24, 27–33, 35, 39, 40, 43–45,
        49, 54, 63, 116
Target namespace, 54–56, 59
TEI. *See* Text Encoding Initiative (TEI)
Text Encoding Initiative (TEI), 10, 54, 79, 109,
        110, 123, 144, 145, 150, 151, 195
Timed Text Markup Language(TTML), 73, 83,
        84, 132
Transduction, 13, 77, 104
Transformation, 13, 75–77, 87, 94, 96–100,
        104, 110, 113, 172, 195, 199, 200
Tree
    processing, 22, 64–66
    regular grammar, 61
TTML. *see* Timed Text Markup
        Language(TTML)
Tunnicliffe, William, 212, 214
Type
    anonymous type, 53, 56
    atomic type, 61
    base type, 57, 59, 119, 120
    built-in type, 54–56, 61, 115–121, 139
    complex type, 53, 56, 57, 59, 61, 114,
        115, 119
    derived type, 114–117
    enumerated type, 44–46, 60
    extension of type, 13, 15, 28, 57, 59,
        119, 156
    list type, 116, 117
    member type, 116, 117
    primitive type, 114–116, 118
    retriction of type
    simple type, 53, 55, 59, 114, 115, 117,
        119, 120
    tokenized type, 44
    type hierarchy, 119–120
    type system, 114, 165
    union type, 117
    user derived type, 116, 117

U
UDDI. *See* Universal Description, Discovery
        and Integration (UDDI)
UML. *See* Unified Modeling Language (UML)
Unicode, 4, 23, 37, 38, 71, 83, 125, 192, 196,
        211, 216, 217
    Consortium, 71
Unified Modeling Language (UML), 89, 176
Uniform Resource Identifier (URI), 32, 47, 48,
        74–76, 80, 153, 154, 159–161, 190,
        211, 213
Uniform Resource Locator (URL), 32, 33
Uniform Resource Name (URN), 32
Universal Description, Discovery and
        Integration (UDDI), 16, 82, 152,
        179, 183
Unparsed entity, 34, 36, 44, 48, 49, 63
Update, 18, 85, 95, 172, 173, 188, 190
URI. *See* Uniform Resource Identifier (URI)
URL. *See* Uniform Resource Locator (URL)
URN. *See* Uniform Resource Name (URN)

V
Valid, validity constraint, 24, 40, 217
Value space, 114–116, 118, 119
Variant, 172, 189, 208
Versioning, 38, 84, 96, 200
Voice Extensible Markup Language
        (VoiceXML), 73, 83, 114, 133
VoiceXML. *See* Voice Extensible Markup
        Language (VoiceXML)

W
W3C Recommendation.
        See Recommendation
WebCGM XCF, 80
Web Computer Graphics Metafile
        (WebCGM), 80
Web Ontology Language (OWL), 73, 80,
        81, 163, 178
Web Services Description Language (WSDL),
        16, 73, 82, 83, 178, 183, 185
Web, the
    Deep Web, 86
    OWL (*see* Web Ontology Language
        (OWL))
    Web browser, 12, 16, 100, 150, 202, 207
    Web communications, 2–3, 22
    Web community, 1, 3, 10, 11, 86, 145, 154,
        155, 162–165, 172, 186, 193
    Web Computer Graphics Metafile (*see*
        WebCGM)

Web enabling, 54, 124, 134, 165, 186, 192, 197, 208
Web publishing, 73, 74, 78, 79
Web resource, 80, 153
Web service, 82, 178, 179, 201
Web syndication, 16
WSDL (*see* Web Services Description Language (WSDL))
Well-formed, well-formedness constraint, 24
Whitespace, 23, 119
Wirth, Niklaus, 216, 217
Working Draft, 36, 71, 72, 196, 211
Working Group, 72, 85, 195, 211, 213, 214
World Wide Web (WWW), 1–3, 12, 21, 70, 71, 77, 80, 85, 86, 88, 135, 152
Consortium, 3, 21, 71
WWW. *See also* Web, the World Wide Web (WWW)

X

XACML. *See* Extensible Access Control Markup Language (XACML)
XForms, 73, 79
XHTML. *See* Extensible HyperText Markup Language (XHTML)
XInclude, 73, 76, 77, 96
XLink, 73, 75, 89, 188, 190
XML
    accessory, 75
    application, 12, 26, 31, 62–64, 75, 76, 208
    base, 73, 75, 76
    database, 188–191, 193–194
    document, 9, 14, 22–25, 27–29, 31, 33–36, 41, 44, 45, 48, 52, 55, 62–64, 66, 74–77, 80, 81, 84, 86, 100, 101, 103, 104, 124, 128, 142, 186, 187, 190, 191

enabled database system, 191, 193, 194
encryption, 73, 82, 83, 179, 183, 201
events, 73, 79
family of languages, 3, 69, 73–84
Infoset (*see* XML Information Set (Infoset))
names, 32, 33, 46, 54, 74, 75
processor, 24–26, 30–32, 34, 35, 43–51, 62–64
signature, 82, 83, 179
specification, 24, 32, 34, 38, 41, 46, 48, 50, 65, 77, 100, 211, 213
transducer, 74, 75
XKMS (*see* XML Key Management Specification (XKMS))
xml:id, 75, 76
xml:lang, 39, 46, 60, 101, 119
xml:space, 46
XSD (*see* XML Schema (XSD))
XSL (*see* XML Stylesheet Language (XSL))
XML Information Set (Infoset), 52, 64, 65
XML Key Management Specification (XKMS), 73, 82, 83
XML Schema (XSD), 13, 17, 21, 42, 52–61, 74–76, 84, 89, 95, 113–121, 123, 139, 154, 156, 172, 174–177, 179, 180, 185, 188
Language, 52–62, 114–116, 120, 156
XML Stylesheet Language (XSL), 13, 74, 76, 77, 96, 97, 102, 104, 124, 126, 193
XPath, 75, 77, 97, 104, 108, 211, 214
XPointer, 75, 76
XProc, 76, 77
XQuery, 13, 32, 71, 72, 74–77, 81, 85, 89
XSLT, 13, 74–77, 87, 94, 96–100, 102, 104, 185, 193